EQUALITIES

EQUALITIES

Douglas Rae

AND

DOUGLAS YATES
JENNIFER HOCHSCHILD
JOSEPH MORONE
CAROL FESSLER

Harvard University Press
*Cambridge, Massachusetts
and London, England
1981*

Library of Congress Cataloging in Publication Data

Rae, Douglas W.
  Equalities.

  Bibliography: p.
  Includes index.
  1. Equality.   I. Title.
HM146.R33   305.5   81-4157
ISBN 0-674-25980-7   AACR2

For Lindblom

Preface

THE OFFICIAL success of equality in American life is just about as irrefutable as the success of General Motors and the Chrysler Corporation recently seemed. Success is evidently corrupting. Yet it is special with ideas, for James Agee was surely saying something specifically true of ideas, of dangerous ones like equality, when he wrote in *Let Us Now Praise Famous Men:* "The deadliest blow the enemy of the human soul can strike is to do fury honor. Swift, Blake, Beethoven, Christ, Joyce, Kafka, name me a one who has not been thus castrated. Official acceptance is the one unmistakable symptom that salvation is beaten again." Our subject is the fate of equality as it is transformed from a furious yet abstract idea into a practicable and concrete maxim of public or social or economic practice. The aim of our book is to chart the main ways in which equality is turned from one thing into many things and turned from something frightening to rich men into something that they unofficially endorse.

The work began as a succession of seminars, stretching back to the fall of 1973. Its form was more specifically shaped by a series of discussions between 1976 and 1978. These involved Douglas Yates, Joseph Morone, Jennifer Hochschild, and me (Carol Fessler joined the project in 1980). Our conversations led to the metaphor of a grammar and to many actual elements in the grammar of equality. It is quite often impossible to disentangle individual contributions to these discussions, and the book is therefore a genuine collaboration. I will nevertheless hazard a few general observations about the contributions made by my collaborators. Yates is to be credited with much of the work's verisimilitude as an account of contemporary politics and policy: he repeatedly compelled me to embellish the text with the truth.

Both Morone and Hochschild often sharpened arguments, displaced my cloudy distinctions with lucid ones, and joined Yates in forcing me to attend to facts (just as Yates quite often joined them in making theoretical suggestions). Hochschild's learning in the psychology and philosophy of justice like Morone's conceptual acuity and knowledge of educational policy, Fessler's in political theory (and notably feminist theory), and Yates's in the reality of American city life were each and all sources of enrichment to the work. Even though I composed nearly all of the text, each of the others is thus recognizable as an author of it. Many others offered advice. We wish especially to thank Bruce Ackerman, Brian Barry, Tony Broh, Jo Beld Fraatz, Jim Fishkin, Amy Gutman, David Mayhew, Richard Medley, and Edward Tufte. The time devoted to my own contribution was granted me by a Yale Senior Faculty Fellowship. Earlier stays with the Center for Advanced Study in the Behavioral Sciences at Stanford and at the Netherlands Institute allowed me to nurture some of the ideas expressed less directly here at a pace permitted by the leisure of a theory class. We are also grateful to Aida Donald and Maria Kawecki for their careful and expert editorial assistance. Typing by Marie Avitable, Carla Berkedal, and Sarah Skubas was most helpful.

Douglas Rae
New Haven

Contents

EQUALITIES

1 Tocqueville's Dread

SUCCESS COMES to political ideas not when they are justified in seminar and speech, but at the moment of their application to life and society. The triumph of Bentham's utilitarianism lay not in its (always mixed) hold on the professoriate, but in its application to society by bureaucrats, economists, and prison wardens. The liberal theory of right finds success not in Locke or Mill, but in the promulgation and enforcement of the laws by which liberal societies are distinctively governed. And so it is with equality. Its success and importance lie not in its crystalline beauty among abstract conceptions, not in its wonderful symmetry, not even in its moral power, but in countless attempts to realize equality in polity, economy, and society. It is this insistent and immediate demand for equality in our lives that vindicates Tocqueville's famous prophecy:

> The gradual progress of equality is something fated. The main features of this progress are the following: it is universal and permanent, it is daily passing beyond human control, and every event and every man helps it along. Is it wise to suppose that a movement which has been so long in train could be halted by one generation? Does anyone imagine that democracy, which has destroyed the feudal system and vanquished kings, will fall back before the middle classes and the rich? Will it stop now, when it has grown so strong and its adversaries so weak? . . . This whole book has been written under the impulse of a kind of religious dread inspired by contemplation of this irresistible revolution advancing century by century over every obstacle and even now going forward amid the ruins it has itself created.[1]

Criticisms of our basic institutions—the state, the family, the market, the school—seldom fail to announce the imminent triumph of equality. The civil rights movement, the women's movement, movements of economic liberation, the demand for worldwide economic redistribution, critical ideologies of Marxist socialism—all these and many more such things vindicate Tocqueville's prophecy.[2] Yet in their very number and variety these phenomena provoke the first of three basic queries about Toqueville's prophecy: *Is equality the name of one coherent program or is it the name of a system of mutually antagonistic claims upon society and government?*

Is equality a plan for a great cathedral, whose walls and buttresses fit together in a progressively more complete and stable structure, each occupying its proper space, the whole consisting in its interlocking parts? Or is equality the blueprint for a contradictory structure—a jester's church—some of whose walls and buttresses can be raised to the sky only as others are leveled to the ground? In the former case, we are justified in viewing equality, as did Tocqueville, as a force, potentially "universal and permanent, . . . passing beyond human control," now menacing "the middle classes and the rich" after having leveled their medieval predecessors. In the latter case, we must instead think of equality as a series of conflicting forces, related in abstract conception yet contradicting one another in practice.

But egalitarianism is neither a blueprint for a cathedral nor a joke about one. If simple models do not suffice, we must construct more complex ones by analyzing the meanings of equality as they appear in actual efforts to promote it.

A second question arises from even a cursory comparison of Tocqueville's vision and the world as we know it: *Everywhere one hears praise for the idea of equality, yet inequality persists. How can we explain the disjunction?* There are, of course, two ready explanations for this—hypocrisy and good faith. In the former view, people talk about equality as an alternative to practicing it; in the latter, they talk about equality in order to practice it. Without denying the importance of human hope and hypocrisy, we think that neither of these views comes very close to the mark. If equality were one thing, or one program of consistent things, then simple-minded notions of good faith and hypocrisy, or of simple adversarial struggle—the party of equality versus the party of privilege—would answer the second question. We could then imagine a history of progressive egalitarianism, overcoming the hypocrisy of its proponents, confronting its enemies, removing one unequal practice after another, erecting first one and then another facet in a final edifice which ultimately would fully transform equality from an idea to a practice.

But this is not to be taken for granted, even as a logical or analytical possibility. It may be that one can without hypocrisy *struggle toward equality while struggling against it.* This more complicated view would not rule out hypocrisy or adversarial relations, but it would make both much more complex, and it would rule out linear, egalitarian progress like Tocqueville's "something fated." This view would converge with the more complicated answer to question one above.

This discussion leads to a third question: *Equality is the simplest and most abstract of notions, yet the practices of the world are irremediably concrete and complex. How, imaginably, could the former govern the latter?* The universal use of "equality" as a category of thought depends upon its very abstractness, its formal emptiness. To assert "X = Y" is to say nothing about X or Y. The claim would stand if both symbols denoted numbers, formal sets with identical elements, the masses of twin planets, two poker hands of the same value. Equality is bereft of descriptive, historical particulars. More definite terms (Indianapolis, Grant's Tomb) are tethered on short ropes to time and place, held down by the narrow limits of their referents. Equality and other formal terms float freely across the layers of time, the points of the compass, the bounds of topical reference. Can we imagine that the simple, formal idea of equality contains enough information, enough specificity, enough texture, to be capable of direct and consistent application to a concrete, complex world? This seeming absurdity should not be taken too lightly given the enormous subtlety with which other abstractions, including the mathematical incarnation of our present idea ("="), are made to blend with complex structures. Shouldn't we expect diversification, even contradiction, as the ideal of equality is applied in one concrete context after another? Couldn't these diversifications sometimes be exploited as weapons of argument, so as to place equali*ties* on two sides of a single concrete dispute?

These are three very tightly linked questions, perhaps three aspects of a single question. We will abandon conscious and direct attention to them until the final chapter of the book, when we will try to answer them, not with categorical truth but with something better than simple dogmatism. We will see that Tocqueville can be read in more than one way as he describes his motive: "dread inspired by the contemplation of this irresistible revolution advancing century by century over every obstacle and even now going forward *amid the ruins it has itself created.*³ Perhaps the revolution's course is more resistible, more elliptical, than Tocqueville imagined, and perhaps some of these ruins are themselves egalitarian in shape.⁴

1.1   From Theory toward Practice

Our fascination with equality lies not in mere theory or established practice, but in the repeated moment of transition from theory into practice.⁵ The importance of this moment is obvious, since it forces an abstraction's sterile form to accommodate life. Trying to make laws or families or universities live up to the doctrine of equality is the point at which we discover egalitarianism as a living conception. Our aim, then, is to ask: *What, when it is brought to life in this way, does equality come to mean?*⁶

We are specifically interested in one main aspect of equality's journey toward life, the way in which that single abstract conception becomes several practical notions. How does "equality" fission into "equalit*ies*"? Of course, the relation of a general abstraction to its particular instance is not remarkable; there is nothing exciting or problematic about the relation between the general color green and the specific greenness of frogs or army jeeps. We do not, then, care about the straightforward relation of a large class to the smaller classes it encompasses. We see no reason to analyze the relation between equality in topics X and Y, or in nations Z and W (where these differ from one another merely as repetitive cases). We are interested instead in something less static, in which notions of equality are divided from one another.

This phenomenon is neither mysterious nor unfamiliar. Consider Allan Bakke's application to the medical school at the University of California, Davis. Bakke expected that his application would be sorted and compared with all its rivals on the basis of some neutral competition. Roughly, he expected equality in the sense that all folders would be judged without recourse to the names, sexes, races, or ethnicities of applicants.⁷ This doctrine is the fossil of an earlier moment in which the general idea of equality had prevailed against vulgar prejudice following the lines of race, sex, ethnicity, and perhaps family connection ("However dull, Smith here is Smith's son"). But a new moment had intervened and created a new notion of equality. This latter notion—actually, as we will see, a swarm of notions—

structured equality as a relation between *blocs* of individuals, not between individuals themselves. It thus shifted attention from individual rights of candidacy (handling folders *without* consideration of race and the like) to rates of admission for blocs of candidates (handling folders *with* attention to race and the like). What is revealed by Bakke's suit and the university's defense (along with the many other commentaries and edicts) is the phenomenon we wish to analyze here, in which specific notions of equality are spawned from the general idea of equality, and come into conflict with one another. Perhaps indeed the idea against which equality must struggle most heroically is equality itself.

Some may claim that the fission of egalitarian ideals, and their contradictions in practice, are special afflictions of the modern west or even of the American civil rights movement. Perhaps the phenomenon is now especially visible, salient, and important. It does not, however, come fresh to the world in our time and season. Here, for instance, is the old Athenian speaking in the fourth century B.C. about the design of an ideal city: "The ancient pronouncement is true, that 'equality produces friendship': the saying is both very correct and graceful. But just whatever is the equality that has this effect? Because this is not very clear, we get into a lot of trouble. For there are two equalities, the same in name, but in many respects almost diametrically opposed in deed."[8] Plato's dispute is quite different from Bakke's case, but its underlying structure resembles a whole series of equalities at issue in contemporary society. Plato's specific case will appear again in modern mold, as we proceed; our point here is simply that equalities have had seasons before our own. The age of our subject may remove some of its glitter, but it also suggests its substance and durability.

1.2   Where Could Equality Be a Straightforward Idea?

The complexity that interests us does not arise *within* the abstract idea of equality but in its confrontation with the world. Our first task, then, is to identify those features of the living world—actual societies and actual persons—that make for complexity in the application of equality. We do this by imagining a society in which equality has one straightforward meaning, and which therefore is devoid of the features that interest us. We concoct this ludicrous society not to see it but to see how it *differs* from societies we know. Each of the differences between the imaginary model and actual societies will then serve as a clue to understanding our subject. This society-made-for-a-straight-forward-notion-of-equality (Society E) is defined by five features:

1. *Unitary social classification.* A unitary society has one class of members, which is never relevantly subdivided,[9] is always distinct from other societies, and is never seen as part of some larger aggregate for purposes of allocation.

2. *Singular allocation.* All things of value in Society E are allocated *once, and for all time,* as if everything were gathered in a single heap one day and divided into inalienable lots for all time by a single decision.

3. *Fine division.* Anything valued by Society E can be divided into identical parts, one per member of society, without relevantly diminishing the total value of the initial lot. Thus, Solomon's baby can be cut into as many pieces as there are members and still have the total value of one whole baby.

4. *Human uniformity.* People are completely alike so far as personal needs, tastes, or vulnerabilities may affect the allocation of values in Society E. The test is this: if a given lot of goods has a given value for any one person in Society E, then it must also have that same value for any other person in Society E. If value is reckoned in utility (though it need not be), everyone in Society E has the same "utility function" vis-à-vis every item of utility.

5. *Dichotomous thinking.* In Society E, all sentences of the form "A is B" are seen simply as true or false. Thus, "Smith is pregnant," "Jones is intelligent," and "That allocation is equal" are each taken to be either true or false, after the fashion of propositions in simple logic. This culture of dichotomous thinking renders all false sentences equally false: the statements "Today is June 5, 1982" and "Today is August 21, 1942" are equally false on June 6, 1982. All nuances of relativity are thus beyond the capacities of this culture.

If all five of these defining features of Society E are satisfied at once, E is unlike any society that we know or could possibly come to know. It must be incomparably provincial, walled off from any larger community (feature 1), yet lacking in any ongoing economy of its own (feature 2)—a combination not easily satisfied. It must be without even a primitive division of labor (features 1 and 4), or sexual differences (feature 4), or a kinship structure (feature 1), or the differentiating effects of age and disease (feature 4). It must be without much intellectual subtlety (feature 5), and its members must value only commodities subject to fine division without loss of value—peanut butter or beer, not houses, paintings, or babies (feature 3). Going on at more length about the contradictions and eccentricities of Society E would be useless; we need only notice how radically E differs from the real societies in which equality must move from theory toward policy and practice.

The interest of this lifeless place is that it is only in a society like it that the abstract notion of equality can be smoothly translated into policy. Given an isolated and indivisible society, once-and-for-all allocation, interchangeable clones, dichotomous thinking, and only finely divisible goods, equality means just one thing: *creating n identical lots of each good available to the society and bestowing one lot of each good on each member of society*. This distribution, and no other, will count as equal. Indeed, given dichotomous thinking, all other distributions will appear equally unequal. Each person thus receives his or her one-nth of every good in society, and stands in a relation of perfect equality to everyone else. For Society E, this is *all* that equality can mean. But equality is a simple and unproblematic notion only in a setting like E, not in any real society.

1.3   Four Sample Cases

We may contrast the false symmetry of this model with actual societies that produced the following tales.

1.3.1   Bad Kidneys

A 1972 amendment to the Social Security Act authorized federal coverage of 80 percent of the costs of kidney treatment for all Americans. It was the first time government had ventured to finance indefinite treatment of a catastrophic disease without limits predicated upon age or income. About fifty thousand Americans a year suffer kidney failure; of these about eight thousand are medically suited for hemodialysis (artificial blood filtration). This therapy normally costs between $10,000 and $30,000 annually, depending on the type of machine, seriousness of the disease, and location of treatment in hospital, clinic, or home.[10]

Between 1964, when dialysis was available to fewer than three hundred kidney patients, and 1973, when the new program went into effect, there were many more candidates than machines. This dramatic scarcity made full and literal equality impossible. The very wealthy usually bought treatment, while others were chosen by "community selection committees" empowered to decide on the relative worthiness of applicants—a Boy Scout leader and father of four might be chosen for dialysis, leaving an alcoholic bachelor to die.[11] This was inequality of life and death, linked to a system of inequality of wealth or community esteem. The system was justifiable only on the (contestable) ground that everyone had an equal opportunity to merit access to a machine (by accumulating wealth or esteem).

Soon after the new law went into effect, enough machines became available so that everyone who could psychologically and physically tolerate the grueling treatment had access to one. Criteria of wealth or attractiveness to the community were no longer relevant. However, new issues arose immediately from the very generosity of this solution to the earlier inequality.

A federal report accused some doctors of delivering routine care to as many as one hundred nonwealthy patients (for which services a doctor could receive a retainer of over $100,000 a year).[12] The owner of one of the largest chains of "dialysis mills," in fact, proposed that he be granted the sole right to treat all the relatively simple and more lucrative cases in New York City, leaving the complicated, costly cases to the city hospitals. He claimed that this would benefit everyone, including city hospitals and taxpayers (his inflated profits would be merely incidental).[13] This generous proposal clarifies by exaggeration: equality between kidney patients does not assure equality or equity in the exchange between their physicians and the paying public.

Furthermore, a government report claimed that doctors were still treating patients unequally in deciding who should start dialysis.[14] The old standards of wealth and esteem were no longer used, but they were replaced by criteria that varied from place to place and from doctor to doctor.[15] Some doctors would rule out patients on the basis of age, judging them too old or too young; some appealed to a standard of general health, ruling out patients with other serious diseases. Instead of receiving free, if arduous, treatment, these patients were left to suffer or die.

These charges turn upon (in)equality—between one kidney patient and another, between physician and taxpayer, between programs of treatment. But they leave open another question of equality: Why should *this* source of suffering be put ahead of others? As *The New York Times* editorialized: "Congress, which voted last year to extend Medicare benefits to patients needing renal dialysis . . . is learning to its dismay that in roughly a decade this provision may require annual expenditures of a billion dollars . . . The point is not that victims of renal disease are unworthy of help, but that Government resources have to be allocated to meeting many needs. If a billion dollars has to go to prolonging the lives of thousands of kidney disease victims, that is a billion dollars that cannot go to eradicating slums, improving education or finding a cure for cancer."[16] Others asked why victims of kidney disease got so much federal money when only tens of thousands each year die of kidney failure, as compared with 350,000 who die of cancer and many more who die of circulatory ailments. The answer was partly political—kidney victims are a highly visible group with a single problem, an obvious need, clear and dramatic results of a proven treatment, and a very highly developed single-issue organization.[17] Their needs were thus politically favored over the needs of others: one inequality (of funding) is thus founded upon another (of political efficacy). Why shouldn't society respond equally to all sufferers and all forms of suffering?

1.3.2   Race and Pay in Baseball

It is commonly believed that baseball offers blacks the same rewards it offers whites. This belief seems well founded: in 1970, the average salary of black baseball players was actually *higher* than that of whites. The difference was considerable and held up across positions on the field. Black pitchers earned, on the average, about $21,000 more than white pitchers, black infielders about $12,000 more than white infielders, and black outfielders about $9,000 more than their white counterparts.[18] Such differences existed among superstars as well. In 1970 seven of the ten players making $100,000 or more were black.[19]

These statistics suggest that blacks have achieved—indeed, have surpassed—equality with whites in baseball. But many black players do not feel that they have been treated equally.[20] They charge that widespread racial discrimination still exists in baseball, and that this racism becomes clear only when salaries are compared *at each level of performance.* Their point is well taken. Although it is true that blacks have on average higher salaries than whites, it is also true that "blacks, on the average, earn less than whites *of equal ability.*"[21] For instance, white infielders who bat around .280 earn approximately

$4,000 more than black infielders with the same average. And at the average level of outfield performance,[22] whites earn about 25 percent more than blacks.[23] This differential persists through all major league performance levels, and actually increases as performance improves.[24] Thus, in 1970 seven out of the ten players earning over $100,000 were blacks, but "Carl Yastrzemski earned $35,000 more than Hank Aaron and Willie Mays, although Yastrzemski had been playing fewer years and had not come close to matching Aaron's and Mays' performances."[25] So, while blacks' salaries compare favorably to whites', blacks have to *surpass* whites in performance in order to earn equal pay. Blacks have achieved (even surpassed) equality of baseball income, but have not achieved equality in pay per crack of the bat.

Notice that the two claims in this tale implicitly agree that racial blocs (not single persons) form the subjects of equality: neither claim opposes inequality of incomes among persons in society or even in baseball. And both claims suppose money to be the appropriate numeraire of equality between races. The contradiction is between equality simpliciter in mean salaries by race, and equality of salary *at each level of productivity* on the diamond.

1.3.3 Language Rights in Canada

In the United States, everyone—Native American, African, Italian, and German alike—is usually compelled to speak English in public transactions. This is, in its way, a species of equality: one and the same language for all. In Canada, and even in some U.S. cities, the issue has a different complexion.

Canada is a bilingual country: English and French are its official languages. All Canadians have the formal right to choose either as their native tongue. English, of course, is the language of the majority. A sizable minority (about 27 percent of the population) claim French as their native tongue.

In Quebec (which is 80 percent francophone) the Parti Québecois gained the majority of the seats in the provincial government in 1976. The party's program stresses the protection of the French culture in Quebec. In pursuit of this aim, the newly elected provincial government passed into law "Bill One"—a bill that purports to make French and *only* French the official language of the province. It requires "that most businesses, professional people and government offices conduct their affairs in French."[26] It also limits the number of students permitted to study English. The bill, reports *The New York Times,* makes Quebec "a French society."[27]

English speakers throughout Canada have, of course, attacked Bill One. They charge that it discriminates against English-speaking Canadians in a land where both English and French have always shared equal status. Why, ask the bill's opponents, should English speakers be forced to speak French in Quebec, when French speakers are allowed their choice of language in other provinces? Why should not all Canadians, English as well as French, have the same right to speak whatever language they choose? Why is equality among languages not enough for the Québecois?

It is not enough, respond the Parti Québecois, because equality among languages is not equivalent to equality among speakers. French Canadians have always suffered a lower standard of living than English Canadians, even in Quebec where they comprise the majority. The French Canadians see language as the chief cause of their inferior position. They feel that "there are penalties attached to being French in Canada," since, they argue, "English is the language in which the most important decisions in Canada are made, whether ... in the scientific, economic, or political spheres."[28] As a result, French speakers are handicapped when forced to compete with English speakers. Their problem was well described in a hearing of the Royal Commission on Bilingualism and Biculturalism:

> Everyone knows that here [Chicoutimi, Quebec] where the population is 98% French Canadian, big business has made English the working language and anyone who wants to work his way up the plant has to use English ... When there are two people at the same level of education entering one of our factories in Quebec, the English-speaking one has no need to learn a second language to earn his living, whereas the other person has to spend hours, even years mastering the second language ... The first one can go ahead and improve himself in the technological field and take advantage of the first promotion that comes up, whereas the other one loses time learning a second language.[29]

Equality of languages has never led to equality of persons in Canada. Perhaps inequality of languages will.

With this third problem, we encounter a new order of complexity. Who is to be equal with whom, in what segments of Canada (judged by place and by class), on what theory about the relation of language and economy? Several nuanced claims are pressed together, even in our radically simplified account of this dispute. The tale's complexity is itself important, for it illustrates the open nature of the social uses of equality: no very simple conception of equality (or of equalities) will account for disputes of this sort. Notice, also, that we have here a new form of egalitarianism: the Québecois refuse to treat the allocation of language rights in isolation from another (more obviously economic) allocation, and they insist that offsetting one inequality with another produces a new relationship of overall equality (or, at least, progress toward overall equality). If English-language managers are so much as permitted to use their native tongue, they will compel Francophone employees to follow suit, and thus perpetuate a long pattern of economic domination. Bill One fights one inequality with another, and does so—in important part—in the name of equality.

1.3.4   The Right to Worship the Christian God

While discussing how seventeenth-century colonists changed in their transition from expatriate Englishmen to Americans, Tocqueville remarks that "nothing is more peculiar or more instructive than the legislation of this time." He speaks more truly than he realizes; a Connecticut law of 1650 illustrates a sharp opposition between two definitions of religious equality. The law reads: "If any man after legal conviction shall have or worship any other God but the Lord God, he shall be put to death."[30]

From the vantage point of the Puritans, this law is perfectly egalitarian. Everyone has an equal right to seek salvation; everyone has an equal obligation to seek salvation in the only correct way, by worshipping the one true God. If a person rejects this right and obligation, even after being once convicted of such a crime, he also forfeits his equal right to life. From the vantage point of a Jew or an atheist, this law is grossly inegalitarian. Only those who believe in the Lord God, as conceived by the lawmakers, have an equal right to worship; nonbelievers or divergent believers have completely unequal—nonexistent, in fact—rights of worship. Only different forms of worship would ensure equal value to the worshippers.

1.3.5   Society E versus the Cases

These illustrative fragments from real societies partly show how actual societies differ from our bizarre model. Let us begin with the egalitarian solution for Society E: *Create n identical lots of each good available to the society and bestow one lot of each good on each member of society.* This would mean that every American would receive about 1/220,-000,000th of the social storehouse of every good, value, or commodity. All would receive identical artificial kidney machines (or equal intervals of hemodialysis therapy from such machines), analogously identical gear for the treatment of heart trouble, cancer, aching feet, bad eyes, psychosis, neurosis, indigestion, and flatulence—for the sick and the well alike, without discrimination among those who suffer from different complaints. This would be the *only* egalitarian solution for a society meeting the description of E. Moreover, we need not discuss medicine alone, for equality in Society E requires a likewise equal division of *every* commodity, including the right and obligation to worship the Christian God, and the right to speak English (or French) regardless of one's native tongue. We could go on in this vein, but the first essential contrast is clear: the egalitarian policy of Society E bears no very striking resemblance to the policies promoted in any actual society.

The explanation for this contrast is, of course, to be sought in more fundamental contrasts, for Society E differs in all five of its constitutive properties from societies with kidney trouble, baseball teams, languages, and God. Here are the essential differences:

1. *Social classification.* Society E is isolated and indivisible, but the societies considered above are divided along many lines: the sick versus the well, renal patients versus other patients, black pitchers versus white pitchers versus shortstops, Anglophones versus Francophones, Christians versus Jews, believers versus atheists. Society E offers one subject for equality; these societies have indefinitely many subjects.

2. *Allocation.* In Society E, everything is to be allocated once, and for all time, but these societies allocate things very differently. First, allocation has a historical flow as goods are produced and called into service; second, many more or less autonomous agencies of allocation operate at any given moment (bureaucracies, hospitals, churches, teams, firms, and so on). In Society E, the problem of equality appears once, and has one solution. In the real world, it appears over and over and has many solutions, each conditioned by the rest.

3. *Divisibility, lumpiness, and so forth.* In Society E, goods can be divided evenly without loss of value. In actual societies, many goods cannot be so divided. Suppose it takes one hundred minutes of hemo-

dialysis treatment to keep people with kidney failure going. If we divide access so that everybody gets ninety minutes instead of one hundred, the value of the shares falls drastically, just as the value of Solomon's baby would if the infant were cut in pieces.

4. *Human differences.* In Society E, there are no relevant differences among persons: a given lot of goods has the same value for all members. If, then, you set a particular value on the right and obligation to speak French, I must value it in the same degree—even if you speak French and I do not. The most profound difference between Society E and living societies may be precisely this, for human differences relevantly affect *every* judgment of value in real life.

5. *Modalities of thought.* In Society E, dichotomous thinking rules out relative differences, such as "this is more equal (less unequal) than that," thus making all things either equally equal or equally unequal. Real societies are not constrained in this way. Grudging tolerance for disestablished faith is, from the minority perspective, more nearly equal than an outright prohibition. A 5 percent racial difference in salaries is more nearly equal than a 10 percent difference.

We have begun by asking how the abstract idea of equality is changed and complicated as it moves toward the concrete world of policy and practice. We have conjured up an artificial society (Society E) in which this transition is smooth and uninteresting; we have seen several cases in which the application of equality to society is less than smooth; and we have reviewed five pertinent ways in which the artificial society differs from the sort of society that deals with bad kidneys, baseball teams, languages, and God. *These five differences each mark out a basic structural problem, and these problems must be anticipated wherever equality is a goal or principle of social policy.* They are: (1) complex social classification, (2) plural allocation, (3) indivisibilities, (4) human differences, and (5) relativity. By the book's end, it should be clear how these five structural facts of any actual society provoke the complex behavior of equality as a guide to social practice.

1.4   Theory to Practice and the Grammar of Equality

These five points of contrast with Society E all represent decisive obstacles to the direct and simple application of equality to actual societies. Each represents a demand for some "middle term," as Kant describes it: "It is obvious that no matter how complete the theory may be, a middle term is required between theory and practice, providing a link and a transition from one to the other. For a concept . . . which contains a general rule, must be supplemented by an act of judgment whereby the practitioner distinguishes instances where the rule applies from those where it does not."[31] The middle term that interests us is the matter of judging the meaning of equality as applied to the circumstances of actual human communities. Confronted with the disjunction between abstract idea and concrete reality, people construe equality to mean first this and then that and then another thing, each construal a judgmental link between theory and practice. *A "grammar" of equality is an account of the ways in which such judgments form coherent patterns of similarity and difference, consistency and contradiction.*[32] It is a *structural* grammar, since it is organized around the five basic structural problems lying between abstract and practical equalities.

Unlike the grammar of a natural language, a structural grammar is not concerned with particular locutions. Thus, we draw no distinction between saying "Speaking French is the equal right of every Canadian" and "Every Canadian has an equal right to speak French." For us, these two statements represent a single demand with an identical underlying structure. Neither are we directly concerned with the topical reference of equality claims. Claims concerned with language and with hemodialysis therapy might have similar structures despite their differing referents. But we *are* concerned with distinctions between sentences that a grammarian might describe as identical. By way of illustration, let us examine the following four claims:

1A. Every Canadian ought to have an equal right to speak French.

1B. Every Canadian ought to have an equal right to speak his native language.

2A. Every sick American ought to have equal acceess to hemodialysis therapy.

2B. Every sick American ought to have equal access to the best treatment for his illness.

A commonsense substantive typology would classify the two upper-row claims (1A and 1B) together, classify the lower-row claims (2A and 2B) together, and draw a sharp opposition between the two pairs thus established. Claims about language in Canada are one thing; claims about medicine in America are another. This is, of course, true, and we do not wish to conflate one topic with another.[33] A grammarian would see all four sentences as essentially identical, since they all contain a subject, verb, and two phrases with infinitive, preposition, and object.

However, a structural grammar calls attention to yet a third way of looking at these claims and others like them. The basic distinctions here run vertically, not horizontally. The left-column statements (1A and 2A) represent one structure of equality, and the right-column statements (1B and 2B) a very different structure. The *structural* difference between 1A and 1B is the same as the structural difference between 2A and 2B. On the left, we are asked to subject all to the "same policy"—French language rights or hemodialysis—as defined by an observer who responded to no pertinent differences among the subjects (What native language? What illness?). On the right, we are asked to adjust allocations to take account of pertinent differences among persons, so as to give each an entitlement to native language rights or therapy whose *value for him or her* is equal to the analogous value granted others. The left-side claims are subject to the ridicule evoked by Anatole France's joke about a law so egalitarian as to permit rich and poor alike to sleep under bridges. The right side claims, which do not promise equal access to hemodialysis whether you have bad kidneys or not, are not subject to the same joke. And the difference is a main structural distinction of the kind we propose to work out in our grammar of equality.

Structural differences thus lead to different equalities. If one takes the side of simple social equality, the right to worship the Christian God—for Puritans, Jews, and atheists alike—counts as equality. And, from this structural viewpoint, rights to worship other Gods are rights to *inequality*. From the opposing view—equality of value to persons—just the opposite is true: the imposition of one religion upon all is a policy of unequal values, flatly contradicting the ideal of equality. The conflict here is not between equality and something else, but between equality and equality: equality of one structural type versus equality of another structural type.

These grammatical distinctions represent human responses to the structural obstacles that life sets between the theory and the practice (or policy) of equality. In Section 1.3.5 we outlined five main structural problems of this sort. The grammatical forms we are looking for represent *culturally developed patterns of response to these structural problems.*[34]

The main point of our cases is not that any one incident unfolds in a particular way, but that whole series of incidents do so. The structural problems repeat, even as context and topic vary. We have already seen three examples of the confrontation between equality and the relevant heterogeneity of persons: differences of health and disease (versus equal medical care), differences of native tongue (versus equal language rights), differences of religious faith (versus equally compulsory Christianity). Despite different topics and references, these stories represent one structural problem repeated in three guises. The basis of our grammatical analysis is that similar structural problems provoke *similarly different* patterns of response. Continuing the three examples just mentioned, we have:

1A. Every Canadian ought to have an equal right to speak French.	1B. Every Canadian ought to have an equal right to speak his native tongue.
2A. Every sick American ought to have equal access to hemodialysis therapy.	2B. Every sick American ought to have equal access to the best treatment for his illness.
3A. Everyone ought to worship the Christian God.	3B. Every person ought to worship the God in whom she believes.

The left-hand responses represent a single grammatical form, the right-hand responses likewise represent a single grammatical form, and between the responses in each pair there is the same difference as that which exists between the responses in the other pairs. The structural problem is, in short, provoking a patterned system of responses, and this patterning is the subject of our grammar.

Things quickly become more complicated, however. Not only do our cases illustrate similar differences, but also they show *different* differences:

1A. Every Canadian ought to have an equal right to speak French.	1B. Every Canadian ought to have an equal right to speak his native tongue.
4A. All major league baseball players ought to have the same salary, regardless of race.	4B. Every major league baseball player ought to have the same salary as others of the same position and ability, regardless of race.

In our earlier comparison, each pair showed the same grammatical difference because it responded to the same structural problem. Here there are two differences, and they are *different differences*. 1A and 1B stem from the problem of heterogeneous needs. The other difference, the focus on racial groups in 4A and on individual abilities in 4B, arises from two distinct views of the social classification problem. Thus, the two pairings represent different differences which have nothing to do with the surface difference of language rights versus baseball salaries. Each of the five structural problems of actual societies leads to its own pattern of responses, its own part of the structural grammar, its own different set of differences.

1.5   Political Economy of Equality

We will be concerned with the grammar of equality partly for the reason already suggested: to clarify the underlying structure of a complex phenomenon. But we would be remiss if we forgot that equality is, or at least used to seem, *dangerous* and *expensive*. If applied without differentiation—without the complexities that concern us— equality would sweep away class differences, level market economies, bleach away the variation of human experience. This was the fate that Tocqueville so dreaded.

The vast majority of human societies have in one way or another been busy with the tasks of equality. Colonial revolutions are commonplace; Marxism-Leninism is by now so institutionalized that it is often an apology for ruling classes; and the emancipation of racial and ethnic minorities is a prime activity of liberal reform. Almost everyone seems somehow a partisan of equality. Yet *in*equality in society is as recognizable today as it was in Tocqueville's time. Equality is perhaps less dangerous and less expensive—one almost says less egalitarian—than it once seemed. This may occur because the grammar of equality allows society to choose facets of equality that evade danger, cut costs, and perhaps indeed vitiate the dangerous ideal before it comes to the point of practice. This suspicion underlies our analysis and will come to center stage again in the book's final pages.

1.6   Conclusion

The next five chapters elaborate on the five parts of the structural grammar of equality that correspond to the five societal structures identified in section 1.3.5. The book's final chapter brings these specific analyses together to answer the three questions raised earlier by Tocqueville's prophecy. We conclude with a discussion of the political economy of equality, and of the implications of the move from equality to equalities as we move from theory to practice.

Two final introductory points. First, simply because we ask sharp questions, we may seem to criticize the ideal of equality itself. Alternatively, simply because we take the ideal of equality seriously enough to write a book about it, we may seem always to endorse it above other political principles. We intend neither criticism of the ideal nor unilateral endorsement of it. The question is not "Whether equality?" but "*Which* equality?"

Second, our grammatical explication of the responses to societal structures does not reduce these responses to causal effects. Rather, it treats them as objects of "subjective understanding," in Max Weber's sense:

> We can accomplish something which is never attainable in the natural sciences, namely the subjective understanding of the actions of . . . individuals. The natural sciences cannot do this, being limited to the formulation of causal uniformities in objects and events and the explanation of individual facts by applying them. We do not "understand" the behavior of cells, but can only observe the relevant functional relationships and generalize on the basis of these observations. The additional achievement of explanation by interpretive understanding, as distinguished from external observation, is of course, attained only at a price—the more hypothetical and fragmentary character of the results.[35]

We are, in short, trying in a fragmentary way to bring out the subjective pattern of dispute and divergence that lies implicit in the consciousness of people engaged in advocacy and argument about the most powerful idea of our time.

2 The Subject of Equality

ANY SOCIETY with a system of kinship, division of labor, different races, or distinct age cohorts, genders, languages, or dialects, even given names, must be a society in which "For whom?" questions matter. For a liberal individualist culture, no question surpasses "For whom?" in naturalness or urgency. Put a little too crisply, any society complex enough to provoke the normative idea of equality in the first place must go on to provoke a series of difficulties centering on the matter of who is to be equal to whom. The subject grammar set forth in this chapter tries to model the answers to this elemental question.

There are three main ways of conceiving the subject of equality:

> *Individual-regarding equalities:*
> Simple subject
> Segmental subjects
> *Bloc-regarding equalities:*
> Bloc-equal subjects

The difference between simple, segmental, and bloc-equal subjects of equality is not in literal content, not in the names of those who are to be equals, but in the structure by which those names are brought together. As these structures change, much more than literal content changes with them.

2.1 Simple Individual-Regarding Equalities

The simplest way to answer the question "Equality for whom?" is to define a class of individuals, and then to demand that each be the equal of all the rest. There is one class of equals, and one relation of equality holds among all its members.[1]

Equality of this sort is very commonly demanded in contemporary life. "One-person-one-vote," for example, defines a class of equal citizens, granting each the same formal right to vote as any other. Any pairwise inequality in the "weight" of votes would count as a violation, no matter which pair of citizens we compared. Equal rights more generally—civil liberties of thought and expression, rights to property, rights against arbitrary arrest, and the like—also fit this mold. So too does the standard example of equality as a prima facie philosophical position: "If I have a cake and there are ten persons among whom I wish to divide it, then if I give exactly one tenth to each, this will not . . . call for justification; whereas if I depart from this principle of equal division I am expected to produce a special reason."[2] In addition, the basic notion of economic equality has (in most cases) the same structure. So do the Golden Rule and Kant's Categorical Imperative. Treat *everyone* as you would be treated; treat *everyone* as an end and not as a means. Even the price mechanism in market systems is partly an instance of simple individual-regarding equality: "2 for 79 cents" is addressed to the whole class of shoppers who happen into the store; it would be "price discrimination" to vary this figure from one customer to another. Both conceptual simplicity and practical application thus suggest that this structure should have pride of place in our analysis.

2.1.1   Implicit, Variable, and Complex Subject Classes

We have written as though the class of equals must be spelled out explicitly. However, as our examples imply, the subject class may be either explicit or implicit. A very important range of examples stems from the operative structure of general rules, laws, norms, and principles. Isaiah Berlin shows this as follows: "All rules, by definition, entail a measure of equality. In so far as rules are general instructions to act or refrain from acting in certain ways, in specified circumstances, enjoined upon persons of a specified kind, they enjoin uniform behavior in identical cases. To fall under a rule is *pro tanto* to be assimilated to a single pattern. To enforce a rule is to promote equality of behavior or treatment. This applies whether the rules take the form of moral principles and laws, or codes of positive law, or the rules of games."[3]

Since society fairly teems with rules, it also teems with subjects for equality. The sign "No Parking" means "no parking for anyone"; we are all equally its subjects. The rules of chess are addressed to the whole class of persons who propose to play that game. Even the constitutional rule that the current president of the United States is entitled to veto congressional legislation sets up an implicit class of equals, albeit a class restricted to those who are or will later become presidents of the United States. Bentham's principle requiring society to serve "the greatest good of the greatest number" requires that all the members of society be counted as equals into this calculation: "each to count for one, none to count for more than one."

Not only may subject classes be implicit or explicit; they may also be fixed or variable. A *fixed* subject class has a definite list of members, as with "everyone currently enrolled in this college" or "the top ten heavyweight contenders as of July 4, 1981." A *variable* subject class has no single, enumerable roster of members; consider, again, the subjects of a general rule.[4] A no-parking sign addresses itself to any motorist who happens by; the statutory laws of a polity address themselves to whomever comes into its territory by birth, land, sea, or air.

The subject structure may remain simple even if the language it uses to classify persons grows complicated. This false complexity occurs when not one but several criteria are used to bound a simple class of equals. Using linking terms like "or" and "and," one could conceive a class of, say, "black females" (each member being black and female), or a class of "blacks and females" (each member being black or female or both). One could go on with any number of classificatory criteria, and still have a simple individual-regarding structure. Thus, for instance, we could define the class of male, Danish, unemployed victims of tuberculosis, and then insist upon equal medical treatment for all of them, pair by pair. That would be a simple individual-regarding equality, even though the language of classification has a fancy composition. The test is not the language used to draw borders around the class of equals, but whether it remains a single class of equal individuals.[5]

2.1.2   Inclusive and Exclusive Subject Classes

Every subject class is an alternative to many rival classes: if we say that the α's are to be equals, why shouldn't we also or instead have said this of the β's? If Smith and Jones are to be equal partners in this barrel of whisky, why not Smith and Rae instead? Or every thirsty soul in town? The utterly simple and sterile Society E is a unitary society: it has one category of member which is never relevantly subdivided; it is always distinct from other societies; and it is never part of some larger aggregate for purposes of allocation (see Section 1.2). Society E could have only *one* class of equals.[6] In less sterile settings, rival classes of equals multiply and compel choices. One main resulting pattern is the comparative distinction between exclusive and inclusive classes.

Recall, for example, our story of bad kidneys (Section 1.3.1). There we had (among other things) a four-step progression: (1) equal access to hemodialysis therapy for *rich* or *virtuous* victims of kidney disease, (2) equal access to hemodialysis therapy for *all* victims of kidney disease, (3) equal access to appropriate medical treatment for all victims of *all* diseases, (4) equal access to remedial measures for *all sufferers*, including those with social or economic, not merely medical, afflictions. As we move from step 1 toward step 4, the boundary of the subject class changes from narrow to broad to very broad, with each class more inclusive than the previous one.

By *inclusionary* equality, we mean a broad class of equals; by *exclusionary* equality, we mean a narrow class of equals. In its strict meaning, this distinction does not refer merely to a numerical relation, but to a relation of inclusion. Class One is inclusionary vis-à-vis Class Two if (and only if) every member of Class One is also a member of Class Two, and some *others* belong to One but not to Two.[7] A weak sense of the distinction is merely numerical. If one hundred individuals fall in Class One and only ninety-nine fall in Two, we have a weak version of this relation even if strict inclusion does not hold. We will use the strict sense for most purposes.

In Western history, electoral suffrage provides the most familiar instance of this distinction. Using an American vocabulary, for instance, we can distinguish: (1) equal votes for *propertied white men,* (2) equality for *white men,* (3) equality for *men,* (4) equality for *persons.* Each class of equals "swallows" the class before it and is therefore strictly inclusionary vis-à-vis its predecessor—the four claims present a neat chain of expansion, and some argue that egalitarianism always means choosing the broader subject.[8]

A more complicated example is suffrage in school bond referenda. The most inclusionary class grants suffrage to all citizens within the school district. One restriction would limit this suffrage to tax-paying citizens (it's their money). Another exclusionary claim would limit suffrage to parents of school-age children (it's their kids who will, or will not, benefit from the bond proposal in question). Both of these categories are strictly exclusionary in relation to the first, full-suffrage doctrine, but neither is strictly exclusionary or inclusionary in relation to the others. Which is *the* meaning of equality, none can say, for each is in its way an instance of this notion.

A more famous and more interesting tale of the same sort arises in the Book of Matthew:

> The kingdom of heaven is like a householder who went out early in the morning to hire laborers for his vineyard. After agreeing with the laborers for a denarius a day, he sent them into his vineyard. And going out about the third hour he saw others standing idle in the market place, and to them he said, "You go into the vineyard too, and whatever is right I will give you." So they went. Going out again about the sixth hour and the ninth hour, he did the same. And about the eleventh hour he went out and found others standing; and he said to them, "Why do you stand here idle all day?" They said to him, "Because no one has hired us." He said to them, "You go into the vineyard too." And when evening came, the owner of the vineyard said to his steward, "Call the laborers and pay them their wages, beginning with the last, up to the first." And when those hired about the eleventh hour came, each of them received a denarius. Now when the first came, they thought they would receive more; but each of them also received a denarius. And on receiving it they grumbled at the householder, saying, "These last worked only one hour, and you have made them equal to us who have borne the burden of the day and the scorching heat." But he replied to one of them, "Friend, I am doing you no wrong; ... Take what belongs to you, and go; I choose to give to this last as I give to you. Am I not allowed to do what I choose with what belongs to me?"[9]

One main message of this parable—the claim of an absolute right to private property—is irrelevant for our purposes. But, even if incidentally, the parable makes an important point for us. Exclusionary equality—a full day's pay only for a full day's work—presents at least as good a case as its inclusionary alternative. Why indeed (on a literal reading) should the eleventh-hour workers be lumped with those who have sweated all day?[10]

The difference between exclusionary and inclusionary claims has two aspects of political and moral significance. First, from an inclusionary viewpoint, exclusionary equalities will generally appear as *in*equalities; conversely, all manner of inequalities can be presented as exclusionary equalities. In Berlin's cake-cutting story, the host might

dine alone and eat the whole cake himself; or he might invite an inti-
mate with whom to share it equally; and so on. Each choice appears
inegalitarian once one compares it to a longer guest-list, but each appears egalitarian in isolation. A better example is provided by South
Africa. By inclusionary standards, as a single national society, it operates according to one of the most repressive and draconian systems of
inequality in existence. If, as the Pretoria government would have it,
we think only about a long series of exclusionary equalities (for example, in the "Republic" itself, in Transkei, in the other "homelands"), and forget about the fully inclusionary view, then the picture
is altered radically. Whether made in good faith or not, this claim is a
primary justification for the dogma of separate development pro-
pounded by the white elite of that society.[11]

Extending the point, equalities within whole nations—the United
States, West Germany, Chad, or Bangladesh—may correspond to
radical inequalities on a world-inclusive basis.[12] The moral dilemma
implied here should, and often does, alarm the proponent of equality
within even the largest of national societies: Why, exactly, are we to
pursue equality only to the Mexican (or Polish) border?

The other main point is that inclusionary equality implies centralization of power for its achievement. In decentralized systems, no
agency can be held responsible for inclusionary equalities. In the limiting case, world-inclusive equalities cannot be achieved partly because there is no central power or authority against which such claims
may be lodged. Less grandly, much of the demand for federal centralization in the United States since the New Deal has been based on the
elementary insight that nationally inclusive equalities—in medical
care, welfare, civil liberties for minorities—can be effected only
through national authority. And part of the difficulty underlying
cases like *Bakke* is that decentralized units such as single universities
attempt to achieve equalities far more inclusive than their authority
(for example, to admit their own students) extends.[13] In general, a
main contradiction for liberal egalitarians is the contradiction between a commitment to decentralized government on the one hand
and to inclusive equalities on the other.

Combining both points—inclusionary equalities seeming to be
more equal, and inclusionary equality demanding centralization—
presents serious philosophical and practical problems. The moral and
ideological bases of egalitarianism do not naturally fit the borders of
governments. Moral argument is universal in form; governments are

not. Moral egalitarianism recognizes no obvious difference between an American and a Mexican citizen; a government sees no practicable similarity between its citizens and the rest of the world. Equalities that were radically inclusive in the nineteenth century—extending to all of a government's subjects—appear very narrow indeed by universal morals. If we are arguing on a high moral footing and the subject of equality is mankind, then "All bona fide citizens of state X have a God-given right to life, liberty, and the pursuit of happiness" sounds silly. Yet, given the existing arrangement of governments, very little can be realistically asserted for any larger group in the name of equality.

A related point governs the problem of equality in market economies. Consider the demand for equalization of incomes within a single firm which must compete against other firms for labor, capital, and buyers. Such a firm faces an obvious dilemma: if it makes wages equal at the expense of its most skillful employees, these may flee to another firm. If, on the other hand, equality is accomplished by bringing marginal workers up to the level of more skillful employees, it may no longer be possible to compete for buyers or capital against efficiently inegalitarian firms. This point provides an almost ineluctable restraint against equality in unregulated market systems.[14]

Compare equality with a less purely relational notion such as minimal welfare. Suppose we had several states or firms and some general idea of minimal welfare (for example, an annual income of at least $1,000). We could pursue this goal separately within each such jurisdiction, and when all had managed this, we could conclude that the required minimum had been reached by everyone, without regard to nationality or employer. The result is *additive* and can be achieved by attending separately to individual communities. There will, of course, be a certain relativity to what counts as minimal welfare in Iran and in Sweden, but the concept still admits of a fixed standard. In contrast, equality is a purely *relational* concept. It is not additive and cannot be accomplished by separate attention to national communities or any other subdivisions of the world. If we established rough equality among relatively wealthy European states—Denmark, Germany, France—and among states less well off—Greece, Spain—we would not have achieved equality for Europe as a whole. This nonadditive property of equality implies that once we have chosen a large class of proper equals, then only equally large governments can effect the transformation in question. In the United States this has, since the New Deal, led to a concentration of some distributive powers in Washington, since equality within Mississippi and (separately) within Connecticut implies nothing about equalization in the country at large.[15] Even within single states there are powerful movements to detach important distributive activities from local government (notably school finance)[16] and concentrate them in larger units to achieve a more inclusive equality.

The distinction between exclusive and inclusive classes is entirely relative. A given class can be exclusive in relation to one alternative and inclusive in relation to another. The class of all men is inclusive when compared to the class of all propertied men, yet exclusive when compared with the class of all persons. The distinction must, therefore, always be rooted in a context, never in a single detached notion of equality. Thus, say, "equality of X for all adult Americans" cannot be classified as inclusionary or as exclusionary by itself; only the relevant alternatives make such a classification meaningful.

Notice that the concepts of inclusivity and exclusivity in no way alter the interior structure of individual-regarding equality. The boundaries of such a class may be changed, but the basic structure remains simple.[17]

2.1.3   The Subject Class as Policy Problem

We have, for the most part, been taking the boundaries of subject classes where we found them in order to analyze the simple individual-regarding structure of the equality relation among their members. Substantively defining the class of equals can, however, present a major stumbling block (or stepping stone) in the transition from equality as an abstract concept to practical reality. Defining a subject class—that is, determining a relation of equality and setting its bounds—is frequently the central problem in formulating a wide variety of public policies.

The centrality of this issue is abundantly clear when equality itself is the policy concern. The boundaries of the subject class have been historically a frequent target of demands for equality, taking the form of demands for inclusion in a class of equals. In the evolution of American public policy, there has been a marked trend toward more inclusive subject classes in response to demands for the rectification of historical inequalities resulting from exclusionary practices. Hence, women long ago established their voting rights; blacks gained access to public accommodations; and more recently the handicapped, the elderly, and, in some government jurisdictions, homosexuals have established claims to equal treatment in employment practices. This is not to say that full inclusion in the target class has been reached by any or all of these groups. It *is* to say that demands for equality have often hinged on the issue of inclusion in a class that is the subject of a certain public (or private) policy.[18]

Other policy issues not concerned with equality per se may also turn on the problem of defining a simple subject class of equals, and, more particularly, of determining how inclusive the class should be. In child custody disputes, should men and women be treated as equals within a simple subject class "parents"? What should be counted as a family unit, given the increased diversity of legal and nonlegal relationships between adults? Although the boundaries of the simple class of "cities" (communities of ten thousand?) may seem to be a petty statistical dispute, it has major consequences in the allocation of government aid.

There is a further complexity in recent policy discourse concerning the problem of inclusion and the definition of subject classes. Even when the *definition* of the class is simple and straightforward, the *identification* of its members may pose significant difficulties. An extreme and bizarre example of the problem of subject identification was presented by the case of Dr. Renee Richards who, after a sex change operation, sought entry as a female player in professional tennis tournaments. Difficulties in subject identification are not always this exotic. Consider the mandatory retirement policy, whose purpose is to require workers to retire when they have reached old age. But does old age begin at sixty-five, sixty-eight, seventy, seventy-five? If the aging process varies among individuals, the class of "workers who have reached old age" cannot be identified by chronological age alone, and any retirement policy that uses such a criterion to identify the members of its subject class will have chronological but not qualitative equals in its class. This problem of subject identification, along with the prior problem of subject class definition, is a tricky step in the translation of equality from a simple abstraction into complex reality.

2.2 Segments and Blocs

Instead of drawing the boundary *around* a class of equals, we might draw a line *within* it. Thus, if the original class of equals were "all

American citizens," we might cleave this into blacks and nonblacks, employed and unemployed, or homosexuals and heterosexuals. Or we might divide the "members" of IBM into categories such as stockholders, executives, union members, and so on. Or Plato might have divided (did indeed divide) the citizenry of his utopian city into classes based on moral quality. By drawing internal distinctions like these, we destroy the simple individual-regarding structure just discussed, and start down a path toward two basic alternative structures.

Recall our story about major league baseball (Section 1.3.2). At no point in that story is there any question of simple individual-regarding equality. It does not suggest that salaries in the major leagues (much less in the American economy) are or should be equal. The issues instead center upon subdivisions among baseball players, based on race, position, and quality of play. Neither does it suggest that there ought to be simple equality *within* the resulting blocs—for example, that Willie Mays should have been paid the same as a rookie black outfielder, or that Carl Yastrzemski should have been paid no more than, say, Bucky Dent. Neither will the real structure of the baseball problem be understood by saying merely that it amounts to a question about a series of smaller classes of equals, such as outfielders batting around .280, pitchers with a 10-5 win-loss ratio, and so on. The story actually turns on two structural alternatives to simple individual-regarding equality, which we call *segmental* and *bloc-regarding*.

Imagine a single class of equals, S, and then divide it into two or more subclasses, X and not-X (for example, white and nonwhite).[19] Now, should we require equality *within* or *between* these subclasses? If we require equality within subclasses, we create a segmental subject structure; if we require equality between subclasses, we create a bloc-regarding subject structure. Each differs importantly from the simple structure with which we began, and the two differ importantly from one another.

2.2.1 Segmental Subjects of Equality

A segmental subject structure is defined by two features: (1) subjects of equality are divided into two or more mutually exclusive subclasses, and (2) pair-by-pair equality is required within, and not between, these subclasses. A segmental structure differs from a simple individual-regarding one in not being "simple"—that is, in not simply defining one class of equals and leaving it undivided. It is, however, very like a simple structure in re-

Table 1. Segmental subjects of equality.

Class S	
Subclass X	Subclass Y
A	D
B	E
C	F

maining individual-regarding; it focuses on pairwise equality inside each segment, just as a simple structure focuses on pairwise equality within its only class. In Table 1, segmental equality requires equality among pairs AB, AC, and BC on the one hand, and among pairs DE, DF, and EF on the other hand. It does not require, and in general we would not expect, equality among pairs (for example, AF) that belong to different subclasses. If the overall class S remains fixed, segmentation diminishes simple equality, because some relations that would have been equalities now need not be so.

Indeed, a major example of segmentation is provided by hierarchical systems of power and authority, in which each tier is explicitly subordinated to the tier above, but is equal within its membership.[20] The military example is simplest: just as a five-star general outranks a lieutenant colonel who in turn outranks a major, there is at least formal equality among five-star generals, among lieutenant colonels, among majors, and so on.

It may even be that segmental equality is required by all systematic forms of inequality. Treating people in a systematically unequal way requires first that they be divided into subclasses, and then that the members of each subclass be treated "equally unequally," hence made equal with each other while remaining unequal with their superiors and inferiors. The segments of equality arise, in other words, to systematize inequality. The law of slavery, dividing freeman from slave, must invest all freemen equally with the status and advantages of freedom, and must invest all slaves with the status and disadvantages of slavery. There may be inequalities within each of the two status categories, but they will not derive from *this* phenomenon.[21] Contemporary "credentialing" systems—that is, systems of mobility based on degrees, certificates, and examinations—are similar structures. These badges and tickets derive their systematic force from their uniformity, from the more or less homogeneous advantages that they confer upon their holders and that distinguish holders from those with greater or lesser credentials.[22] Only by bestowing more or less uniform advantages do these insignia work as the basis for systematic inequality.

Note that systems appearing to provide very broad and simple equality may *mask* actual patterns of segmentation. Thus, on a Marxian analysis, the legal system of capitalism offers the appearance of universal rights to everyone. All are entitled to sell their property and to buy the property of others, to offer their labor as a commodity for sale and to buy this precious commodity from others. Whereas medieval society publicly and forthrightly stated the line of segmentation between lord and serf,[23] capitalism masks an analogous division between bourgeois and proletarian with the appearance of universal equality. The rights *are* equal; the inequality is just a question of having the property, the actual and potential means of production, to buy labor rather than to have one's own labor bought.[24]

Just about any systematic division of labor in society creates a ground for segmentalism. In the simple case of baseball, positions on the field are bases for one form of segmental equality—equality among shortstops, among catchers, and so on.[25] In larger economies occupational positions are important determinants of income and prestige, so that these benefits are more evenly distributed within a given occupation than, on average, between occupations. Indeed, class inequality in late-industrial societies may be based on occupational lines rather than classical Marxian ones, thus following function in production, rather than control over the means of production.[26]

Similarly, the provision of many public services is organized on a principle of segmental equality, where individuals are fragmented into statistically segmented subunits by government programs that aid categories of people defined by age, sex, family status, nature of employment (or unemployment), military service, health, geographic location, and the like. Any two individuals may find that they receive quite different government aid streams, depending on their particular combination of such demographic characteristics. Tax burdens are also distributed on a basis of segmental equality. The existing system of income taxation sorts individual taxpayers into a series of tax categories based on factors like number of dependents, level of medical expenses, and mortgage interest deductions, and then reassembles the pieces and slots the taxpayer into the appropriate adjusted gross income tax bracket along with her peers.

Note that the results of programs like these, which emphasize

equality within segmental structures, sometimes resemble simple individual-regarding equality between two sorts of people with very different tastes and needs. Thus, to divide medical patients by their diseases, and then to give each disease-segment the treatment it most
needs, may approximate an overall equality for the total group of
sufferers. And, while the construction of short drinking fountains for
grade schools and tall ones for colleges may have the appearance of
segmental structure (discriminating between children and adults), it
may be a subtle form of simple individual-regarding equality: it depends on one's understanding of the value-structure implicit in the
problem.[27]

2.2.2   Bloc-Regarding Equalities

Although there is a radical difference of structure between simple and
segmental equality, both are individual-regarding: they are alike in
always requiring that someone be someone else's equal. But these
structures do not exhaust the possibilities. Whereas segmental structures demand equality *within* subclasses, bloc-regarding (or, for variety, "bloc-equal") structures demand equality *between* subclasses. Formally, *bloc-equal structures are defined by two features: (1) the subjects of
equality are divided into two or more subclasses, and (2) equality is required between subclasses (blocs) and not within them.* The first desideratum distinguishes bloc-equal structures from simple ones, and the second distinguishes bloc-equal structures from segmental ones.

A classic example of bloc-equal structure is the majority opinion
in the American Constitutional law case *Plessy* v. *Ferguson* (1896). The
case was a test of Louisiana's "Jim Crow" law requiring that railways
"provide equal but separate accommodations for white, and colored,
races."[28] Setting aside questions of racism and good faith, notice the
kind of equality embraced by the court's majority which upheld the
Louisiana statute. The overall quality of black ("colored") and white
accommodations must be equal. No particular individual, black or
white, need be accommodated equally to any other, but the two
blocs, each taken collectively, are to be so treated. This is a classic
bloc-equal structure, and it stands in diametrical opposition to the
dissenting opinion of Justice John Harlan, for whom the Constitution
is "color blind" and thus unable to define racial blocs: "[It] neither
knows nor tolerates classes among citizens . . . The law regards man as

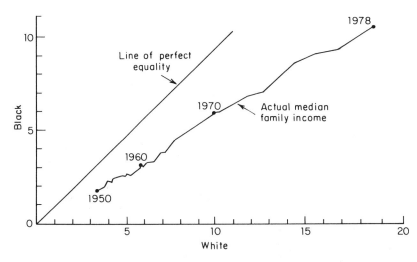

Figure 1. Median family income by race of head, 1950–1978, in thousands of current dollars. (*Source:* Dorn, *Rules and Racial Equality*, p. 33; and U.S. Department of Commerce, Bureau of the Census, *Current Population Reports*, P-60, no. 120 [November 1979], table 1.)

man and takes no account of his color."[29] Harlan was plainly arguing for simple, individual-regarding equality.

Next, consider the figures and tables below, all of which suggest familiar American patterns of inequality (nurtured in part by the heritage of *Plessy*). Figure 1 plots the relationship between black and white median incomes (per household) for the period 1950–78. Figure 2 plots unemployment rates by race from 1960 to 1979. Despite worthwhile nuances of interpretation, both clearly indicate that Gunnar Myrdal's "American dilemma"[30] persists: being black roughly doubles the rate of unemployment, and costs something over $5,000 per annum in median income (an expensive luxury, blackness).[31] Table 2 compares the median income of women to that of men at approximate five-year intervals from 1955 to 1978. The shocking feature here is the *diminishing* relative income of women over this period: with the exception of the last, each datum is a little worse than the one before. Table 3 presents a similarly dismal progression: as educational attainments increase, the "sex gap" increases—that is,

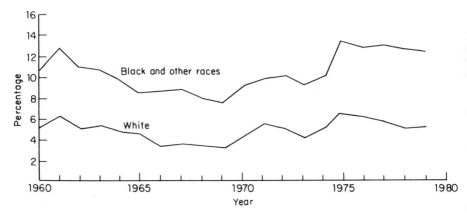

Figure 2. Unemployment rates, 1960–1979. (*Source:* Dorn, *Rules and Racial Equality,* p. 43; and U.S. Department of Labor, Bureau of Labor Statistics, "Employment and Earnings," vol. 27, no. 5 [May 1980], chart 11.)

the difference between medians grows from less than $3,000 for minimal education to almost $7,000 for college degree holders.

Let us assume (quite safely) that these data are meant to document some unmet requirements of equality. Then—to see why we have a new underlying structure to reckon with—let us ask what sort of equalities it would take to satisfy these demands. Roughly, they are: (1) black incomes being on average (or on median) equal with

Table 2. Median income for women as a percentage of median income for men, 1955–1974.

Year	Percent
1955	64
1960	61
1965	60
1970	59
1974	57
1978	59

Source: Data for 1955–1974 are from U.S. Department of Labor, Women's Bureau, *The Earnings Gap between Women and Men,* p. 6, cited in Boles, *The Politics of the Equal Rights Amendment,* p. 49. Data for 1978 are from David E. Rosenbaum, "Working Women Still Seek Man-Sized Wages," *New York Times,* July 27, 1980, sect. 4, p. E3.

Table 3. Median income for male and female workers, by education, 1974.

Educational level	Women's median wage	Men's median wage	Difference
Less than eight years elementary school	$5,002	$ 7,912	$2,890
Eight years elementary school	5,606	9,891	4,285
Four years high school	7,150	12,642	5,492
Four years college	9,523	16,240	6,717

Source: U.S. Department of Labor, Women's Bureau, *The Earnings Gap between Women and Men,* p. 10, cited in Boles, *The Politics of the Equal Rights Amendment,* p. 48.

white incomes, (2) black unemployment rates being equal with white ones, (3) women's incomes being on average (or on median) equal with men's incomes, (4) women's educations bringing on average (or on median) the same economic advantages as men's educations. The essential point is this: *the full and complete achievement of these equalities would not imply the fulfillment of any simple (or segmental) equality.* Black and white median incomes, for example, might be precisely equal, yet there could be tremendous inequality among blacks, among whites, and within the society as a whole. The same point holds for all four examples, and for all other examples of bloc-regarding equality, whether by race, sex, age, native tongue, or sexual preference, and whether aimed at the distribution of income, power, prestige, or leisure. Bloc-regarding equality asks for something very different from individual-regarding simple and segmental equalities.

The extent of this difference can hardly be exaggerated. Imagine an island society with ten members who live in relative equality. Using bananas per day as a numeraire, the initial distribution is this: sixty apiece for five persons, and forty apiece for five other persons. It turns out, sadly, that the five advantaged persons are all women, and the five disadvantaged persons are all men. Now notice, before we get around to reform, that there is perfect segmental equality within each gender, and that the inclusive, simple equality covering all ten individuals is violated, but not very violently (the biggest gap is twenty bananas). Now a men's liberationist demands that the median attained by the two blocs be made equal, and your authors go around redistributing bananas from person to person until the reform is effected, as shown in column 4 of Table 4. Note that we have been

Table 4. Equality among members of an island society (in bananas per day).

Person	Sex	Pre-reform	Post-reform
A	Female	60	105
B	Female	60	95
C	Female	60	50
D	Female	60	40
E	Female	60	10
F	Male	40	60
G	Male	40	55
H	Male	40	50
I	Male	40	20
J	Male	40	15

thrifty, wasting not a single fruit (five hundred in all, before and after redistribution). We have also *fully* satisfied the bloc-regarding equality in question: the median income for women (in the person of C) is fifty, and the median for men (in the person of H) is also exactly fifty bananas. Sexual inequality has been perfectly rectified. But notice that: (1) inequality among women, formerly nonexistent, is now very serious; (2) inequality among men, formerly nonexistent, is now very serious; (3) overall inequality in the whole population of ten, formerly constrained between narrow limits at top (sixty) and bottom (forty) now spreads much farther (from ten to one hundred five units); (4) not one banana has been transferred from women to men; all transfers have occurred within the two sexual blocs.

Point 4 speaks to an important detail—the problem of measuring central tendencies—but this is not our main point.[32] What concerns us here is the strict independence between bloc-regarding equality and the two other main forms discussed in this chapter. Points 1 and 2 indicate that a reform fully satisfying a demand for bloc-equality can destroy segmental equality. And point 3 shows how the resolution of this same demand for bloc-equality can diminish simple equality in the same population. It would be wrong to say that all policies answering to the demand for bloc-regarding equality will work against these other equalities. We simply wish to show that this is a logical possibility, which means that bloc-regarding equality is in no sense *equivalent* to the other forms of equality already introduced.

Finally, note a special difficulty raised by bloc-regarding equality in a society like the United States—one with many simple inequali-

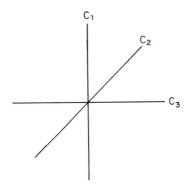

Figure 3. Pinwheel effect of bloc-regarding equality.

ties and many markers that could be bases of bloc formation. What we may call the "pinwheel effect" then leads to the sort of trouble that underlies affirmative action, *Bakke,* and *DeFunis.*[33] Suppose we have a number of cross-cutting cleavages, C_1, C_2, C_3, and so forth. These might designate class, race, sex, religion, age cohort, or sexual preference. We satisfy a bloc-regarding claim based on C_1 so that inequalities fall equally on both sides of the vertical line, C_1 (see Figure 3). But someone else sees C_2 as the primary cleavage, demanding equality along that line, and yet another party sees C_3 as the basic line along which equalization must occur.[34] In carrying out our C_1 plan, we obviously may fail to satisfy the other two demands, and may actually exacerbate the inequalities that they seek to remove. Thus, if B and W mark races, while M and F mark sexes, a racial emancipation of the fullest proportions might look like that shown in Table 5.

At least in logic, then, bloc-equality by race could wreck bloc-equality by sex. More probably, one equality would merely fail to promote the other.[35] If enough cleavages are invoked, and crosscut

Table 5. Results of full bloc-equality by race.

	Least advantaged					Most advantaged				
Status quo	M	F	M	F	M	F	M	F	M	F
	B	B	B	B	B	W	W	W	W	W
Emancipatory result	F	F	F	F	F	M	M	M	M	M
	W	B	W	B	W	B	W	B	W	B

one another, *only simple equality can be a joint solution for all the would-be bloc-equalities.* If there are no simple *in*equalities, then there can be no inequality of incidence by race, sex, sexual preference, religion, age, and so on. Where simple inequalities remain, it is always possible to identify some criterion as a basis for further bloc-equalization.[36]

2.3   Two Roads to Emancipation

Nothing as complex as the question "Equality for whom?" can lead to one answer, yet we suggest that a particular configuration of choices may be especially important.

Suppose one begins with an era of systematic inequality based upon conspicuous and fairly permanent markers, such as race, sex, and language. One can (and society does) use these markers to tell "winners" from "losers." Presumably, this system of inequality will also (for the reasons given in Section 2.2.1) approximate segmental equality: losers will be in one class and winners in another. (Things will, of course, actually be much more complicated, but we are describing an ideal type in order to accentuate a central issue.) Many actual historical systems correspond roughly to this idealization, including the United States before the Civil War, South Africa today (homelands notwithstanding), perhaps the slave systems of ancient Greece, and some schemes of male domination within families. The class structure of industrial capitalism may also bear more than a metaphorical resemblance to this model, even if one must resort to subtleties of accent or dress to distinguish winners from losers.

2.3.1   Rotating Winners and Losers

Now imagine that an emancipatory movement arises in the disadvantaged bloc and begins to gain leverage over this system—leverage enough to alter it in some relevant ways. Such a movement will then face a choice (which may or may not be understood) between two divergent roads toward emancipation. One sets foot upon the first by taking the existence of some advantaged class, hence also of a disadvantaged class, as given. In that case the reform movement will *aim merely to diminish the unfavorable incidence of the old inequalities upon those who bear the stigmata of former losers.* It will, to alter a phrase from the era of Vietnam, change the colors of the slaves. This is bloc-regarding egalitarianism, and its eventual end is a *rotation* of simple inequalities, so that fewer victims are members of the once disadvantaged bloc—defined by race, sex, language group—and so that more and more victims are drawn from the formerly advantaged bloc.

We might begin with a distribution of persons in classes so that Bloc X constitutes an advantaged class and Bloc Y constitutes a disadvantaged class. Bloc-equal egalitarianism would transfer persons in Bloc X into the disadvantaged class through downward mobility for some X's, while elevating some persons from Bloc Y into the advantaged class. This would not necessarily change the extent of inequality between classes or the distribution of persons among classes—that is, the total population of the advantaged class and of the disadvantaged class could remain fixed. One would, in effect, redistribute the incidence of simple class-based inequality without affecting its extent.

2.3.2   Simple Equality of Subjects

The other road to emancipating the disadvantaged bloc is begun by supposing that the underlying inequalities can *themselves* be overturned. One need not change the composition of an underclass if no such class is to exist. This is the road to simple inclusive[37] individual-regarding equality. It is not that a proper share of former underlings, or children of underlings, will be moved up to an advantaged class, but that this class will itself be dissolved. This is apparently the path of radical egalitarianism, though we will see that it is neither as unambiguous nor as uncompromisable as it first appears.

2.3.3   The Consequences of Emancipation

Even if we take the path of simple equalization, we do not know what the precise social consequences will be for the formerly advantaged and disadvantaged. All individuals could be raised to the level previously enjoyed by the advantaged—or, more likely, the level of the rich could be lowered, the level of the poor raised, and a uniform level established somewhere between the previously existing extremes. Or everyone could end up at a level below that previously enjoyed by either the rich or the poor.

To gauge the practical consequences of the other road to emancipation—the rotating of winners and losers—the structure, scale, and range of the goods being reallocated must be taken into account. Rotation of women into previously all-male positions has different consequences for emancipation when the position is corporate president rather than prison guard. Rotating winners and losers through school desegregation has a different emancipatory impact when the range is restricted to a single school district or extended to all schools nation-wide.[38]

But even with the greatest conceivable range and scope of alloca-tion, two major sticking points remain. First, emancipating one group does nothing for another—allowing some blacks to enter the ranks of the winners does not touch the status of women, except as they hap-pen to be women as well as black. Second, solving even a multitude of emancipatory problems (of women, blacks, the elderly, the handi-capped, religious groups, and so on) will still leave many inequalities. Emancipation by rotation is a zero-sum transaction; for every winner there is a loser. Emancipation by rotation does not change the social structure in which some win and some lose—it merely changes the names of the winners. Bloc-equality does not address the claims of simple equality.

There is, however, a case in which bloc-equality does achieve simple equality. The distribution of two goods may be linked in such a way that equalizing the first across blocs equalizes the second on a simple, individual-regarding basis. The sense of racial superiority and inferiority that is fostered by racial bloc-inequalities in income, for example, might be entirely eliminated by bloc-equalization of in-come. Inequalities in income remain, but are no longer distributed unequally between racial blocs. Thus the linked good, pride of race, becomes equally distributed on a simple, individual-regarding basis throughout the society.

2.4   Implications for Public Policy

In spite of the sharp analytical differences between simple, segmental, and bloc-regarding equalities, these are often conflated and com-mingled in actual practice and policy. Subject classifications vary from one policy to another: the subject in some policies is simple, as in the case of draft registration; sometimes segmental, as in the case of emergency aid programs for home heating expenses; and sometimes bloc-regarding, as in affirmative action programs. Sometimes two structurally distinct subjects are combined, as in revenue sharing leg-islation that includes a concern both for segmental equality (among different-sized jurisdictions) and for bloc-regarding equality (in the treatment of minorities and other low-income groups).

Let us turn now to the important special case of equality in American public education.

2.4.1   Equal Education for Whom?

An early equality doctrine in education invoked a simple individual-regarding equality—namely, free public education for all American children.[39] Later, there were various moves toward segmental equality, such as the creation of vocational schools designed for the "terminal student" not headed for higher education, the development of tracking systems and programs for the handicapped and, more recently, special programs for the gifted (the so-called Excellence Movement).

A fundamental departure from simple individual-regarding equality, which has generated most of the confusion and debate in educational policy, came with the separate-but-equal doctrine originating in *Plessy* v. *Ferguson*.[40] The structure of the Supreme Court's decision in this case was plainly bloc-regarding, the test of equality being whether the facilities provided for blacks as a group were equal in quality to those provided for whites. In *Brown* v. *Board of Education*[41] the Court overturned *Plessy,* finding that *separate facilities* could not provide *equal education* for blacks and whites, but nonetheless persisting in the application of a bloc-regarding test of equality.

Since *Brown,* the bloc-regarding principle of equality has been widely applied. Schools have been desegregated in the face of *de jure* segregation; busing programs have been implemented in the case of *de facto* segregation; affirmative action plans have been established in government, education, and industry; and some institutions of higher education have implemented admission policies that involve numerical quotas for blacks and other minorities.

This last application of the bloc-regarding principle came under attack in Bakke's complaint against the Medical School of the University of California at Davis.[42] Whatever clarity and consistency may have existed in the definition of the subject of educational equality since *Brown,* it was thrown into disarray with the *Bakke* decision. That decision outlaws numerical quotas for minority admissions, which constitute a strong application of the bloc-regarding principle.

But the decision allows some consideration of racial identification as a factor in admissions, which reconstitutes the bloc-regarding principle in weaker form.

The Court's way out of the contradiction inherent in its simultaneous acceptance and rejection of a bloc-regarding principle is the appeal by Justice Lewis Powell to the doctrine of "diversity"—the admission of students who "exhibit qualities more likely to promote beneficial educational pluralism."[43] It is difficult to find concrete meaning in the doctrine of diversity, and we are not the first to point out its oddities, ambiguities, and perversities.[44] Following the analysis of this chapter, it can be given three different interpretations, conforming to each of the three structurally distinct subjects in our grammar of equality. First, the doctrine of diversity may be read as requiring a more inclusive simple individual-regarding subject class. That is, in an all-white school, or an all-male school, or in a college of students all under the age of twenty-four, the simple subject class of "students" could be redefined so as to include blacks, women, or older students, thereby diversifying the student population. On a second construction, diversity might entail a form of segmental equality. This argument would run as follows: education is improved when the student body is a mixture of men and women, blacks and whites, city dwellers and farmers, athletes and poets. But because the *Bakke* decision shuns specification of the numerical proportion of any particular group in the class, its operative force would be segmental equality. That is, treat athletes equally, alumni children equally, foreign students equally, minority applicants equally, within each segmental pool of roughly similar applicants. Finally, diversity may be interpreted as a weak construction of bloc-regarding equality—weak because diversity casts so wide a net and the prescriptions for providing equality for diverse blocs are so tentative. All sorts of blocs must be considered: racial, sexual, geographic, blocs based on different academic proclivities, foreign blocs, and so forth, all of which fit into our pinwheel of bloc classification described above. Attention to one bloc classification may conflict with attention to another, and within this analytic framework there is no way to determine the priority of attention to be given to one bloc or another, except as diversity dictates.

What, then, does the diversity doctrine accomplish in the face of the specific challenge to a program of bloc-regarding racial equality at U.C. Davis Medical School? It may provide a useful camouflage, permitting consideration of many different blocs (playwrights, Alaskans, Polish Americans, older students) while in reality opening a wedge to justify a bloc-regarding principle of *racial* equality. On the other hand, diversity may be a subtle and unintended move toward simple individual-regarding equality. If we proliferate enough blocs for consideration in admissions, the only practicable policy would be simple individual-regarding equality, whereby all applicants are evaluated by the same standard. Or it may be an equally unintended move to vitiate any drive toward greater equality of any kind: a doctrine that means everything may mean nothing.

2.5 Summary

Without summarizing the whole of this chapter, we shall repeat and collect the main points of structural definition:

Simple individual-regarding equality. A claim of equality for one class of equals, each to be the equal of every other.

Inclusionary equality. A claim of equality X is inclusive by comparison with a claim Y if X adds some individuals to Y's class of equals while subtracting none from it.

Exclusive equality. A claim of equality Y is exclusive by comparison with a claim X if Y subtracts some individuals from X's class of equals while adding none to it.

Segmental equality. A claim of equality for two or more classes of equals, equality being required within each class and not between classes.

Bloc-regarding equality. A claim of equality for two or more subject classes, equality being required between these classes (blocs) and not within them.

The most fundamental divergence among subjects concerns the first, fourth, and fifth of these types. The essential differences among

Table 6. Essential differences among three types of equality.

	Simple individual-regarding	Segmental	Bloc-regarding
How many classes?	1	≥ 2	≥ 2
Equality within or between classes?	Within	Within	Between

these are shown in Table 6. The "subject grammar" responds to only one range of problems and thus models only one distinction among equalities: we might agree completely in answering the question "Equality for whom?" and yet disagree profoundly on the other features of that equality.

3 The Domain of Equality

IN OUR IMAGINARY Society E of Chapter 1, perhaps the most bizarre feature was this: all things of value in Society E are allocated *once, and for all time*—as if everything were gathered in a single heap one day and divided into inalienable lots for all time by a single decision. This is a political economy without history or future, and without the slightest failure of centralization. As a result, we confront *one* allocative choice, confined to a single thin slice of time. The question "Equal what?" is always foreclosed by the answer, "Equal everything." One would, for simple subjects, simply give each subject one-nth share of every good. One would, for segmental subjects, make sure each good was equally divided within each segment. One would, for bloc-equal subjects, produce an overall bloc-to-bloc equality in dividing each good.

This chapter is about circumstances in which the question "Equal what?" is more complex. In such cases, equal shares in a bottle of whiskey are distinguished from equal shares in the barrel whence it springs; equal tax rates on income are distinguished from tax rates that make incomes equal.

Answers to the question "Equal what?" refer to *domains of equality*—that is, to the *classes of things that are to be allocated equally*. Usually, natural language terms of kind (corn, whiskey, jobs), of quantity (gallons, bushels, dozens), of special reference (this, that, those), and of time (this year's, June's) are used to sketch out the boundaries for any given domain of equality. These, of course, lead to widely different classes of goods marked out for allocation and thus to wide variation of literal content. But here we are interested in structure, not topic. Thus, we may distinguish our analysis of domain structures from a direct classification of topics. One author, for instance, suggests that "contemporary political debate recognizes four types of equality: political, legal, social, and economic."[1] This is a way of answering the "Equal what?" question: equal political rights or powers, equal legal standing or advantage, equal social status, equal incomes, and so on. It is, however, a topical or literal answer, not a structural one. The structural patterns mapped by a grammar for the domain of equality are logically and phenomenologically independent of topical reference.

By reducing all allocative phenomena to a single event, Society E represses two basic facets of the question "Equal what?" These are: (1) broad versus narrow domains, and (2) global versus marginal versus straightforward domains. Most of this chapter deals with these two dimensions. Society E also hides a third phenomenon, in which allocation in one domain causally influences allocation in another domain (a point that we take up in the latter part of this chapter and extend in chapter 4).

3.1   Breadth versus Narrowness

Just as the subject of equality may be either inclusive or exclusive, its domain may be broad or narrow. Let us compare some arbitrary domain I with an arbitrary domain II. Domain I is broad in relation to II if, first, everything in II is also in I, and, second, some of the things in I are in II.[2] This is a strict definition, and thus defines a limiting case; it may be approximated by less rigorous differentiations that permit less brittle comparisons. Under the strict definition, domain I is broad in relation to domain II where, say,

I = 100 tons of gold and 1 peanut;
II = 100 tons of gold.

And on this same strict definition, we have no broad-narrow relation in the following case:

I = 100 tons of gold;
II = 1 peanut.

Since there is no strict inclusion relationship, we cannot strictly consider the former broader than the latter. But this second comparison suggests a more flexible, and therefore more useful, interpretation for the broad-narrow comparison. If two domains can be placed on some single scale of value upon which the affected parties agree, and domain I is agreed to contain a greater total value than domain II, we may consider it broader in this extended sense. The scale of value might be defined in utilities, or in labor equivalents, or simply in cash.[3]

This distinction is neither beautiful nor elegant, but it is relevant and important. It draws attention to an old and persistent difficulty which must be faced by all proponents of equality. A hint of this difficulty is found in the following passage from John Locke's *Second Treatise of Government:*

> Though I have said above . . . *That all Men by Nature are equal,* I cannot be supposed to understand all sorts of *Equality: Age* or *Virtue* may give Men a just *Precedency: Excellency of Parts and Merit* may place others above the Common Level: *Birth* may subject some, and *Alliance* or *Benefits* others, to pay an Observance to those to whom Nature, Gratitude or other Respects may have made it due; and yet all this consists with the *Equality,* which all Men are in, in respect of Jurisdiction or Domain one over another, which was the *Equality* I there spoke of, as proper to the Business in hand, being that *equal Right* that every Man hath, *to his Natural Freedom,* without being subjected to the Will or Authority of any other man.[4]

Here is the age-old difficulty: if *this* is to be divided equally, why *only* this? If, as Locke advocates, rights before the state are equal, why not, as Locke fears, also divide everything else on that same principle? If cakes at tea are to be cut equally, why not also serve up equal shares of the host's silverware? If votes are to be equal, why should other aspects of life in democratic society not follow that same pattern of distribution? If schools are to be equally open to all, why not hospitals and colleges and golf courses? When, and why, should society stop by distributing only some things equally?[5]

This is not only an important practical question, and thus a source of grammatical variation in applying equality to practice, but it is also an important patterning criterion among ideologies. Market liberals (corresponding roughly to American "conservatives") are not so much *anti*egalitarian as they are *narrowly* egalitarian. Milton Friedman, Murray Rothbard, and Robert Nozick[6] do not oppose equality, for the very heart of their appeal is a universal—that is, equal—distribution of formal property rights and certain civil and political rights. But they oppose the *broadening* of equality beyond the narrow limits of this domain. Leftward ideologies, no matter how various in other respects, all seek to broaden the domain to which equality is to be applied. All forms of Marxian thought resist narrow equality.[7]

Marx and his successors argue that narrow equality leaves the weak at the mercy of the strong, and thus lets the strong use a form of equality to cover and justify inequality of accumulation and exploitation.[8] It is thus, we think, quite wrong to construe this central ideological conflict as pitting "liberty" against "equality." Rather, it is "equal liberty" against "equal life in society," or "equality in the narrow" against "equality in the broad." This is perhaps too simple, but it comes much closer to the actual line of division.[9]

The same patterning shows up frequently in less grand public policy debates. Thus, for example, our hemodialysis therapy example (Section 1.3.1) is problematic partly because of a progressive broadening in the claims for equality. When hemodialysis machines were scarce, so that kidney patients without one were left to die, mere equalization of this therapy was at issue. When this had been accomplished, the domain broadened to health care for kidney disease and other afflictions such as cancer and heart trouble. Finally, the claims spread to cover afflictions of health and of other sorts of suffering such as poverty and pollution. And this brings us back to the essential underlying issue: If *this* is to be equally distributed, why *only* this? A limiting case occurs when the subject becomes more and more inclusive while the domain becomes broader and broader, bringing one finally to the total world economy: equal everything in the world for everyone in the world.[10]

We turn now to a related but subtler distinction.

3.2 Straightforward, Marginal, and Global Domains of Equality

Let us define a *domain of allocation* as the class of things that a given agent (or agency) presently controls for the purpose of allocation. The limits of this domain may be *de jure* or *de facto*. Uncertainty and ambiguity may, and quite often do, cloud the definition of such domains: whether, for instance, a given piece of property lies within a domain of allocation may depend upon whether it will be stolen or carried off by a flood, or whether a government agency suddenly faces a large shortfall in its expendable resources. The domain of allocation *defines the range of resources with which a given agent can act upon a demand for equality.* No claim to equality can be meaningfully addressed to an agent who controls no means for its satisfaction.

Let us further define a *domain of account* as the class of things over which a given speaker seeks equality. It might be the cake after dinner, or the U.S. Gross National Product over the next century, or the $10.00 that is in my pocket as I leave with two children to see a ballgame. The domain of account is always, for a given speaker in the language of equality, a *de jure* conception: it is the domain she says ought to be divided equally. And its boundaries may be as far-flung as her imagination permits.

Notice that these two categories ordinarily have different locations in society. A domain of allocation is attached to the agent *to* whom a demand for equality is addressed, and a domain of account is cited by the agent *from* whom such a demand issues. This distance is an important source of structural divergence: *Does X's domain of allocation cover Y's domain of account?* By "cover" we mean "contain all the elements of."[11] If the covering relation holds, then the agent receiving a demand for equality can (if he chooses) respond straightforwardly, by making an equal allocation over the full domain of account. We will thus call a claim to equality *straightforward* in this respect if its domain of allocation covers its domain of account. If a domain of allocation contains $10.00, and two children demand an equal division yielding $5.00 each, straightforward equality is available as an alternative. If the kids demand, say, $5,000,000 each, straightforward compliance is not available. And if the parent also wants an equal share for himself, straightforward equality is attainable only at the narrow plane of $3.33.

Whether this covering relation holds is jointly dependent upon relations among four things: a domain of allocation, a domain of account, a subject, and the level of equality. The same domain of allocation can cover one domain of account and not another—can cover the demand for equal slices of cake, but not the demand for equal slices of Europe. Likewise, a domain of allocation may suffice to cover a given domain of account for an exclusive subject, but not for an inclusive subject—we can manage equal cake at X ounces per serving for these ten guests, but not for all the residents of New Haven. Moreover, some subject structures—segmental and bloc-regarding ones—may permit meager domains of allocation to stretch further than they would for simple individual-regarding subjects. This occurs because both allow us to retain inequalities that fall within blocs or between segments and are therefore permitted by the corresponding structures.[12]

No failure of coverage can occur so long as equality is kept com-

pletely relational or "distributive," utterly distinct from "aggregative" considerations, to use Brian Barry's terminology.[13] Thus, the
demand for equal X can always be satisfied by *no* X at all, provided
everyone alike gets nothing and the beneficiaries have in mind no aggregative constraint. Even equal slices of Europe can be allocated
from Douglas Rae's private holdings on that continent under these
circumstances. (See Section 6.3 for more on the *level* at which equality
is achieved.)

The more problematic cases, in which equality passes less directly
into application, occur when (1) a domain of allocation fails to cover
the apposite domain of account, and (2) the residue of things in the
domain of account not covered by the domain of allocation is unequally divided.[14] Under this very general class of conditions, straightforward equality is unattainable, and the consequent ambiguity leads
to a new series of structural variations. Let us introduce this series by
imagining a ridiculously plain society with two simple subjects of
equality, A and B, one commodity, grapefruit, and a third agent, C,
who is not a subject of equality but is required to bring about equality between A and B. Initial holdings in grapefruit are as follows: A
has 0; B has 50; C has 50. C's 50 fruits are her domain of allocation,
but she is required to effect an overall equality, for all 100 grapefruits,
between A and B. The 50 fruits belonging to B are the source of trouble, for they are counted in the domain of account but *not* in C's domain of allocation. These fifty fruits explain why one domain does
not cover the other, and illustrate an uneven division of the residue.
Now C has two conspicuous solutions, neither of them obviously correct, leading to these two end-states:

A has 25   A has 50
B has 75   B has 50

The one on the left results from what we will call *marginal* egalitarianism, since C has simply divided her available fruit equally, without
attention to the unequal division of the residue between domains of
allocation and account, and A and B are left with the same 50-fruit
inequality with which they began. In general, *marginal equalities equalize domains of allocation, yet leave domains of account unequally divided because
they ignore the residue between the two domains.* The end-state on the right
is an instance of *global* egalitarianism. It equalizes the total domain of
account (50-50), though it does not necessarily equalize the domain of
allocation. And, in general, *global equalities promote equalization of a full
domain of account, probably through unequal division in a domain of allocation.*

Before continuing, we should note that there are two distinct forms of globalism. One corresponds to the common speech idea of *compensatory inequality,* and we will use that name. The other form challenges the disjunction between power and accountability, between domains of account and domains of allocation. At some hazard of being misunderstood, we will call this second form *redistributive* (short for redistribution of domains). In our example, compensatory inequality would entail C's giving A all 50 of her own fruits to make up for—compensate for—B's initial holding of 50 (that is, $0 + 50 = 50 + 0$). The redistributive form of globalism would have C confiscate B's 50 fruits, thus increasing her domain of allocation to 100 fruits, and permitting a return to straightforward equality (that is, $50 = 50$). The two forms seem equivalent only because the example is artificially simple.[15] We will say more about this in Section 3.2.1.

Consider now a somewhat more worldly example, in which we are operating a government committed to "small" taxes. A 5 percent sales tax or a 10 percent income tax would be permissible, as would an X-dollar capitation. If the domain of account is also "small," so that it is covered by these levies, we have straightforward domain structures. But what if the domain of account is much larger, seeking equality, or some approximation of it, in full after-tax incomes? From the perspective of such a large domain of account, these small taxes, with equal percent or dollar rates, are egalitarian, but only in *marginal* form. That is, they divide a domain of allocation equally, but this domain is itself marginal in relation to the domain of account. Your tax of 5 percent (or X dollars) may be equal to your landlord's tax of 5 percent (or X dollars); it may nevertheless fail utterly to promote overall equality between the two of you.[16]

Marginal equality is defined with respect to (often small) changes from the status quo, with the *changes* being equal in magnitude for all. Global equality is defined with respect to holdings above zero, with their *amounts* or end states being equal. Salaries in an ordinary firm or university provide a clear illustration. Begin with the rather unequal initial salaries for persons or occupational strata X and Y shown in Figures 4, 5, and 6, and marked as X_1 and Y_1. If we ignore the inequality between these two base figures, and allocate a given sum of incremental dollars equally, then we define equality by the relation,

$$X_2 - X_1 = Y_2 - Y_1$$

where X_2 and Y_2 represent salary figures for the following year. This

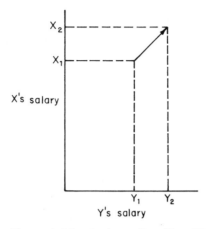

Figure 4. Marginal equality: $X_2 - X_1 = Y_2 - Y_1$.

is accomplished by the policy corresponding to the arrow in Figure 4. If X's initial salary were \$100,000 and Y's were \$1,000 and we had a "raise budget" of \$1,000, the new salaries would become \$100,500 and \$1,500. This is a straightforward equality if Mr. Y chooses not to expand the domain of account beyond the stingy budget for raises; once he does so, it is merely marginal, that is to say, inegalitarian[17] from a global perspective. The global view accords no legitimacy to initial salaries, and simply requires that salaries become equal: $X_2 = Y_2$. This could be accomplished by a policy of compensatory in-

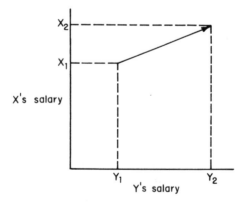

Figure 5. Global equality via compensatory inequality: $X_2 \simeq Y_2$ and $Y_2 - Y_1 > X_2 - X_1$.

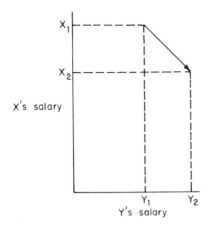

Figure 6. Global equality via redistribution: $X_2 = Y_2$.

equality, which moves toward an equal end-state with unequal marginal increments. If Y is to catch up with X, his raise $(Y_2 - Y_1)$ must exceed X's raise $(X_2 - X_1)$, as shown in Figure 5. A more radical method of achieving global equality is depicted in Figure 6. By this redistributive policy, the residue between the initial salaries of X and Y is assimilated into the domain of allocation, which then covers the domain of account, and global equality is achieved by a straightforward equal division. We return to these strategies of achieving global equality in Section 3.2.1.

The difference between marginal and global equalities is general to all allocative situations where the domain of account exceeds the domain of allocation, *except where an initial state of full equality exists.* If it happens that initial endowments are fully equal, then any marginal equality must coincide precisely with global equality. If $X_1 = Y_1$, then we may infer from $X_2 - X_1 = Y_2 - Y_1$ that $X_2 = Y_2$. Put simply: adding equally to two equal sums must produce two larger but still equal sums. The distinction between marginal and global equality therefore arises only *after* inequality has been introduced into society—which is, of course, quite common.

Note that a fine opportunity for a bogus version of compensatory inequality exists here. Suppose X is earning $50,000 and Y is earning $5,000. X (who sets salaries) finds himself smitten with guilt, and gives unequal raises, granting poor Y 20 percent and permitting himself only 10 percent. This would, of course, raise Y's salary by $1,000 and keep X's raise down to \$5,000, which is a profitable form of compensatory inequality indeed.[18]

Politically, the marginal/global distinction will generate real tension—hence contradiction and conflict—whenever certain features combine:

1. government agendas are limited, or functionally divided, so that resources are allocated piecemeal;
2. allocative processes not now on the government's agenda (that is, markets) generate (or permit the development of) inequalities; and
3. someone makes the more general social allocation function as a main domain of account.

These are common features, whose combination characterizes the modern state. Under their joint impact, government may: (1) seek marginal equality by promulgating policies with equal net incidences on each subject, or each bloc of subjects;[19] (2) aim at global equality, by trying somehow to offset the effect of existing inequalities generated outside government (or by past government policies);[20] or (3) aim somehow to compromise between these positions. What it cannot do is to *reconcile* them.

Even greater conflict is likely when government becomes committed to global equality but continues to rely upon capitalist markets for production. It is logically and empirically possible for the government's domain of allocation to provide compensatory inequality— through progressive taxation, say—*and* for overall economic inequality to remain constant or even increase. It is like running against an escalator; one may progress, or stand still, or even slip backward, depending on the *relative* velocity of the running (government egalitarianism) and the escalator (the market's countervailing effect).[21] For example, if unemployment worsens, reducing more and more pre-tax incomes toward a limit of zero, then a progressive unemployment insurance may coincide with growing inequality as its clients become more numerous, so long as their incomes are kept below their pre-unemployment levels.

In America, public efforts to achieve global economic equality have been conspicuous for their rarity. Apart from the progressive income tax and certain housing subsidies, American government has implemented few income-equalizing policies. Rather than provide additional income to its poorer citizens, government tends to provide services, such as health care, job training, day care centers, and legal assistance. Policies that do involve direct payments (unemployment compensation, Aid to Families with Dependent Children, food stamps) tend to be ameliorative rather than equalizing in aim, designed to prevent severe economic hardship. The service strategy constitutes an indirect and uncertain approach to economic equality and may benefit the service deliverers more than the recipients; income supplement policies provide equal minimal security against economic disaster. Neither strategy attempts to achieve a global economic equality.

3.2.1   The Methods of Globalism: Compensatory Inequality and the Redistribution of Domains

Like jumping past one's own shadow, global equality seems impossible. The defining predicament is that a domain of allocation, providing means of action, fails to cover a domain of account, providing requirements for action. How can one satisfy the wider demand with the narrower means? There are two main ways to manage this leap across one's shadow: *compensatory inequality* and *redistribution of domains*.

Compensatory inequality is the division of a domain of allocation unequally, so as to offset other inequalities that lie outside this domain but inside a larger domain of account. In our earlier example (Section 3.2) this would mean dividing C's fruit allocation unequally (50 for A, 0 for B) so as to compensate for B's initial 50-fruit advantage. It would also be illustrated by the unequal raises diagrammed in Figure 5 above. This approach earns its name by "compensating" for goods *outside* one's domain of allocation, and by "unequally" dividing goods *within* one's domain of allocation.

More sophisticated examples abound. Project Headstart, under which children from disadvantaged families are given compensatorily unequal early educations ("headstarts") is a clear case. The progressive income tax is justified by, among other things,[22] compensatory inequality: by taking more from those who make more, the tax man makes up for the inequalities produced in market competition. The demand that blacks should receive compensation now from whites for the enslavement of their forebears is a grammatically identical claim;[23] so are some versions of affirmative action and school busing. Busing makes up for the segregating, unequalizing effects in education of racial income inequality and the *de facto* housing segregation that it helps to generate.[24]

The trouble with compensatory inequality—"inequality in the name of equality"—is that it seems akin to "killing for peace" or "lying in the name of truth." Public authority sometimes acts as if this analogy really held good, as it may on occasion. Consider Section 703 of the 1964 Civil Rights Act, written to head off such an analogy: "Nothing contained in this title shall be interpreted to require any employer . . . to grant preferential treatment to any individual or to any group because of the race, color, religion, sex, or national origin of such an individual or group or on account of an imbalance which may exist with respect to the total number or percentage of persons of any race, color, religion, sex, or national origin employed."[25]

We should in fact pause here to note an especially vexing structural combination, pointed out in this legislation, of *bloc-regarding subjects and compensatory inequality.* By pursuing this combination, one may promote the most remarkable inequalities among persons. Suppose we divide subjects into two blocs, α and β, with α's generally better off when we begin a program of compensatory inequality on behalf of the β's. Now let us also reasonably assume that not *every* α benefited from the bloc-regarding inequality, and that not every β was a victim of it. By analogy, not every white was rich and not every black was poor before the 1964 Civil Rights Act. If we distinguish W's ("winners") from L's ("losers"), the Wα and Lβ groups are the typical cases, but Lα and Wβ groups, though relatively scarce, do exist. Now if we engage in compensatory inequality, favoring β's indiscriminately at the indiscriminate expense of α's, then we will have made the inequality between exceptional sub-blocks *worse* than it was to begin with. We will have further depressed the Lα's and further advanced the Wβ's—that is, inflicted further losses on some losers and handed further winnings to some winners. This would correspond to taking something away from the poorest whites to give it to the richest blacks. This is simply and absolutely *unjustifiable in the name of equality,* and results from the pernicious combination of two otherwise respectably egalitarian structures.[26] It is nevertheless wrong to throw out all compensatory inequality simply because one subtype is pernicious. In circumstances of great initial inequality and relatively marginal domains of allocation, *only* compensatory inequality can lead to global equality, and this may be a proper goal.

The strategy of compensatory inequality, however, swims against a strong tide. Inequalities are continually being generated in the economic domain outside public control; inequalities are generated by previous public policies with an inegalitarian thrust, and by present public policies (such as exclusionary zoning laws) that reinforce existing inequalities. And the effect of compensatory programs may be greatly diluted by other forms of public spending. For example, allocations are frequently made to exclusionary, geographically based subject classes, as when a congressman obtains a new federal office building, dam, or senior citizen center for his district. This spending pattern is only occasionally a form of compensatory inequality, as when the allocation is made to an economically depressed region like Appalachia or the South Bronx. The expensive class of transfer or insurance programs like social security and medicare, and programs that financially assist the relatively affluent, like subsidies to farmers and insured loans for college students, also dilute the effects of programs of compensatory inequality.

As a political matter, compensatory strategies seem especially prone to generate public controversy. Although overshadowed by nonegalitarian programs in aggregate public spending, compensatory programs often suffer from their visibility. In a small community, special school programs for slow learners are very noticeable. Busing programs are not only noticeable, they are often inflammatory, as is affirmative action hiring in a small factory, or special college admissions policies for minority groups.[27]

The alternative to compensatory inequality is a *redistribution* of domains, which requires either that domains of allocation be enlarged to cover domains of account; or, conversely, that domains of account be deflated to be covered by extant domains of allocation; or both. The effect of each maneuver is to regain or to approximate straightforward equality, in which domains of allocation cover domains of account (Section 3.2).

The main case is enlarging domains of allocation so that they cover full domains of account. This is most simply done by confiscating the holdings that create unequal residue between the two domains, adding them to the original domain of allocation, and imposing straightforward equality in the expanded domain of allocation.[28] We might thus simply confiscate B's 50 grapefruit and go forward; or we might declare whole salaries open to negotiation, rather than merely tacking on marginal raises; or we might socialize the means of production in a market system so as to permit equal division of the means of consumption (though this would not, as we understand it, be Marx's view). A central element of Marx's attack upon liberal constitutionalism belongs to this category, as Miliband indicates:

> [There exists] a fundamental distinction which Marx drew at the very beginning of his political life between "political emancipation" and "human emancipation." Political emancipation, by which he meant the achievement of civic rights, the extension of the suffrage, representative institutions, the curbing of monarchical rule, and the curtailment of arbitrary state power in general, was by no means to be scorned. On the contrary, it should be welcomed, Marx wrote in his essay *On the Jewish Question* in 1843, as "certainly a big step forward," and as "the last form of human emancipation *within* the prevailing scheme of things." The stress is Marx's own and is significant: it points to a major Marxist theme, namely that human emancipation can never be achieved in the political realm alone, but requires the revolutionary transformation of the economic and social order.[29]

According to Marx, then, a central flaw in liberal constitutionalism is its marginality—its formal equalities of right, and its inattention to the nonformal inequalities that lie beyond and beneath them in the underlying capitalist economy. Equality within the former provides merely political emancipation; Marx's global conception of human emancipation is defined over both domains—state and economy—conceived as a single, highly integrated whole. He is arguing that liberalism wrongly divides the two domains and he insists that society's domain of allocation must be expanded to meet his sweeping domain of account. He is anxious most of all to insist that liberal constitutional reforms must not substitute for analogous changes in the political economy.

To a remarkable degree, the central issue confronting liberal- and social-democratic states is precisely this division of domains. The old French *poujadistes,* the Danish Glistrup movement, the American "Proposition 13" movement, "supply-side" economics, the "libertarianism" of Robert Nozick—all demand that domains of account be reduced. They also resist the tendency of the state and its bureaucracy continually to expand the domain of public allocation and diminish the range of market decision. But this century-long expansion is a response to the crisis-generating disjunction between narrowly equal citizenship and broadly, often devastatingly, unequal subjection to unregulated market allocation. We believe that experience confirms Marx, for the central embarrassment of liberal capitalism is precisely the effects of this disjunction between domains.[30]

3.2.2   Proportionate Equality and Compensation for Productivity

Compensatory inequality distributes a good unequally in order to *off-set* a preexisting inequality. A good may also be distributed unequally in order to *preserve* an inequality.[31] This, paradoxically, is also a form of equality, what Aristotle called "proportionate equality." "The just must be equal," said Aristotle, but "if persons are not equal their [just] shares will not be equal."[32] This, in fact, constitutes equal treatment, since "there is no inequality if unequals are treated in proportion to their mutual inequality . . . Equality is of two kinds—numerical and proportional to desert."[33]

The principle of proportionate equality requires that the ratio of the merits (measured on some standard) of two persons, A and B, determines the relative size of their respective shares (a, b) of some good being distributed—that $A/B = a/b$, or that $a/A = b/B$. If potatoes were being distributed among individuals according to their body weight, and A weighed 100 pounds while B weighed 500, then B would receive five times as many potatoes as A. If A got 10, B would get 50, an apparently unequal distribution. But each receives 1 potato for every 10 pounds of body weight; potatoes are distributed in *equal proportion* to each. While compensatory inequality may have given more potatoes to A than to B in order to compensate for A's relative thinness, proportionate equality does not ameliorate the existing inequality, but instead preserves it as the justification and the measure of the final inequality in potato distribution.

The essential principle of distribution here is: "to each according to his deserts." As Aristotle is quick to point out, this requires a way of measuring and comparing deserts, and "not everyone would name the same criterion in deserving."[34] If equals are to be treated equally (and unequals unequally), it must be determined *who* are the equals (or unequals); this takes us back to the problem of drawing boundaries around a simple or segmental subject class discussed in Chapter 2.[35]

Many criteria may be used to make proportionately equal distributions. Aristotle mentions free birth, noble birth, wealth, and excellence,[36] and generally refers to functionally relevant criteria as in his familiar example of giving the best flutes to the superior flute-players.[37] A sales tax charges each buyer in proportion to the cost of his purchase. Candles are put on a birthday cake in proportion to the age of the guest of honor. Basketball teams are awarded points in proportion to the number of times they put the ball through the basket.

A particularly interesting case of Aristotle's principle of proportionate equality emerges immediately when we turn our attention to the production side of life—that is, the actual creation or collection of things to be allocated. This arises when productive contributions are unequal. If Ms. X contributes 90 units to a domain of allocation and Mr. Y contributes merely 10 units, and the whole lot of 100 units constitutes the domain of account, global equality would be achieved by a straightforward equal division of 50 units apiece. But if the extent of contribution were taken to be the criterion of desert, the principle of proportionate equality would dictate that Ms. X receive 90 units and Mr. Y receive 10—that is, $90/90 = 10/10$, and each would receive in equal proportion to contribution.[38] The 50-50 distribution makes the *action* of distribution equal; the 90-10 distribution makes the *transaction* of production and distribution equal.

Proportionate equality, which matches inequalities of distribution to prior inequalities of production, is not ordinarily conceived of as egalitarianism.[39] Compensation for productive contribution has, of course, an illustrious pedigree in liberal economic thought and ideology (for example, the theory that market systems match incomes to marginal productivity), and an even longer history in human culture (for example, the story of the workers in the vineyard recounted in Section 2.1.2).[40] When viewed as compensation, proportionate equality comes to look like a species of compensatory inequality—one gives unequal payments to compensate for inequalities in producing the thing paid out.[41] It is also, in a sense, global rather than marginal equality—equality for the whole production-distribution cycle, not just for its distributive phase. But despite these structural kinships with redistributive measures, its effect is to legitimate most or many inequalities endemic to market systems.

A structurally identical notion flourished among nineteenth-century socialists, most notably Robert Owen, Pierre Joseph Proudhon, and Louis-August Blanqui—three figures who otherwise agreed about little.[42] The idea was to price all commodities and services as linear functions of the labor-time required for their manufacture or provision, and to reward producers according to the resulting ratios.

This is a moral judgment resembling the medieval notion of just price, and is quite distinct from the use of the labor theory of value by more scientific analysts like Ricardo and Marx. Note, however, how different the implications of these systems are from the implications of market liberalism. All members of an economy approved by these authors would have equal net returns for their work: X hours of work done for others would imply X hours of work done by others for the worker in question. It was correctly argued that this equality does not obtain in market systems with unequal stocks of capital.

3.3   Causally Linked Domains of Allocation

What seems most artificial about compensation for productivity is the close causal relationship between productive capacity and other, unequal allocations—of capital, training, genetic advantage. If these are unequally distributed, and lead to unequal productivity, why should this determine yet another unequal pattern of allocation?[43] Our interests here are primarily analytical, so the important feature of this problem is its causally linked domains of allocation.

We have so far spoken as if it were possible to distribute one thing and then go on to an unfettered distribution of another thing. But often causal strings run from one allocation to another—from political influence to tax benefits to greater political resources to more political influence; from desirable genes to favorable socialization to success in a competitive labor market to marriage with someone else with desirable genes. The great power of classical economists—Smith, Ricardo, and most of all Marx—was their delineation of intricate causal chains linking all distributive outcomes to their antecedents in productive activity and power over productive activity. These lessons may be inconvenient to remember, and we need not belabor them here. We do, however, need to recognize that a whole complex of structural problems for equality arises from the existence of causal determinations linking one domain to another.[44]

Let us, before we close the chapter, examine a devilishly ironic instance of one allocation affecting another. Turn back to bloc-equal subject structure for the moment, and consider rates of capital sentencing among convicted murderers in Florida between 1973 and 1977. The shocking datum is this: during these years, whites were *more* apt to be sentenced to die than blacks. Under this progressive policy of compensatory inequality, only 2.3 percent of blacks received capital sentences while 3.2 percent of whites were so sentenced.[45] Before leaping to a rash interpretation of these few facts, notice that most murders are racially segregated: blacks killed blacks and whites killed whites in about 90 percent (4464 of 4823) of the cases studied. Furthermore, killing white people is a lot riskier than killing blacks—about ten times as risky, with capital sentencing rates of 5 percent for white corpses and only 0.5 percent for black corpses. The latter two facts jointly explain the first fact: blacks kill blacks, the courts are less vengeful about black corpses, and black killers thus profit a bit in relation to white ones. And this patterning has additional origins in the social and class segregation of society at large. To pick out one domain of allocation and to ignore its causal antecedents is risky indeed.

In the next two chapters we will deal more systematically with causally related domains of allocation. In Chapter 4, we analyze the rough-hewn relation in ordinary language between "opportunities" and "results." In Chapter 5, we discuss the relation between externally observable allocations and internally sensible allocations of satisfaction, attainment, and so on. Both are essentially relations of *partial determination:* opportunities and the like partly determine competitive success and its kin; external allocations partly determine internal satisfaction and its kin.

3.4   Summary

A *domain* is the class of things to be allocated, and we distinguish *broad* from *narrow* domains according to extent: a domain is strictly broader than another if it includes everything in the other plus something else. Narrowness is defined by the converse.

We also distinguish between a *domain of allocation,* which an actor *can* divide in response to a demand for equality, and a *domain of account,* which an agent thinks *ought* to be so divided. The former may, or may not cover the latter; when it does, a *straightforward* equality is possible. *Under straightforward equality, the full domain of account is equally divided.* This is not always possible, or is not always admitted as possible. Marginal and global equalities present alternative responses to situations in which domains of allocation fail to cover domains of account (though we do not want to say that they exhaust the class of possible responses). *Marginal equality allocates only a domain of allocation equally, when this fails to cover a full domain of account and when the residue of the domain of account is unequally distributed: these residual inequalities are thus left in place.* The two global responses refuse to leave these residual inequalities alone. *Compensatory inequality divides a domain of allocation unequally so as to offset inequalities beyond its own boundaries. A redistribution of domains either enlarges the domain of allocation or diminishes the domain of account, so as to restore a straightforward arrangement.*

Were all processes of allocation collapsed into a single act at a single instant in time, all of the above would likewise collapse into a single egalitarian structure. That does not happen in actual fact.

4 Equalities of Opportunity

How could an American essay on equality get this far without reference to "equal opportunity"? How have we overlooked the most distinctive and compelling element of our national ideology? In Emerson's words, "the genius of our country has worked out our true policy,—opportunity. Opportunity of civil rights, of education, of personal power, and not less of wealth; doors wide open. If I could have it,—... invitation as we now make to every nation, to every race and skin ... hospitality of fair field and equal laws to all. Let them compete, and success to the strongest, the wisest and the best."[1] The operative word is "opportunity," which tames "power," "rights," and "wealth." *These* are not to be shared equally: success to the strong*est*, the wis*est*, and the *best* implies at least relative failure for the less strong, less wise, and merely good, to say nothing of the weakest, most foolish, and worst. Opportunities of power, right, and acquisition are to be equal; power, right, and acquisition themselves are not.

Yet we learn little merely by noting the gulf between "equal X" and "equal opportunity for X." It is a real and important difference, but one that in itself requires no new analysis here.[2] It has already been analyzed precisely in Edwin Dorn's *Rules and Racial Equality,*[3] roughly as follows: the claim that equal X has been achieved is falsified by observing that X is unequally distributed; the claim that equal opportunity of X has been attained is not falsified by the observation of X's being unequally divided. This fails, of course, uniquely to define equal opportunity, but it fully distinguishes it from direct equality itself.

Nor does it help much to point up the self-serving merits of meritocracy from the viewpoints of elites—that is, from the perspective of winners who wish to congratulate themselves for having won, and to damn losers for having lost. It is an apology of some force and great comfort, but it is merely one among many, since the advantaged "have always felt the need to justify [inequality] . . . if for no other reason than to try to convince those who have less that they should accept this fact with relative docility."[4] Without denying this ideological slant to the notion of equal opportunity, we wish to take a quite different tack here.[5]

Our starting point is the third difference between our mythical Society E and any actual society. In Society E, all valued goods and social roles can be divided evenly without loss of value. In actual societies, many goods and roles cannot be so divided without the value of the shares falling drastically. Consider a first-place ribbon, the love of the man of your dreams, the job of chief executive officer—these things either cannot be subdivided and distributed or lose most of their value if they are. An equal allocation of such goods is impossible. In these circumstances, societies must devise more complex rules to decide how indivisible goods are to be allocated. Equal opportunity is one such rule with egalitarian claims.[6]

But when one looks further, one quickly sees that "equal opportunity" is not a very useful concept, because it blurs at least two conceptions.

4.1   Prospect-Regarding and Means-Regarding Equalities of Opportunity

Let us distinguish an end-good X from both the *prospect* of attaining or acquiring X, and some *means* for attaining X. The former is defined by a probability, or probability function:[7] Smith has a .5 chance of getting into medical school, Jones has a .000001 chance of getting to be president of the United States, Yates has a .01 chance of winning the Connecticut State Lottery, and so on. The latter is defined by institutional and material instruments that might help someone attain or acquire X: a box of tools, a set of skills, a series of legal rights, a system of rules permitting one to pursue X in one way or another. These two domains, equally distributed, define the two principal forms of equal opportunity.

1. *Prospect-regarding equal opportunity.* Two persons, j and k, have equal opportunities for X if each has the same probability of attaining X.[8]

2. *Means-regarding equal opportunity.* Two persons, j and k, have equal opportunities for X if each has the same instruments for attaining X.

Since these utterly different conceptions are easily conflated in ordinary argument, let us begin with a list of settings in which each is exemplified.

1. lottery, bingo, drawing lots, flipping coins, opening fortune cookies;
2. decathalon, boxing match, I.Q. test, poker game, weight-lifting contest.

The first list consists of practices under which prospects of success are equal for all, since each lottery ticket has the same chance of being drawn, each bingo card is equally likely to fill a row, one face of a coin is just as apt to land "up" as the other face, each diner has an equal prospect of opening a happy cookie (all fortune cookies are happy). The common feature here is that *nothing about the people affects the result.* Randomization rules out the effect of differing talents and differing developments or adaptations of talent. This is one reason why prospect-regarding equal opportunity is rare in practice, the Civil War and Vietnam era draft lotteries being exceptions.[9] The means-regarding practices in the second list all provide equal rules and equipment to each contestant—equal means—in order to reveal unequal talents, resulting in *un*equal prospects of success. Every entrant in a decathalon is scored on the same system of standards; every boxer must stay within the same kind of ring and eschew the same illegal punches; every subject of an I.Q. test answers the same questions; every poker player draws from the same deck, forming hands with the same *a priori* odds; every weight lifter meets the same resistance from gravity. These equal means are used to demonstrate unequal speed, agility, punching power, wit, cunning, muscle—so as to create, systematize, and legitimate unequal prospects of success. The purpose and effect of these equal means is *not equal prospects of success, but legitimately unequal prospects of success.*

It is significant that these two forms of equal opportunity are seldom sharply distinguished from one another. The practice of means-regarding equal opportunity is almost forced upon society by the logic of industrial and bureaucratic labor markets (see Section 4.2).[10] Such equality does combat vulgar ascriptive prejudice, such as racism, in the selection of labor forces. But the ideological power of equal opportunity does not lie in this fact; rather it lies very largely in the prospect-regarding variant, in the wish and hope that the children of yesterday's losers may become tomorrow's winners, or, more exactly, in the belief that their birth-date prospects may become equal to those of other infants who are luckier in their choice of parents. This is, of course, seldom true, as any responsible study of social mobility reveals.[11] But it may have great ideological power if means-regarding equal opportunity becomes confused with equality of prospects. To see how this blurring occurs, let us look more closely at means-regarding equal opportunity, which is more important to practice and more complex than prospect-regarding equality.

4.2   Means-Regarding Equal Opportunity

Means-regarding equal opportunity is completely consistent with the logic of market societies, with bureaucratic rationality, and indeed with all the main features of late industrial society. Members of a labor force sort themselves out in competition for the best positions, and are treated neutrally in order to avoid mistakes in which worker skills do not match job requirements. This system reveals quality even in unlikely people, which enhances efficiency. It also preserves and promotes class equilibrium, in which the revolutionary toxin feared by Pareto is flushed out: "It is not only the accumulation of inferior elements in a high social stratum which harms society, but also the accumulation in the lower strata of superior elements which are prevented from rising. When, at the same time, the upper strata are full of inferior elements and the lower strata full of superior ones, social equilibrium becomes highly unstable and a violent revolution is imminent. In a way, the social body may be compared to the human body, which soon perishes if the elimination of toxic matter is prevented."[12]

Pareto, of course, is a supreme proponent of means-regarding equal opportunity, and of the competitive market society to which it is so well suited. Means-regarding equal opportunity requires that values (like jobs and places in school) be *un*equally distributed. Generally, this is so because these values are lumpy or indivisible: there can only be so many good jobs in a firm, and there is only one best job. Not only, we are told, is it necessary that these prizes be unequally distributed, but it is also desirable, for two reasons. First, they provide incentives for hard work, investment in "human capital," and other behaviors that promote the common good (on a utilitarian construction of the good). Second, these unequal outcomes stabilize class relations: one can both co-opt the most able people from the underclass, and blame losers in the upper class for their losses. What is essential is that the rules of competition be utterly impersonal. The competitors are not equal in their talents (thus prospects) and will soon be unequal in their achievements. But the rules by which they are sorted out give equal terms of judgment to all. Note that the aims of this doctrine are mainly utilitarian,[13] not egalitarian. It is a doctrine for promoting total welfare by protecting the interests of the strong.

It is by historical relativity that this doctrine looks most egalitarian. If we begin with a system of racist (or anti-Semitic, or anti-X) assignment, and if some of its victims would win under impartial rules, means-regarding equal opportunity appears to promise a move toward a more egalitarian society. This is why nondiscrimination, defined as impersonal competition, plays a main role in bloc-regarding doctrines of equality for women, blacks, Hispanics, and others, even though it fosters inequality between gifted and ungifted women, strong and weak blacks, more and less talented Hispanics.

4.3 Equal Means and Unequal Prospects

Means-regarding equal opportunity is consistent with its prospect-regarding alternative only rarely—when differences among persons are unknown, nonexistent, or irrelevant. As soon as people are knowably different in their capacities to use the tools given them, equal tools reveal and legitimate unequal talents. These talents can then be the bases for unequal distributions of other values. If a person's prospects for success depend jointly on her means and her talents, and if talents are strictly unequal, then equal means imply unequal prospects and equal prospects may be attained only through unequal means. This general point, applicable to school or trial court or industry or athletic field, is illustrated in Figure 7. Suppose we simplistically quantify means as the domain available for allocation. The amount granted a given person is shown on the horizontal axis. We quantify prospects for success along the vertical axis, and think of individual talents as curves converting means to competitive capacity. Person A is more talented than person B in the following sense: at any level of means, A has a better prospect for success than B. This is strict inequality of talents and it is shown by the fact that the curves of tal-

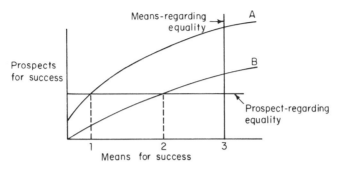

Figure 7. Means-regarding and prospect-regarding equalities of opportunity for two persons with strictly unequal talents.

ent never intersect. *Given strictly unequal talents, every policy of means-regarding equal opportunity must violate equality of prospects, and every prospect-regarding equal opportunity must violate equality of means.* In Figure 7, we show one means-regarding policy (granting amount 3 to each), and one prospect-regarding policy (granting amount 1 to A and amount 2 to B). The point is not that these policies *happen* to be different, but that they *must* be different: any program of means-regarding equality of opportunity must generate unequal prospects and vice versa, given strictly unequal talents.[14]

Two additional points arise. First, in this instance the grammar of equality turns in upon itself, giving two angles of vision for a single phenomenon, or, in the metaphor of language, two locutions with the same message. Prospect-regarding equality here is a special case of compensatory inequality, as defined in Section 3.2.1. We have a global domain of account entailing both talents and means, and a marginal domain of allocation (means): we compensate for inequalities beyond our control—unequal talents—with inequalities within our control, granting unequal means to A and B. This common form of inequality is at least superficially expensive for society because it squanders means on the less able and inhibits the Paretian process of circulation noted earlier.[15]

Second, the simplification underlying this analysis highlights relations of quantity and represses relations of qualitative difference. Our curves represent A as B's quantitative superior, and define a relation of strict inequality of talent between these two persons. Likewise, their prospects of success are contrasted simply by differing altitudes on the vertical axis. What all this leaves out is the variation in kind that characterizes human talent and aptitude. By repressing variation, we miss a vital point: *inequality of talents is not a phenomenon of nature, but a phenomenon of nature as mediated and reified by human culture.* Nature creates a wide variety of human capacities; culture picks out certain of those capacities to treat as relevant or important. Culture creates the concept of intelligence, produces an I.Q. test to measure it, and thus casts aside other features of individuals—even other kinds of intelligence.[16] Inequalities of talent are not simple facts of nature. Of course some people *are* more talented than others—but only *after culture has set standards that cooperate with nature to create such differences.*[17] Means-regarding equal opportunity is not a chimera or a lie, but neither is it as innocent as our simplification suggests.

Consider the following. Suppose we are teaching children to read, and we find two kids who differ in the kind of instruction that works best for them. One learns best by visual instruction, the other by phonic teaching. If we are dogmatically committed to equal teaching, or to means-regarding equal opportunity in learning, we may decide that every subject that is taught should be taught in the same way and to the same extent to every pupil. This view dominated in nineteenth-century education[18] and remains a common assumption. It is, however, dangerously naïve in a way that dramatizes our point. Suppose we follow this dictum and administer equal phonic education. One student will then seem more talented than the other, and we will have reified that inequality through equal, uniform instruction. Had we chosen visual methods, precisely the opposite inequality of talent would have appeared, and we might have simply attributed each outcome to the work of nature without ever seeing our own hand in the event. The underlying phenomenon is not quantitative inequality of talent, but qualitative diversity of need and aptitude; we would have turned the latter into the former, and thereby *generated* a "natural" inequality.

This point suggests a larger insight expressed admirably by John Schaar:

> The usual formulation of the doctrine—equal opportunity for all to develop their capacities—is rather misleading, for the fact always is that not all talents can be developed equally in any given society. Out of the great variety of human resources available to it, a given society will admire and reward some more than others. Every society has a set of values, and these are arranged in a more or less tidy hierarchy. These

systems of evaluation vary from society to society: soldierly qualities and virtues were highly admired and rewarded in Sparta, while poets languished. Hence, to be accurate, the equality of opportunity formula must be revised to read: equality of opportunity for all to develop those talents which are highly valued by a given people at a given time. When put this way, it becomes clear that commitment to the formula implies prior acceptance of an already established social-moral order.[19]

Let us illustrate this with another acute simplification. Suppose that society can adopt any of N criteria for advancing persons to favored positions, that each criterion is linked with appropriate means for the use of one's talents, and that an apposite range of talents appears, like so:

1. criterion 1, criterion 2, criterion 3, . . . criterion N
2. means 1, means 2, means 3, . . . means N
3. talent 1, talent 2, talent 3, . . . talent N

Means-regarding equal opportunity speaks only to the distribution of instruments within a given cell in row 2. Once society reaches this level of specificity, basic inequalities have already been created. Imagine that for each criterion people's talents range from great acuity to full oafishness (even these words imply a choice). If, and only if, talents are identical or strictly unequal *can the choice of criteria be neutral in its effect on competitive outcomes.* Thus, if person A is more talented than B by every criterion, then A would be better served than B by any criterion: the choice of criteria is neutral in effect on the outcome of a competition. The more interesting case occurs when neither person is strictly superior, so that B excels A by certain criteria and A excels B if other criteria are adopted. The person who is quick at addition may be slow at sprinting, and the choice of criteria for success—good arithmetic or good running—affects the outcome of a competition. The choice of criteria in a society, or sector of society, will be *neutral only if every pair of subjects are identically talented or stand in a relation of generalized superiority-inferiority on all criteria.* Under *any* other circumstance, the selection of criteria is itself an act of unequal allocation, favoring some persons over others. This powerfully limits the egalitarian claims of means-regarding equal opportunity, and suggests the deep rift between equal prospects and equal means.

4.3.1   A Rawlsian Compromise

We are dealing, then, with a basic division—between equal prospects and equal means—and a series of consequent difficulties. Is it possible, despite all this, to generate a single conception of equal opportunity that makes fundamental sense, that enjoys the moral appeal of prospect-regarding equality as well as the businesslike advantages of means-regarding equality? And one that works even while actual attainments are left unequal? We might quickly renounce this possibility but for the judicious effort of John Rawls in *A Theory of Justice*.[20] Rejecting the doctrine of "careers open to talent," which is simply a thin version of means-regarding equal opportunity, Rawls proposes a doctrine of "fair equality of opportunity," by which "positions are to be not only open in a formal sense, but . . . all should have a fair chance to attain them."[21]

This sounds as if Rawls would like both a thin version of means-regarding equal opportunity *and* some fair or equal distribution of prospects—a combination that we have just shown to be extremely hard to attain. However, he goes on to explain that fair equality of opportunity means that *"those with similar abilities and skills should have the same life chances.* More specifically . . . those who are at the same level of talent and ability, and have the same willingness to use them, should have the same prospects of success regardless of their initial place in the social system, that is, irrespective of the income class into which they are born."[22] He then embeds this notion within his larger conception of maximin justice, requiring that society be structured in such a way that "the higher expectations of those better situated . . . work as part of a scheme which improves the expectations of the least advantaged members of society."[23] In Rawls' version of equal opportunity, then, positions are formally open to all, people of equal talents have equal prospects regardless of their starting place in society, and the overall system is structured in a way that maximizes the prospects of those least favored in the natural distribution of talent and in initial social position.

Two structural features distinguish Rawls' view: (1) the pursuit of both means-regarding and prospect-regarding equalities, and (2) the definition of equalities *within exclusionary subjects* (see Section 2.1.2), namely, within classes of individuals matched in their talent and ability (and willingness to apply these). Not everyone must have equal opportunities; only everyone in a given ability class must have equal opportunity—in both senses. This suggests a segmental structure,[24] with many exclusive talent strata (perhaps alphas, betas, and so forth), equality inside each, and inequality between each and all the rest. The degree of inequality between talent strata would presumably be dictated by what maximizes the prospects of the lower stratum.

This compromise advances understanding less than may be imagined. First, it is silent and evidently naïve about the phenomenology of talent—that is, about the maze of choices beneath any society's notion of talent. What does it mean to say that children with different needs or different talent profiles are, or are not, at the same "level of talent and ability"? It means much less than Rawls—and most of us—seem to think.

The poverty of fair equality of opportunity is revealed less in what it ignores than in what it proposes. Rawls would require equality of opportunity only among those in the same talent stratum. If he were taken at his word, we could have both unequal means *and* unequal prospects among persons in different strata. He gives, moreover, no idea how to define these strata apart from the equalities with which they are associated; yet if they are not conceived and constructed independently, the whole requirement is circular, and *any* personnel assignment meets the test.

4.3.2   Ignorance and the Ideology of Equal Opportunity

The ideological (or moral) appeal of equal opportunity is vitally connected to its prospect-regarding form,[25] but its practical implementation is almost always means-regarding. There must, if this is true, be some link between equal means and equal prospects that escapes the analysis so far. We have been attending to talents and other traits that are, at least by hypothesis, known or knowable. Yet the vital connection turns upon what is unknown or unknowable.

Consider, for example, majority rule, which provides equal opportunity in that everyone gets the same means (one vote)[26] to promote his preferences. But is majority rule also a system of equal prospects? If we knew what issues would arise, and which persons would have which preferences, thus which majorities would form and determine outcomes, we would certainly *not* think that majority rules provide equal prospects for enacting one's preferences.[27] If we knew all this, no distinction between prospects and results would remain, and (barring a wildly improbable accident) results would be unequal (since those with more common views would find majorities on their side more often than others). The concept of prospects, thus of equal prospects, *requires ignorance of the facts that determine future events.* In addition to majority rule, this is true for the general range of practices for which equal opportunity is realized, asserted, or imagined.

Imagine that we enjoy full knowledge of the talents of every infant, of the ways and degrees to which these talents will be developed, of the criteria for success that society will adopt, of the intervening events (sickness, trauma, and so on) that may deflect individual courses of action, and finally of the distribution of means for advancement. We can thus see what will happen to each child as she matures and is evaluated by society and its agencies. Do we now see equal prospects? We do not, for we see directly ahead to the unequal results in store. Will equal means strike us as giving equal value to persons? No. Here, as with majority rule, ignorance is vital. In a world of perfect knowledge, there are no prospects, thus no equal prospects, and equal means simply effectuate unequal results.

4.3.3   Marginalism and Means-Regarding Equal Opportunity

Most if not all forms of means-regarding equal opportunity are marginal (or may be so understood by their critics). Recall from Section 3.2 that a marginal equality divides some things equally while leaving related inequalities in place. In the present case, some means of success are equalized while others, which affect the use of the first, are allowed to fall unevenly. We believe this to be a very general truth about means-regarding equalities of opportunities. Bernard Williams puts the point as follows:

> Suppose that in a certain society great prestige is attached to membership in a warrior class, the duties of which require great physical strength. The class has in the past been recruited from certain wealthy families only; but egalitarian reformers achieve a change in the rules by which warriors are recruited from all sections of society, on the results of a suitable competition. The effect of this, however, is that the wealthy families still provide virtually all the warriors, because the rest of the populace is so under-nourished by reason of poverty that their physical strength is inferior to that of the wealthy and well-nourished.[28]

The open-entry competition, with its equal rules for testing strength, is a specimen of means-regarding equality, and it is means-equal so far as it goes. The trouble is, of course, that other means such as nutrition are properly included in the domain of account, yet are excluded from this domain of allocation. It is in that way marginal, as are most forms of means-regarding equal opportunity in modern societies—schooling, labor markets, procedural rights in courts, or bureaucratic proceedings.

In fact, the fair race of life resembles a tournament more than an open contest, the selection rule being: "When you win, you win only the right to go on to the next round; when you lose, you lose forever."[29] Educational tracking is frequently structured in this way, so that there is only downward movement between tracks. Students who do poorly in the early grades are assigned to a slow track in higher grades. Those in a slow track are assigned to a vocational training course in high school; those in a fast track who do not perform well in high school are dropped at the level of college admissions. Early losses cannot be recouped. Rather than a single race, there is a sequence of races, the starting places in each determined largely by the results of the previous race. Means-regarding equality of opportunity in any one of these successive competitions is marginal in respect to the tournament overall.

This is not a merely contingent feature of such equality, for it follows not from some accident but from a fact that lies at the very core of equal opportunity. Such equality is meaningless if it does not produce unequal payoffs, which can usually be converted to further means of success the next day or in the next generation.[30]

A more interesting line of thought begins by asking whether truly global means-regarding equal opportunity might not eventually converge with prospect-regarding equal opportunity. One would have to include a great deal under the domain of means—for example, genetic endowments (cloning equals?), the family (raising children under common conditions), schooling (a perfectly standardized curriculum for genetically standardized children). With these draconian measures, equal means would lead toward equal prospects. At the limit, that would be *too* true, for there would no longer be demonstrable differences among persons upon which to base further inequalities of allocation.[31]

Finally, we come to the most profound danger of equal opportunity systems. In a system of competitive advancement based on equal opportunity, where do success and failure come from? They come from within persons, and must ultimately become stigmata of salvation and damnation, of dignity and its absence. And from this viewpoint, the better and more global the equality of opportunities, the deeper the threat to personal dignity—of both winners and losers.[32]

4.4   Bloc-Regarding Equalities of Opportunity: Nondiscrimination and Quotas

What happens if one continues to insist upon equality of opportunity but shifts from a simple subject to a bloc-regarding one? Not equal opportunity for all persons in a society, but equal opportunity for X's vis-à-vis non-X's in that society—blacks versus whites, women versus men, heterosexual versus homosexual? How, in other words, does transforming the subject structure alter the meanings of equal opportunity? The answer is that it does make a difference, but it makes a different difference depending on whether one is using means-equal or prospect-equal opportunities.

4.4.1   Means-Regarding Equality between Blocs

To a society committed to means-regarding equal opportunity, the introduction of a bloc-regarding subject implies a doctrine of *nondiscrimination:* the means of advancement for one bloc are to be equal with the means of advancement for another bloc. This is, in basic structure, contained within a simple individual-regarding equality of the same means-regarding type: one merely adds that inequalities between the blocs in question must *especially* be avoided. If a Scholastic Aptitude Test score of 600 will get a white male into Yale, make sure that a score of 600 earns admission for a black female. Notice the logical weakness of such a rule: assuming good faith adherence to simple opportunity to begin with, a demand for nondiscrimination would add *no new* requirement. For we could already have said, "If an S.A.T. score of 600 will get someone into Yale, it should get anyone else in as well."

Practically, of course, the rule is not that weak, since such systems often and notoriously operate in bad faith toward certain blocs of the population—blacks, Hispanics, women—and must be altered for that reason.

One can, of course, comply with a doctrine of nondiscrimination in a way superficial enough to defeat its purpose. One may no longer limit the number of Jews admitted to Princeton or Yale by discriminating against Jews, but simply by limiting the number of persons from New York City. One may not exclude women from a police force, but simply exclude persons less than six feet tall. One may not exclude ghetto blacks from a school but rather exclude persons whose vocabularies differ from those of the Educational Testing Service staff.[33] One may, in short, gerrymander the talents and criteria discussed in Section 4.3 so as to discriminate among blocs without discriminating among blocs. Thus the 1964 Civil Rights Act, as construed by the Supreme Court in a landmark decision, "proscribes not only overt discrimination but also practices that are fair in form, but discriminatory in operation. The touchstone is business necessity. If an employment practice which operates to exclude Negroes cannot be shown to be related to job performance, the practice is prohibited."[34] The larger and vaguer doctrine of affirmative action, set out originally by John Kennedy's Executive Order 10925 and extended in Lyndon Johnson's Executive Order 11246, aimed originally at just this point.[35] Its idea was to insist upon good faith compliance with nondiscrimination without disturbing the old system of means-regarding equal opportunity for simple subjects.

Notice also that this doctrine of affirmative action is perfectly in tune with the businesslike efficiency of (marginal) means-regarding equal opportunity.[36] One could use a test that was hard on blacks or women, provided only that the test was hard on them for reasons of efficiency or business necessity. There is no hint of prospect-regarding equal opportunity for persons or for blocs of persons. And yet, there remained the difficulty of proving that a firm or university really had eschewed discrimination and really had chosen only those tests necessary to efficient operation. What better proof could be imagined than the actual success of afflicted minorities? And what could be more obvious than to measure their per capita, or per applicant, rate of success in order to draw inferences about discrimination? Referring to the Executive Orders just mentioned, Daniel Bell writes that "the initial intention of the Executive Order[s] was to eliminate *discrimination*. But discrimination is difficult to prove, especially when the qualifications required for a job are highly specific. And the government's test became: are the members of the minority groups to be found in employment, at every level, in numbers equal to their proportion of the population? Or, if women earned 30 per cent of the Ph.D.'s, are 30 per cent of the faculty women?"[37] Thus we arrive at quota representation on *inferential grounds*. In the case of marginal, means-regarding equal opportunity in the form of nondiscrimination, proportional representation of blocs becomes an inference ticket for compliance. It is not that quotas are themselves demanded as a form of equality, but that quotas allow government to infer and enforce another form of equality—nondiscrimination.

But this inference is in a major way confused, for it conflates marginal and global forms of means-regarding equal opportunity (recall Section 4.3.3). The quota inference might read as follows:

> *Test I.* The (marginal) means of advancement controlled by a given agency are being disbursed without discrimination between two blocs if and only if members of these blocs succeed at approximately equal per capita (or per applicant) rates.

Thus, a United Nations Commission of Inquiry that looked at the results from the 1980 Winter Olympics (shown in Table 7) would conclude that, by Test I, discrimination had occurred. But it would be absurd for the commissioners to infer that the Olympic officials at Lake Placid had discriminated in favor of athletes from Liechtenstein or the U.S.S.R. at the expense of competitors from Cuba or China. And the reason for this absurdity is instructively clear. The officials did not control enough of the relevant means of winning—snow in one's back yard, for instance—to be held responsible for the resulting inequality. So too, though somewhat less obviously, is it wrong to hold the officials of a given firm, government agency, or university accountable under Test I. Test I is, quite simply, a garbled version of another test, namely:

> *Test II.* The *global* means of advancement, controlled by a given agency and other agencies, or not controlled by anyone, are being disbursed without discrimination between two blocs if and only if members of

Table 7. Results of the 1980 Winter Olympics.

Country	Medals	Population	Ratio of Medals to population
Liechtenstein	4	24,000	1:6,000
U.S.S.R.	23	200,000,000	1:9,000,000
U.S.A.	12	240,000,000	1:20,000,000
France	1	53,000,000	1:53,000,000
Cuba	0	10,000,000	1:∞
China	0	1,000,000,000	1:∞

these blocs succeed at approximately equal per capita (or per applicant) rates.

It follows from actuarial wisdom that quota-like equality among blocs should follow from a *fully global equality of means,* which is exactly what means-regarding equal opportunity virtually never entails. Test II is itself free of confusion, but is not the test imposed or imagined in recent practice. The confusion arises because under Test I agencies whose domains of allocation for means are marginal are expected to achieve the outcomes that would occur if they had much more global means to allocate.

Notice that this analysis does not excuse or dismiss discrimination. It simply tells us that Test I's numerical goals, targets, or quotas are improper inference criteria for discrimination. The trouble with Test I is, of course, as simple as it is irremediable, for it holds people responsible for allocative patterns over which they have no control: it inflicts a very broad domain of account on agents controlling narrow domains of allocation (compare Section 3.2). Because it does this indirectly, indeed obliquely, the resulting absurdity may escape notice by vehement opponents of discrimination, but it remains an absurdity nonetheless. This does not mean that quotas are themselves absurd, which is a more complicated matter; it simply means that Test I quotas are confused inference criteria for discrimination. Could any quota properly test for discrimination? Yes, if the observer possessed an *independent* test of qualification. If (as with the recruitment of a track team) there existed some simple and public test (for example, a 9.6-second 100-meter dash), then one could begin to draw inferences about discrimination between blocs as their success rates per qualified applicant diverged from identity. Such cases are rare and are not the cases for which Test I was devised.

Test I has never really been fully institutionalized, but in many places it serves as a polite obfuscation upon which policy proceeds. What it obfuscates is the possibility that we may want bloc-regarding equality even if this violates means-regarding equality. It would entail such a violation whenever the blocs in question were unequally served by history and by social influences beyond the direct ken of government (or a university or firm). These are, of course, precisely the circumstances—of blacks, Hispanics, women—that raise the question to begin with.[38]

4.4.2   Prospect-Regarding Equality between Blocs

Quotas *can* assure prospect-regarding equal opportunity between blocs. We can make sure that an anonymous black eighteen-year-old has the same probability of becoming a Harvard freshman as does a nameless white eighteen-year-old, that a randomly chosen female has the same likelihood of serving on the federal bench as does a randomly chosen male, that a French-speaking Canadian has the same odds for advancement in Molson Breweries as does an English-speaking colleague. While ambiguity will remain about the definition of proper blocs and of proper ratios—based on whole populations, or on applicant pools, or on client pools[39]—the essential method is simple: to equate rates of success (admission, promotion, and so forth) for blocs.[40] If blacks constitute, say, 15 percent of the relevant population, then the black quota is to be 15 percent, and so on for each bloc. The effect is to make bloc identities actuarially irrelevant: neither color, nor sex, nor anything of the sort has predictive value in a properly tuned quota system of this sort.

This achieves a sort of functional color blindness to replace Justice Harlan's simpler doctrine of color blindness in *Plessy* v. *Ferguson.*[41] It makes color, sex, and ethnicity irrelevant to the mechanism of social selection, not by totally ignoring them but by paying exactly the necessary amount of attention to them in setting quotas. It may help to think about this from the perspective of the historical era in which vulgar prejudice governed all important processes of selection. In a limiting case, it would simply have been stated—or even have been unnecessary to state—that only white male Protestants need apply. This would combine means- and prospect-regarding inequalities and would make them indistinct. Removing the discriminatory procedure, making it metaphorically color blind, would directly augment the means-regarding opportunities of the disadvantaged and would therefore appear to improve their prospects of success. This is, quite simply, too simple. And its excessive simplicity is what masked the difference between these two choices for equalizing opportunities.

Note that prospect-regarding quotas are compatible with means-regarding equality *within* blocs. An agency can simply set up distinct pools of places, one pool of the right size for each bloc, and then insist upon a direct means-regarding equality of opportunity within each pool. Though the rationale may have been confused, this was exactly the mechanism used by the Davis Medical School in the *Bakke* case.

Allan Bakke's complaint was that he had done better while losing in the advantaged pool than others had done while winning in the disadvantaged pool. And that is, of course, hardly surprising, for there would be no point to these mechanisms if they were consistent with simple means-regarding equality across blocs.

Why, then, do quotas of this sort raise such a ruckus? Because these quotas embody not one but three contradictory equalities at once: equal results versus equal opportunity,[42] equal means versus equal prospects, and bloc-regarding versus individual-regarding equalities.[43] What more can one ask from one policy?

4.5 Summary

We have proposed yet one more distinction, between prospect-regarding and means-regarding equalities of opportunity, with these definitions:

1. *Prospect-regarding equal opportunity.* Two persons, j and k, have equal opportunities for X if each has the same probability of attaining X.

2. *Means-regarding equal opportunity.* Two persons, j and k, have equal opportunities for X if each has the same instruments for attaining X.

These are, as the analysis shows, more complex and less easily confused than some would imagine.

5 The Value of Equality

THE MOST profound difficulty for egalitarianism in all its forms arises from the persistence of human diversity: If people are different, how are they to be made equal? The problem is not that people are distinguishable—by gender or race, say—and therefore not equal in the most literal sense. Nor is the essential difficulty that some people are "better" or "worse" than others. The difficulty is instead that people differ in their needs, tastes, vulnerabilities, capacities, moral commitments, and life histories. These are differences that can make "equal" treatments of persons "unequal" and, no less important, may make "unequal" treatments of persons "equal." These are the differences that lead Tawney to say that

> equality of provision is not identity of provision. It is to be achieved, not by treating different needs in the same way, but by devoting equal care to ensuring that they are met in the different ways most appropriate to them, as is done by a doctor who prescribes different regimens for different constitutions, or a teacher who develops different types of intelligence by different curricula. The more anxiously, indeed, a society endeavours to secure equality of consideration for all its members, the greater will be the differentiation of treatment which, when once their common human needs have been met, it accords to the special needs of different groups and individuals among them.[1]

Tawney here advocates a particular solution, which we term *person-regarding* equality. This solution describes the left-hand (A) formulae in the following examples:

1A. An equal right for every Canadian to speak his native language.

1B. An equal right for every Canadian to speak English.

2A. An education equally suited to the talents and interests of every child.	2B. An equal scientific education for every child.
3A. A tax exacting an equal sacrifice at each income level.	3B. A tax of X dollars for everyone, rich and poor alike.

The right-hand (B) formulae illustrate a contrasting structure which we entitle *lot-regarding* equality.

The very rough idea of lot-regarding equality is that each person should derive as much value from her lot as she would from her equal's lot. It involves one person comparing many lots of goods. If, say, my education has a value of 7 International Value Chits for me, then you and I are lot-equal if your education would also have a value of 7 I.V.C.'s for me. Lot-regarding equality may thus be defined by the fact that people will neither gain nor lose by switching lots with one another. Such equality is violated when lots differ so as to permit gain or loss through changing places. Thus, if we both value money in the same general way (that is, more is better), and you have a dollar while I have a dime, we are not lot-equal; a redistribution in which we both finished with 55 cents would leave us lot-equal.

Equal holdings of 55 cents would *not* imply that we were equally well off if there were relevant differences between us (such as your needing a 56-cent pill to stay alive). Attaining the relation of person-regarding equality is a quite different thing; it requires that I should derive as much value from my lot as you derive from yours.[2] This might require me to get just 55 cents while you get that 55 cents plus a further 56 cents to buy your pill. Or it might mean that you would attend a preparatory high school, consistent with your aims or aptitudes and convictions, while I attend a vocational high school, consistent with my aims or aptitudes and convictions.

5.1   Person, Lot, and Value

The feature of our mythical Society E that represses the structural pattern about to be analyzed is its human uniformity: people are completely alike so far as personal needs, tastes, or vulnerabilities may affect the allocation of values in Society E. The test is this: if a given lot of goods has a given value for any one person in Society E, then it must also have the same value for any other person in Society E.[3] Notice that this uniformity does not entail that people are indistinguishable from one another, or that they are equally good. It instead implies that *personhood is irrelevant to the valuation of lots in society*. If every child is, for instance, allowed to speak English at school, then the value of this entitlement should be independent of the child in question: if it is valuable in some given degree for an English-speaking child, it should be of the same value to children who speak Spanish or Chinese. If all of us are to be taxed $1,000, the value (disvalue) of this burden should be the same for all: either there are no rich and poor, or the poor carry their burdens much more lightly than the rich. In Society E, then, people are relevantly uniform so that they all view a given lot of goods in the same way.

Formal analysis permits us to analyze Society E more precisely and show how it differs from actual societies. Suppose we have two persons, P_i and P_j. Society bestows a lot (an allocative outcome) upon each, L_i and L_j. The result is that P_i has L_i, while P_j has L_j. In Society E, both P_i and P_j would value L_i in exactly the same way, and they would both value L_j in the same way. To illustrate this point, let us shorten our notation by using V to represent value, and continue the subscripts from above, so that we have the following four terms:

1. V_{ii}: the value of i having i's lot
2. V_{jj}: the value of j having j's lot
3. V_{ij}: the value of i having j's lot
4. V_{ji}: the value of j having i's lot

The first subscript thus denotes personhood, and the second subscript denotes the lots assigned to persons. The essential feature of Society E thus becomes $V_{ii} = V_{ji}$ and $V_{jj} = V_{ij}$, since the value of i's lot must be the same for i as it is for j and the value of j's lot must be the same for her as it is for i.

Notice that this condition does not rule out inequality, but simply requires a particular kind of inequality. *Inequality must arise from differing lots, not from differing human needs and proclivities.* Suppose, then, that V_{ii} and V_{ji} are the value of i's mansion (a value that is, in Society E, equal for him and for j), while V_{jj} and V_{ij} denote the value of j's hovel (again a value equal for i and j). This former value is much greater than the latter, so an inequality exists. But it centers upon the difference between a mansion and a hovel—between one lot and another, not between one person and another.

If and only if a society were like E, in that all people valued the same house to the same degree, could we ignore the distinction between lot-regarding and person-regarding equality. We could ignore it because these two forms of equality would be the same thing. All identical lots would be equally valued by all people; thus i would not envy j, and vice versa, *and* i would value his lot as much as j values hers. Another way in which Society E might efface this basic difference would be to allocate value (for instance, utility) directly. There might thus be a pot containing one thousand Standard International Utiles, and the lots would consist in such utiles. If this were so, then it would be impossible (by definition) to distinguish between lot-regarding and person-regarding equalities.[4] Note, however, that value (or utility) is always a predicate of something else, so that this remains an imaginary example. Lots are always to be understood as things having a causal or determinative relationship to value, and value is always to be understood from the viewpoint of persons.

5.2   Lot-Regarding Equality

Lot regarding equality requires that, for any pair of equals i and j: $V_{ii} = V_{ij}$, and $V_{jj} = V_{ji}$—which is to say that term 1 equals term 3 and term 2 equals term 4 in the scheme just outlined in Section 5.1. The test is whether Mr. i is as well off with his lot as he would be with Ms. j's lot (term 1 = term 3) and whether the converse holds for j— whether she is as well off with her lot as she would be with i's lot (term 2 = term 4). A lot-equal class of persons will therefore be free from envy: i will not wish he could trade his lot for j's, and j will not wish she could trade hers for i's.[5]

Lot-regarding equality can always be attained by making lots identical: the same boots for every soldier, the same draft liability for young men and women alike, the same housing for every family, the same hours and terms of employment for all. There will be one law for all without privilege or exception, one vote for each, one liberty shared equally and exercised identically by all. In the limiting case, every good in society will be divided equally among all members— that is one-nth of every good for all n members. This identity is sufficient to lot-regarding equality, since identical lots for i and j straight-forwardly rule out gains or losses from switching lots—out of the frying pan into the frying pan, as it were.

Although sufficient, identity of lots is not logically necessary to lot-regarding equality. However, the instances in which different lots satisfy this requirement are rare. There may exist tolerance for some quantitative differences: although you have more money than I do, the difference is negligible, so we are equals for all practical purposes.

Another case, perhaps more interesting, occurs when unequal lots imply equal misery: you have two ounces of rice to my one, but five ounces are required to survive. Yet another instance occurs when individual tastes have a particular symmetrical form best relegated to a footnote.[6] But the main and dominant form of lot-regarding equality is identity, because it requires very little knowledge of other people.

5.2.1 Lot-Regarding Equality and Economic Theory

Lot-regarding equality requires no knowledge of other persons, and can thus be attained without violating the famous stricture of Pareto's *Manual:* "Take a man who is eating a chicken; someone wishes to demonstrate to him that he would experience more pleasure if he ate only half of it and gave the other half to his neighbor. He replies: 'Certainly not; I have already tried that and I assure you that I experience more pleasure by eating the whole thing than by giving half of it to my neighbor.' You can call him wicked, you can insult him, but you cannot prove to him logically that he does not experience that sensation. *The individual is the sole judge of what pleases or displeases him.*"[7]

This unremarkable insight has played a considerable role in the ideological history of our century, particularly in excluding egalitarianism from neoclassical economic argument. It is the ground for banishing interpersonal comparisons of utility, and once these are banished people may assume equality and inequality to be unknowable states of affairs. All we can know about others is that they like more, or less, for themselves. Thus, a business executive earning $500,000 per year may employ a gardener at 1 percent of that salary; in the dimly illuminated halls of neoclassical thought, we are not entitled to infer that the executive is better off than his gardener. Perhaps the gardener is better off; perhaps the executive is better off; perhaps they are equally well off. We simply cannot tell which, for any such telling would entail an interpersonal comparison of utility.[8]

A considerable strength of lot-regarding egalitarianism is that it can be attained and demonstrated without such comparisons. If we ask the executive whether he would trade his lot for the gardener's, and he answers no, or yes, or indicates indifference, that is an *intra*personal datum. If we then make the same inquiry of the gardener, again getting back an *intra*personal answer, we can draw inferences about the existence of lot-regarding equality between these two. This is precisely the basis for the Foley-Varian criterion of economic equity,[9] and it appeals to economists precisely because it avoids the interpersonal comparisons ruled out by Pareto. The point may be underscored by looking again at the defining equations: $V_{ii} = V_{ij}$ and $V_{jj} = V_{ji}$. In each instance, personal identity is a constant: Mr. i alone enters into the first equation and Ms. j alone enters into the second. Lot-regarding equality is thus in the strictest analytic sense consistent with the Paretian stricture against interpersonal comparisons of utility. Notice, finally, that the strategy of identity offers a very quick route to the attainment of lot-regarding equality if we make the (interpersonal) assumption that no individual can have a strict preference between two identical lots.

It might therefore seem that lot-regarding equality would find a natural home in neoclassical economics. However, market exchange economies that seek efficient production seldom satisfy lot-regarding equality (or even the less exacting standard of Foley-Varian equity).[10] Although it takes many subtleties to explain this fact, the fact itself is clear; in market economies, incomes will be unequal and will permit their holders to buy envy-inducing bundles of commodities.

The economists thus confront an ideological bind. Equality (of a person-regarding sort) is unknowable—hence out of bounds—within the Paretian framework.[11] Yet this same framework encourages lot-regarding egalitarianism, which is profoundly at odds with the market order to which this tradition has always been devoted. It would probably require that everyone get the same bundle of commodities,[12] and that some forms of exchange be ruled out—lest some acquire bundles envied by others.[13]

We would be remiss to leave this topic without noting a further feature of modern economic experience, namely the dominating role of commodities in capitalist markets. For Max Weber this was a matter of impersonality: "The market community as such is the most impersonal relationship of practical life into which humans can enter with one another. This is not due to that potentiality of struggle among the interested parties which is inherent in the market relationship . . . The reason for the impersonality of the market is its matter-of-factness, its orientation to the commodity and only that."[14] The homogeneous commodity takes center stage, and effaces the individual personalities of its maker, its consumer, its seller, and its purchaser. For Marx this phenomenon is "commodity fetishism," and is encapsulated thus: "The relation of the producers to the sum total of their own labor is presented to them as a social relation existing not between themselves but between the products of their labor . . . There it is a definite social relation between men, that assumes, in their eyes, the fantastic form of a relation between things."[15]

Neither Marx nor Weber implies that market participants are lot-regarding equals.[16] But they do point out a central metaphor of liberal-capitalist culture: the effacement of individual differences in the homogeneity of commodities. And this metaphor closely resembles the form taken by lot-regarding egalitarianism in the liberal theory of the public order. For, like commodities, our formal votes, rights, and legal statuses tend often to be indistinguishable from one another.

5.2.2   Lot-Regarding Equality and Liberal Democracy: Votes and Liberties

Lot-regarding equality has the very great political advantage of being publicly demonstrable. Since it depends on no knowledge of individual differences, personhood indeed being irrelevant to it,[17] it perfectly fits the liberal formula of equal citizenship. The power of this fit may be captured by looking briefly at some features of the liberal public order.

The doctrine of "one man one vote" is an essential element of liberal representation and of its majoritarian sequela. As Dahl and Lindblom write, "Unless government policy responds to the preferences of the greater number, the preferences of some individuals (the lesser number) must be weighted more heavily than the preferences of some other individuals (the greater number). But to weight preferences in this way is to reject the goal of political equality."[18] The metaphor of equal weights is common, and its exact meaning is brought out by Kenneth May's axiom of "anonymity."[19] May says that we should always be able to permute the identities of the voters without ever altering the result. Suppose that you have voted for X and I have voted for not-X. X wins. Now we switch identities so that my vote goes for X and yours goes for not-X. If "anonymity" obtains, X remains victorious, because any alteration of the result would imply that personal identities mattered to the result by being weighted differently. It is the votes, the lots, that are equal, and they are equal without attention to the names of the citizens. While the actual details of voting can become very intricate indeed,[20] the lot-regarding formula for liberal electoral laws remains constant: I have nothing to gain by trading my ballot (or my district) for yours.

Of course, votes and other political rights are intimately linked to inequalities of influence, wealth, security, status, and happiness among the actual persons who hold those rights and cast those votes.[21] It is, for example, said that Charles Seymour, late president of Yale, voted in eight consecutive elections for president of the United States without once picking a winner. This does not, however, imply that this vote was weighted less than equally—that his lot as a voter was unequal. Or, again, the rights of property probably serve the Rockefellers and the Mellons better than they serve you, but this does not mean that your right is less a right than theirs: an equal right to property, as the saying goes, is not a right to equal property. Like all the important instances of lot-regarding equality, these rights are indifferent to the identities of their beneficiaries, just as commodities are indifferent to the identities of those who buy and sell them. They are purposefully inattentive to special needs of individuals. Imagine, for example, an eccentric voter whose views are known to be consistently unpopular: should equal voting rights permit him two votes, or perhaps two million votes, to make up this liability? Not at all, for his equal lot is to have one vote just like everyone else's. Or imagine a worker whose skills command a market price of exactly zero dollars a year: setting aside taxes, he is as entitled to keep whatever he can accumulate as is speculator Bunker Hunt. If the state or society wishes to give him money or goods, that is a further question, and his right of property will *then* protect these acquisitions. But they are not implied by his right of property. Again, a simple lot-regarding equality.

5.2.3   Lot-Regarding Equality and Rules

Lot-regarding equalities correspond exactly to Felix Oppenheim's stipulation of equality: "A and B are treated equally by C, if C allots to A and B the same specified benefit (e.g., one vote) or burden (e.g., one year's military service) or the same amount of some specified benefit or burden (e.g., salary, tax burden). If A is let to vote but not B, if A is drafted but B is exempted, if A receives a higher salary than B, then A and B are treated unequally in these respects."[22] This stipulation reminds us of Isaiah Berlin's point, which we noted in Section 2.1.1: "All rules, by definition, entail a measure of equality. Insofar as rules are general instructions to act or refrain from acting in certain ways . . . they enjoin *uniform behavior* in identical cases. To fall under a rule is *pro tanto* to be assimilated to a *single pattern* . . . This applies whether the rules take the form of moral principles and laws, or codes of positive law, or rules of games."[23]

All rules capable of enforcement without attention to individual subjects—their mind-states, needs, chosen ends, and so on—are archetypically lot-regarding. Everyone's subjection to rule X is identical with everyone else's subjection to it, provided only that the rule is impersonally formulated and scrupulously enforced. Thus, for example, the rule against theft applies to everyone lot-equally, whether they be rich or poor, fat or starving. The biblical prohibition of adultery applies equally to those with richly sexual marriages and to those with arid ones.

5.2.4   Lot-Regarding Equality and Equality of Income

For many egalitarians, equalization of incomes[24] is the sine qua non of equality—the completion of the long journey from ideology to practice. There is much to support this view, for money is the root of many ugly differences and the lack of it occasions much suffering.[25] Here, however, we ask only whether such equality would fit with the lot-regarding equality we have been analyzing. The answer is a qualified yes: equal incomes correspond *in themsleves to lot-regarding equality* (*1*) *before they are used in exchange and* (*2*) *after they are disassociated from work.* Qualification (1) rests upon the potential violation of lot-regarding equality through exchange, illustrated thus: Mr. i trades more shrewdly, drives a harder bargain, and ends up with a bundle of goods superior to stupid Ms. j's ill-chosen bundle, so that both would prefer i's final market basket. In this not improbable case, the incomes will be lot-equal, but the commodities for which they are traded will not be. Qualification 2 has two main parts, both associated with work. First, incomes provide marginal, not global, equality in respect to life at work if jobs are unequally attractive. To provide global equality, incomes must, in the fashion of Adam Smith, be adjusted to offset differences in work satisfaction.[26] Thus, equal incomes for a garbage collector and a college professor are lot-equal in themselves, but the professor would presumably enjoy a global advantage if work satisfaction were counted in. The second part of qualification (2) is that incomes would remain equal over time only if either they were never used to purchase the work of others or if this work were always paid for in equal quantities at equal prices. In all other cases (and these are implied in the very idea of money income—that is, freedom of disposition to others in exchange for work and its products), we must expect an indefinite series of lot-regarding inequalities.[27] Income equality thus fits the exactions of lot-regarding equality only with eggshell fragility.

5.2.5   Insensitivity of Lot-Regarding Equality

Equal lots imply nothing about equal well-being. By ignoring individual differences, lot-equal allocation blinds us to variations of need, character, capacity, and so on.[28] These failures of vision may be quantitative or qualitative. In regard to differences of degree, even if income equality is at least briefly lot-equal, Albert Weale points out that "variations in individual welfare functions may mean that individuals will experience large variations in welfare on the same income because their circumstances require greater expenditure in order to achieve the same level of satisfaction. An obvious example would be the comparison between a physically handicapped person and someone who is not handicapped. The former has greater needs than the latter, if they are to achieve the same level of well-being."[29] A similar observation and analysis leads Amartya Sen to formulate "the weak equity axiom," as follows: "Let person i have a lower level of welfare than person j for each level of individual income. Then in distributing a given total of income among individuals including i and j, the optimal solution must give i a higher level of income than j."[30] This is "weak" in not requiring income differences sufficient to attain equal welfare (as would be prescribed by full-fledged person-regarding equality), but in requiring them merely to approach it. It corresponds to compensatory global equalization (see Section 3.2.1), as distinguished from redistributive equality. Strong or weak, however, the axiom illustrates the quantitative insensitivity of lot-equality.

Lot-regarding equality may be even more insensitive to qualitative differences, as examples throughout this book demonstrate. The uniform manufacture of right-handed can openers, scissors, door handles, pens, and toilet paper racks is lot-equal, but insensitive to the needs of left-handed persons. Similarly, uniform language rules or rules of worship are lot-equal, but insensitive to the needs of linguistic or religious minorities. It is this sort of thing that inclines people to seek equality among persons—which is not to say that this alternative equality can be neatly and demonstrably attained.

5.3   Person-Regarding Equality

Formally, person-regarding equality is defined as: $V_{ii} = V_{jj}$, for all pairs of equals i and j—which is to say that Mr. i should be as well off with his lot (V_{ii}) as Ms. j is with her lot (V_{jj}). This is the equality aimed at by giving dialysis to a person with bad kidneys, and aspirin to a person with a headache. It is the equality that proposes French-language rights for Francophones and English-language rights for Anglophones. It is the equality that produces right-handed scissors for right-handed persons and left-handed ones for southpaws. It is person-regarding because it takes account of persons and their differences.

Identical treatment can be relied upon to produce person-regarding equality only among clones with identical biographies. For real persons who differ in their needs and vulnerabilities, their convictions and plans, their capacities and personal histories, *identical treatment* constitutes *person-regarding inequality*. Thus, to give identical pianos to a pianist and a guitarist does not promote equality between persons. To issue boots of size 8D to everyone, whatever the size and shape of their feet, satisfies lot-regarding equality but violates person-regarding equality. The way to attain equality between different persons is not to treat them alike but to treat them differently.[31]

The importance of the difference between person-regarding equality and lot-regarding equality increases with the extent to which people differ from one another,[32] and with the value of the goods being allocated.[33] In an entirely homogeneous community the difference would never arise, but as communities become differentiated we must more and more often acknowledge the two forms of equality as fundamentally distinct. Even a society living at the edge of subsistence, under strict discipline of conformity, will manifest human differences. An industrial civilization with a liberal state and a competitive, consumption-oriented culture will reveal painfully obvious differences among persons—in their bodily traits, abilities, tastes in wine and food, the nature and extent of their ostentations, the size of their dental bills, the I.Q.'s of their children, the cost of their divorces, *ad infinitum*. In these circumstances, it is easy to see the meaning of person-regarding equality and difficult to imagine its attainment (or the *demonstration* of its attainment).

This difficulty arises because person-regarding equality requires interpersonal comparisons of utility (or of value in some other sense).

The formula itself ($V_{ii} = V_{jj}$) shows this requirement, since both persons are implicated in the "equals" sign. The test of lot-equality depends upon *one* person, with her wants and needs, placing the same value on two lots in an allocative pattern. Person-regarding equality depends on *two* persons—eventually on many such pairs—setting equal value on their own lots. It is precisely this sort of comparison that Pareto and Robbins[34] wish to say cannot be made. The proponent of person-regarding equality thus faces a challenge that is avoided by his lot-regarding colleague.

Since all interpersonal comparisons are not of one kind, we may roughly distinguish among three bases for them. First, *utility-based* comparisons address subjective states of satisfaction in individual minds. The individuals in question are ultimate authorities on their own mind states; no one but Yates can say how much he enjoys an ice cream cone. Second, *ends-based* comparisons address publicly announced ends or aims, to which individuals commit themselves. Once announced, ends are socially verifiable and the individual enjoys no privileged authority about his own commitments. Third, *needs-based* comparisons address those individual requirements that are determined by knowledgeable third parties. A physician may discern that Hochschild needs yellow pills; this suggestion may be right or wrong, but its defining trait is that the needs-bearing subject enjoys no special authority on this question. These three categories do not exhaust all the possibilities, and no doubt overlap. They mark three approximate points on a scale in which authority passes from the individual's unrivaled monopoly (utility) to a social sharing of authority (ends) to the hands of an observer or expert (needs). As may be guessed, comparisons grow easier, but more dangerous, as we travel between these points.

5.3.1   The Possibility of Utility-Based Person-Regarding Equality

Let us begin with a simple case. Suppose we are dividing a pie between two persons, and we want to cut the portions so that each will attain the same satisfaction from his or her piece. In pursuit of lot-regarding equality, we could simply cut the pie in two equal halves. But in pursuit of person-regarding equality, we must consider the beneficiaries. Since pie-eating is a utility-based practice if ever there was one, we must find out how much pleasure each person would derive from each bite of the pie. This knowledge can be obtained only by talking with Mr. i and Ms. j to find out about their mind-states (or tongue-states). Ms. j says that she will derive great pleasure from even a single crumb. Mr. i, on the other hand, says that nothing short of the whole pie will in the least satisfy his wants. Perhaps he is engaged in strategic manipulation, or perhaps he is stuck with a relentless sweet tooth.[35] Regardless of their reasons, we will be led to give Mr. i most of the pie. But will we *know* that we have attained equal utility between these two persons?

Now consider Ms. j's cousin Rumpelstiltskin. We endeavor to gratify his wants at a level equal to everyone else's. But our efforts never suffice, and he is always turning blue with rage at our failure to acknowledge his endlessly urgent wants and to provide the enormity of the material required for their satisfaction. The satisfaction of his wants would require an expenditure equal to the cost of all others' wants—and this merely to attain equal gratification for him and *each* of the others. At some point, we will wonder about the little man's sincerity, but his sincerity is not open to verification: Rumpelstiltskin is the sole and ultimate authority on his wants and satisfactions.

Next, consider two reasonable people, both utterly honest, both anxious to attain person-regarding equality in dividing a ten-dollar bill. Assume that there are no needs-based differences between the two (for example, neither is handicapped). Consider, first, a five-five split. This will imply equal utility only if the two have relevantly identical utility functions for money (roughly, equally expensive tastes). Consider then the general case of a split in which one person gets X and the other gets 10-X. This will lead to equality only if the expensivenesses of their tastes are in the same proportion as X to 10-X. Can we imaginably know this to be true or false?

Edward Thorndike has (perhaps unwittingly) demonstrated the intractability of such comparisons in his effort to find a measure of utility in money. He asked a panel of young recipients of relief in the 1930s how much money they would require in order to "do or suffer" a series of unpleasant experiences. The median dollar amounts turned out as shown in Table 8. Suppose now that we have two respondents, one asking $100 to eat an earthworm, and another seeking $100,000 for the same act. The *dollar* ratio is 1000 to 1. Do we learn anything interpersonally about the level of utility attained by each? No, we learn something about each person's *intra*personal tradeoff between money and the avoidance of worm-eating: although Thorndike's

Table 8. Measure of utility in money.

Unpleasant experience	Recipients' median requirement
Have one upper front tooth pulled out	$ 4,500
Have a little finger of one hand cut off	200,000
Choke a stray cat to death	10,000
Have to live all the rest of your life on a farm in Kansas, ten miles away from any other farm	300,000
Eat an earthworm six inches long	100,000

Source: Thorndike, *Human Nature and the Social Order*, p. 82.

printing of central tendency figures (medians) suggests interpersonal knowledge, this suggestion is false.

The trouble with utility-based personal equality is that each individual is the ultimate authority in all questions bearing upon his wants and satisfaction. This implies two difficulties: (1) *strategic manipulation* in which persons *lie* about their wants and satisfactions,[36] and, failing dishonesty, (2) *dialogic failure* in which there exists no grammar, no system of rules for conversation, by which people *can* understand one another's wants.[37] In the words of William Stanley Jevons: "I see no means whereby such comparison can be accomplished. Every mind is inscrutable to every other mind and no common denominator of feeling is possible."[38] This is a grave difficulty. We must, and do, make *rough* comparisons everyday, but they lack the rigor that would withstand unsympathetic argument.

The foregoing criticisms do not rule out rough and ready egalitarian good will toward diverse wants and tastes. We plausibly imagine that a *more* equal (and higher) level of utility will be attained by granting shoes that fit each person's foot rather than inflicting size 8 shoes on everyone. We assume that people will be more and more equally pleased if they choose their own ice cream instead of eating a single flavor chosen by the central authorities. Fully and precisely equal Standard International Utiles are thus not attained by all, but something more like equal utility is attained by recognizing diverse wants than by ignoring them.

5.3.2   Ends-Based Person-Regarding Equality

Instead of viewing people as passive receptacles of pleasure, we may view them as active authors of ends and purposes. Lot-regarding egalitarianism accepts discriminatory choices among ends, so long as all must equally pursue a given end or hierarchy of ends, such as the worship of God, or the development of square-cornered tomatoes. However, in person-regarding egalitarianism people are conceived as equal in their status as authors of (different) ends and purposes. This is a central tendency of liberal philosophy from Locke and Kant to Robert Nozick, Charles Fried, and Bruce Ackerman.[39] Here, for instance, is Ackerman's "principle of neutrality," which is a constraint on the giving of reasons for one's exercise of power in a "liberal dialogue": *"Neutrality.* No reason is a good reason if it requires the power holder to assert: (a) that his conception of the good is better than that asserted by any of his fellow citizens, *or* (b) that, regardless of his conception of the good, he is intrinsically superior to one or more of his fellow citizens."[40] Part a illustrates ends-based personal equality. The full relativism of this criterion is revealed in Ackerman's book, as "Commander" applies neutrality to a distributive argument between "A" and "Q."

> A: I should get some of this manna.
> Q: Why should you get it rather than I?
> A: Because I'll use it to build a great cathedral (or . . .).
> Q: But I too have a purpose in making a claim for the manna. I want to keep my belly warm.
> COMMANDER: What is it, then, about your purposes, A, that differentiates your claim from Q's?
> A: Easy. It's better to build cathedrals than warm bellies.
> Q: No it isn't.
> COMMANDER: Well, I'm afraid that Neutrality prevents me from recognizing either of your assertions as admissible in political conversation.
> A AND Q: Why?
> COMMANDER: Because no citizen may rightfully expect others to recognize that he has the legitimate authority to define the goals that everyone must work to achieve. Neutrality denies the legitimacy of a power relationship when such a thing must be said in its rational defense.[41]

This doctrine, and the larger structural type it illustrates, may seem to absolutists an appalling invitation to the worst of human pursuits, and in the fullness of time it may well be rejected along with similar liberal conceptions.[42] But our task is not to justify or condemn ends-based egalitarianism—simply to point out its existence and character.

Notice that this is a narrow or *marginal* form of egalitarianism, for it deals only with the *admissibility* of ends, not with the actual attainment of, or instruments for attaining, those ends. Mr. i's ends are just as admissible as Ms. j's. It may turn out that j pursues the square circle with little success while i pursues winning backgammon with full success, but success is irrelevant to ends-based equality. Furthermore, ends-based equality ignores, but would have no conceptual difficulty in adding, a more global equality aimed at the attainment of ends. This would commit us to whatever lot-regarding *in*equalities are required to attain ends that are more modest or extravagant than the national average. The very best topologists might thus be hired at great expense to work out j's very special circle, while little help would be needed for i's more modest aim. The equal status of their ends is simply a different matter from inequalities in success rates or in the allocation of means needed for success.

Notice also that ends-based equality implies nothing about equal utility. Someone may actually try to make himself miserable, and utility is itself only one among many ends that are on equal footing with one another. And the problems of interpersonal knowledge associated with utility are reduced and simplified in the matter of ends. So long as each subject can articulate her ends and purposes, natural language provides appropriate means of communication. And it is possible for listeners to correct a person about ends in a way that listeners cannot correct the beneficiary of utility.[43]

Once articulated, ends may be *detached* from specific individuals. Equal status for a given end does not depend on any one person's subscription to it. Thus, academic freedom, for example, attempts to promote equality between dissenting and established opinion without asking who articulates which opinion. That Jones had given up his Marxism changes nothing for the protection of Marxian teaching or for the more general doctrine of academic freedom. The solipsisms associated with utility-based equalities bear indirectly or not at all upon ends-based ones.

The real difficulty for ends-based equality is its collision with bureaucratic uniformity of treatment. This lot-equal system dominates in public education, as revealed by every family with peculiar values trying to cope with a uniform curriculum. This is illustrated by the 1972 Supreme Court case *Wisconsin* v. *Yoder*.[44] The Amish choose to withdraw their children from school at an early age in favor of practical work, and as a protection against the assimilationist forces of standard education.[45] Wisconsin law demands school attendance through age sixteen for all children. The state view is simply lot-regarding; the Yoder view is based on equality among ends, and favors a school system open to the ends of all, including those who wish to withdraw their children before age sixteen. The Amish family won the case on several counts, among them the view that: "Wisconsin's requirement for school attendance to age 16 applies uniformly to all citizens of the State and does not, on its face, discriminate against religions or a particular religion. A regulation neutral on its face may, in its application, nonetheless offend the constitutional requirements for government neutrality if it unduly burdens the free exercise of religion."[46] Here, we believe, the Court acknowledges a form of ends-based equality that has played an important role in the history of liberalism.

Notice that such equality has distinct limits. It is, first of all, unattainable when one of two ends is intolerant of the other: permitting both a tolerant and an intolerant creed is to favor the former and to reject the latter. Religious toleration in western European societies has in this way been flavored by Protestant pluralism at the expense of Catholic catholicism. The resulting arrangement cannot quite count as equal so long as any faith-in-one-faith, be it Roman Catholic or Leninist, is party to the deal, for no such faith can be served by pluralism in the way that pluralists are served by it.[47] By a similar paradox, a doctrine of ends-based person-regarding equality must acknowledge the equal status of egalitarian and antiegalitarian aims alike.

Frequently, conflicts of ends arise due to shortages of space or other resources. Fishermen and water-skiers cannot simultaneously pursue their separate ends on the same small lake, and, on the American frontier, sheep-herders pursuing their aims undermined the attempts of ranchers to achieve theirs. In such cases, the pursuit of one end forecloses the possibility of achieving another, and simple toleration of all ends does not result in ends-based person-regarding equality. A way out of such conflicts may lie in partitioning. We could, for example, reserve part of the lake for fishing, part for water-skiing, part for swimming, part for sailing, and part for biological research. People could then sort themselves out among these areas according to their aims and purposes.[48] The limit of this strategy, of course, lies in anarchy and utter atomization, where each individual is a community unto himself. Equality for all ends would lead to a paralyzing *immobilism* in which no end having social content could be attained.

5.3.3 Needs-Based Person-Regarding Equality

The real power of person-regarding equality appears in response to socially intelligible differences of need among persons. These needs may be based on differences of body or health, life history or present circumstance, aptitude or vulnerability. All that is required is that the needs be open to public perception, not confined to private whim.[49] Consider Gregory Vlastos' well-known hypothetical example of needs-based equality:

> Suppose, for instance, New Yorker X gets a note from Murder, Inc., that looks like business. To allocate several policemen and plainclothesmen to guard him over the next few weeks, at a cost a hundred times greater than the per capita cost of security services to other citizens during the same period, is surely *not* to make an exception to the equal distribution required by the equal right of all citizens to the security of their life and person; it is not done on the assumption that X has a greater right to security or a right to greater security. If the visitor from Mars drew this conclusion from the behavior of the police, he would be told that he was just mistaken. The greater allocation of community resources in X's favor, we would have to explain, is made precisely *because* X's security rights are equal to those of other people in New York. This means that X is entitled to the same level of police-made security as is maintained for other New Yorkers. Hence in these special circumstances, where his security level would drop to zero without extra support, he should be given this to bring his security level nearer the normal.[50]

The idea is that different services—differing in quantity or quality or both—may be justified in order to meet unequal needs equally. This is not to say that everyone will attain an equal level of pleasure or utility, but that each will have her needs served equally. Perhaps *no* service could make a crippled child as happy as her healthy friends, but her special needs may nonetheless require special services equal to and different from those of her playmates. Even if a mentally retarded boy will never derive the same utility from schooling that his bright brothers derive from it, schooling equally suited to his needs should still be provided (even if it is more costly than ordinary schooling).

Here is the kicker of Marx's slogan "From each according to his ability, to each according to his needs":[51] outsiders may decide on needs. An individual may thus be held to need X even if he denies that he needs X or opposes X or indicates that X will greatly diminish his utility.[52] It is thus quite possible for the authorities—political or scientific, radical or reactionary—to sail highly coercive paternalism under the flag of needs-based equality. This is the very insignia of B. F. Skinner's behavioral engineering,[53] and the chilling implication of the following speculation by Abraham Maslow:

> It turns out that chickens allowed to choose their own diet vary widely in their ability to choose what is good for them. The good choosers become stronger, larger, more dominant than the poor choosers ... If then the diet chosen by the good choosers is forced upon the poor choosers, it is found that *they* now get stronger, bigger, healthier, and more dominant, although never reaching the level of the good choosers. That is, good choosers can choose better than bad choosers what is better for the bad choosers themselves. If similar findings are made in human beings, as I think they will be, we are in for a good deal of reconstruction of all sorts of theories ... Only the choices and tastes and judgments of healthy human beings will tell us much about what is good for the human species in the long run. The choices of neurotic people will tell us mostly what is good for keeping a neurosis stabilized, just as the choices of a brain-injured man are good for preventing catastrophic breakdown, or the choices of an adrenolectomized animal may keep *him* from dying but would kill a healthy animal.[54]

If needs are thus to be ascertained only by the "good choosers," we must plead for the old inequalities.

Another advantage, and danger, of needs-based equality occurs when some members of society determine what they themselves, as well as others, need. For example, increasing a society's supply of goods through efficient use of talents and resources seems desirable. Such efficiency may require a division of labor, in which case "everyone of whom a given function is required may claim ... the conditions necessary to its performance ... Thus different functions imply different special needs."[55] However, who determines how difficult or important a job is, and what its doer needs to do it? The danger to equality in this version of needs-based equality is evident in Andrew Carnegie's paean to wealth: "Great inequality of environment, the concentration of business ... in the hands of a few, and the law of competition between these ... [are] not only beneficial, but essential for the future progress of the race . . . It follows that there must be great scope for the exercise of special ability in the merchant and in the manufacturer who has to conduct affairs upon a great scale."[56]

This elite-supporting version of needs-based equality is not limited to market capitalism. Edmund Burke argues that the tasks of governance require special wisdom and expertise, and that future leaders need special resources: "To be bred in a place of estimation to see nothing low and sordid from one's infancy; . . . to stand upon such elevated ground as to be enabled to take a large view of the widespread and infinitely diversified combinations of men and affairs in a large society; to have leisure to read, to reflect, to converse; . . . to be habituated in the pursuit of honour and duty; . . . these are the circumstances of men, that form what I should call a *natural* aristocracy, without which there is no nation."[57]

And yet to reject need as a basis of person-regarding equality would turn equality into a monstrous parody of itself. It *is* egalitarian to provide medical services to the sick and not to the well. The reason for this is not that sick people especially prefer such services (though they may) or that they choose health as their end (though they may). The reason is that they especially *need* medical help. Or consider fuel rationing applied with lot-regarding impartiality to homeowners in Alaska and Florida, to commuters and homebodies alike. The trouble with this is not that Alaskans especially like fuel oil, or that commuters have a yen for gas; it is that they need more of these fuels than other people need. These judgments of need are not incontrovertible, and they may conflict with judgments of want. Still, they play an essential part in deciding what is equal.

5.4 An Intersection Among Equalities

In societies with great individual-regarding inequality—great economic inequalities among persons—it is frequently argued that redistribution should begin at the top and flow to the bottom, so that more basic needs are met. A hundred dollars taken from a yachtsman and given to a poor mother is transformed from a nautical toy to a sack of potatoes for hungry children. This idea of the diminishing marginal utility of income[58] is based on the hypothesis that people first satisfy their most basic needs, and turn to progressively less basic needs as their budgets expand. It assumes that people are in this rough way "good choosers." Programs with this general shape are advertised everywhere and practiced more or less imperfectly in many places. The central idea of social democracy, the point of the welfare state, the pious hope of public charity, the ostensible purpose of progressive taxation—all of these are shaped around this notion of downward redistribution from the less basic needs of the rich to the more basic needs of the poor.

Our point here is that this kind of redistribution stands at an *intersection* among equalities. Three distinct strands of egalitarianism lead toward it. It is, first, an instance of person-regarding egalitarianism based on the satisfaction of needs. It takes account of the different needs of poor and rich and responds differently to each so as to respond equally to both: given the greater or more basic needs of the poor, the greater share of resources must be directed toward their satisfaction so that it becomes more nearly the case that $V_{ii} = V_{jj}$, where i is poor and j is rich. Paretians rightly observe that this action cannot be vindicated through utilitarian comparisons. Common sense and Anatole France[59] suggest that it can be vindicated on needs-based comparisons.

A second path leading to redistribution is only obliquely egalitarian, in that all moralism, including utilitarianism, is universalistic about its subjects: each to count for one and none to count for more than one. Peter Singer had indeed named this form of utilitarianism "equal consideration of interests."[60] If we are allowed interpersonal comparisons, and if it is true that the utility of material things, or of income, diminishes continuously at the margin, and if the total to be divided is fixed,[61] then it can be shown that we can always increase total utility by downward redistribution. The lost utility of the formerly rich will always be less than the gained utility of the formerly poor. This means, also, that a program designed to give equal marginal utility to all must give more in material goods to the rich than to the poor—we can buy the poor for cheap.[62] This is an old and endlessly criticized argument, stretching back to Hume and reaching the present era in the capable hands of Abba Lerner.[63] A third strand, which is not fully defined until the next chapter, would conceive this redistribution as a step toward global, lot-regarding equality. By diminishing differences of lot (say, income), we diminish grounds for envy, and make it more nearly true that $V_{ii} = V_{jj}$ for once-poor i and once-rich j. This, too, is a reason for the broad program of economic redistribution.

This point of intersection has two claims upon our continued attention. First, it suggests that structurally antagonistic equalities *may* find expression in common practice. So far as this is true, egalitarians may agree on their practical demands without agreeing on their reasons for them. This would hold true for any coincidence or intersection, not just for the one now under discussion. Second, and more interesting, it may happen that some equalities diverge from one another because other inequalities exist. If these other inequalities were diminished, then the contradictions in question might likewise be diminished. This seems true specifically for the inequalities alleviated by economic redistribution. Diminishing these inequalities may diminish the extent of divergence among other equalities—for instance, the distance between bloc-regarding and individual-regarding subjects, or between means-regarding and prospect-regarding equalities of opportunity. But this anticipates the work of our final chapter, and an intermediate task remains to be accomplished.

5.5 Summary

The essential distinction drawn in this chapter separates lot-regarding and person-regarding equalities. The former is defined by the formula $V_{ii} = V_{ij}$,[64] and by the corresponding fact that Mr. i would gain or lose no value in giving up his lot in favor of Ms. j's. Identical lots are a sufficient but not a necessary condition to this. Person-regarding equality is defined as $V_{ii} = V_{jj}$. Mr. i derives as much value from his lot as Ms. j derives from her lot. This requires a form of interpersonal comparison that is unnecessary for lot-regarding equality, a fact that limits the prospect for demonstrable person-regarding equality. This limit seems most damaging when comparisons are based on utility, less damaging when they are based on ends and needs.

6 Relative Equalities

THE FIFTH and last feature of our mythical Society E of Chapter 1 was "dichotomous thinking": all propositions are seen as either wholly true or wholly false without shades of differentiation. Just as people are or are not women, they are or are not tall, intelligent, or honest. Just as political societies are or are not members of the European Economic Community, they are or are not prosperous, just, or free. This type of thinking naturally simplifies the transformation of any ideal into practice by reducing its existence to a yes-or-no proposition: freedom or its absence, prosperity or the lack of it, justice or no justice—and equality or no equality.

Table 9, for instance, shows some possible divisions of one hundred apples between two persons. Dichotomous thinking would sort these alternatives by labeling allocation V equal, and I, II, III, and IV unequal—and, in effect, equally unequal. It would fail to distinguish between absolute inequality (allocation I) and progressively increasing equality as we move along toward IV. However, our society, unlike Society E, can distinguish I from IV; this chapter will explore a few main structural distinctions that arise from this and associated nuances of degree.[1]

Table 9. Possible divisions of one hundred apples between two persons.

Subject	Allocation				
	I	II	III	IV	V
Person i	100	99	75	51	50
Person j	0	1	25	49	50

Table 10. Sample allocations.

Subject	Allocation	
	I	II
Person i	100	7,000
Person j	50	5,000

We examine three main items. First, we discuss the difference between absolute and relative equality. Second, we identify several distinct notions of relative equality and examine the ways in which they relate to one another—for instance, in deciding which of the two allocations in Table 10 is more equal than the other. Depending on the notion of relative equality applied, each allocation is more equal than the other. We will investigate the possibility of ordering the different notions of relative equality by their stringency or fidelity to the root notion of equality to determine whether a plausible yet complete ordering of relative equalities is possible. Last, we will look at the relation between a commitment to equality and the *level* at which equality is to be established. Is our egalitarianism strict enough to prefer allocation V in Table 11? If not, then it is apparently necessary to embed equality in a larger system of allocative principles, or to embrace some theory that does this for us. Each of these issues arises from the fact of nondichotomous ideas, and each is treated in a section of this chapter.

6.1   Absolute versus Relative Equalities

By absolute equality we mean that every pair of individuals (or blocs) who are supposed to be equal at all are fully equal. If the subject structure is simple, then every pair of individuals must be fully equal; if the subject is bloc-regarding, then every pair of blocs must be fully equal.[2] We will here concentrate upon the central case of simple individual-regarding equality. Notice the two-fold character of absolute equality: (1) every

Table 11. Sample allocations.

Subject	Allocation				
	I	II	III	IV	V
Person i	2,000	200	20	2	0
Person j	1,000	100	10	1	0

pair of subjects must be covered, and (2) every such pair must be fully equal. The former governs extent and the latter governs degree. One might thus complain that some equals had not been made equal, or that some equals had not been made equal enough. The two complaints are independent and both must be answered by absolute equality. Notice that such equality may be highly marginal, or may deal with a very narrow class of equals, or may deal with means and not prospects, or may deal with lots and not persons: it is absolute only by its extent and its degree within the prior structure of subject, domain, value structure, and so on. One could thus have absolute equality in the division of a packet of chocolates between a pauper and a titan of industry, even if only the titan liked chocolate, even if all other aspects of life conspired to compound the pauper's misery: the absolute equality would be absolutely trivial, but absolute nonetheless. It may indeed be that absolute equality arises *mainly* where the class of subjects is exclusionary or where the domain is marginal or both.

By relative equality we mean that one allocation is more nearly equal than another, by being more extensive or more intensive or both. "More extensive" means covering more of the subjects who are supposed to be equal. "More intensive" means that, for a given pair of would-be equals, something closer to absolute equality has been attained. Again, these are independent considerations to which we will give independent consideration. They are also capable of interactive complexity when one has hubris sufficient to construct an index for relative equality in all its aspects (see Section 6.2.3).

Relative equality is more important than absolute equality, since it is more readily useful in our lives. Absolute equality is often impossible, or is possible only at a very low level. This is particularly true when a person-regarding value structure prevails and some persons suffer great handicaps. Only by highly inefficient investment in the handicapped can equality be approximated, and under no policy can it be attained. Or, quite distinctly, some goods such as praise, victory, and distinction can be divided unequally or not at all. Most important, society may want relative equality without so much as contemplating absolute equality. This is surely true in taxation and incomes policy for most if not all Western systems, as well as in policies to mitigate inequalities in health, education, transportation, housing, and the like. And we may embrace marginal equality, say, in the allocation of political rights or minimal incomes, conceiving this as a way of making the global condition of life more equal than it once was, yet without seeking the eventual attainment of absolute equality. Thus, the idea of relative equality is especially worthy of our attention.

6.2   Relative Equalities

A typical situation for egalitarian reform is a not-so-equal allocation and a demand for some alternative that will be more nearly equal. But what is to count as more nearly equal? This may hinge on the number of putative equals made actually equal (Section 6.2.1), or on the degree to which pairs of equals approach absolute equality (Section 6.2.2), or on some combination of these (Section 6.2.3).

6.2.1   The Extent of Equality

Suppose we have N putative equals.[3] Then an allocation becomes more and more equal as the number of actual equals approaches N. To begin with, suppose a society claims that all adults should have the right to vote, but intimidation prevents 15 percent of the adult population from exercising this right. If this number is cut to 14 percent (or even to 14.999 percent), relative equality may be claimed for the new arrangement. This is the first and simplest version of relative equality: the more equals, the more equal.

Felix Oppenheim proposed a closely related view:

A distribution of benefits is the more egalitarian, the larger the class of persons who receive it, as compared with the number who are excluded. Universal suffrage which excludes only minors and aliens is more egalitarian than a system which excludes Negroes in addition. Disenfranchising women is more inegalitarian than disenfranchising Negroes if the latter constitute less than half the population, but less inegalitarian if the majority is colored . . . On the other hand, a rule which allots *burdens* is the more egalitarian the larger the class of persons on whom it is imposed.[4]

Oppenheim's view appeals to shared experience, but courts a contradiction. Benefits and burdens are sometimes defined by mutual alternation: a benefit is the absence of a burden, a burden the absence of a benefit. If so, then the first half of Oppenheim's criterion will contradict the second and vice versa. Suppose we have the two allocations shown in Table 12, in which 1 denotes a benefit (or absent burden) and 0 denotes a burden (or absent benefit). Since allocation II dis-

Table 12. Two allocations of burdens and benefits.

Subject	Allocation	
	I	II
Person i	1	0
Person j	0	1
Person k	0	1
Person l	0	1
Person m	0	1

burses a benefit more widely than allocation I we must conclude that it is more equal. Since I disburses a burden more widely than II, we must conclude that it is more equal. But surely both of these views cannot hold true at once! Oppenheim evidently intends that burdens and benefits be considered separately in applying this criterion.

A different way to think about the problem is to think of *pairwise* relations among putative equals. Suppose the class of such equals consists of Messrs. i, j, k, and l. Absolute equality exists since, say, each suffers the same burden. Each pairwise relation is an equal one: i is equal with j, j is equal with k, and so on. We can develop a tableau such as the one in Table 13, where one denotes a pairwise equality and zero a pairwise inequality. The blanks are redundant comparisons, and the implied measure is the number of ones divided by the number of nonredundant comparisons (that is, by $n!/2[n-2)!]$ for n putative equals). Here the answer is $6/6 = 1.0$, which is the maximum value and corresponds to absolute equality. Now suppose we rearrange things so that Mr. j is privileged while i, k, and l remain one another's equals, as shown in Table 14. The answer is now $3/6 = 1/2$. When both k and l enjoy a benefit while i and j do not, the tableau becomes the one shown in Table 15, with the result $2/6 = 1/3$. By inventing a different level of benefit or burden for each person, we

Table 13. Pairwise relations.

Subject	Subject			
	i	j	k	l
Person i		1	1	1
Person j			1	1
Person k				1
Person l				

Table 14. Person j privileged, while i, k, and l remain equals.

Subject	Subject			
	i	j	k	l
Person i		0	1	1
Person j			0	0
Person k				1
Person l				

Table 15. Persons k and l privileged.

Subject	Subject			
	i	j	k	l
Person i		1	0	0
Person j			0	0
Person k				1
Person l				

Table 16. Sample allocations.

Subject	Allocation	
	I	II
Person i	10	1
Person j	11	1
Person k	12	1,000,000

could make every pair unequal and thus define the minimum for this measure to be zero. This is, in fact, a well-known measure of homogeneity used in political science, economics, biology, and other subjects.[5] It may be as good a definition for the extent of relative equality as will be found, but it, like all other such definitions, is subject to a decisive critique.

The flaw in these measures is that they rest upon an overly simple, indeed dichotomizing, view of allocation. This is easily seen by comparing the two allocations in Table 16. Thinking in merely nominal terms, allocation I contains no equality and II contains some equality (since i and j are equals). In the measure described above, I = 0, and II = 1/3. But surely allocation I is more nearly equal than II. The problem is, of course, that we have so far failed to note the degree of equality or inequality within given pairs of putative equals.

6.2.2   The Degree of Equality between Two Subjects

Now we examine just one pair of individuals (or blocs) who are supposed to be equals, and ask how equally they are treated under two allocative outcomes, so as to decide which outcome is more equal. The rules we use to answer such a question constitute criteria of relative equality, and four such rules command our attention: (1) maximin criterion, (2) ratio criterion, (3) least difference criterion, and (4) minimax criterion. We will take up each singly, commenting briefly upon its peculiarities, and then bring the four together to see how they relate to one another within shrinking, constant (or redistributive), and expanding economies.

The maximin criterion says that any allocation that improves the position of the less advantaged subject is more equal ("maximin" standing for "maximizing the minimum"). This criterion, praised elsewhere as a principle of justice,[6] judges relative equality by saying that what gives more to those with less must be more equal. This is the elemental feature of social democracy that most clearly links it with egalitarianism. It often corresponds to our intuitive notion of egalitarian redistribution. In Table 17, II is more equal than I, and II would be recommended by the maximin criterion. You may wonder whether this is not coincidental, since the lowering of the advantaged person's entitlement coincides with the raising of the disadvantaged person's entitlement. But note that, as in III, raising j's take from 20 to 50 while leaving i's at 80 would also be preferred under a maximin test—which seems reasonable.

The ratio criterion says that any allocation that increases the ratio between the lesser entitlement and the greater is more equal. The question is: What fraction of the advantaged subject's take goes to the disadvantaged subject? Thus, in the sequence of allocations shown in Table 18, the fraction in question moves from zero to one as we move from absolute inequality toward absolute equality. This corresponds very closely with our intuition, and avoids the obvious promiscuity of maximin as

Table 17. Egalitarian redistribution.

Subject	Allocation		
	I	II	III
Person i	80	50	80
Person j	20	50	50

Table 18. Sample allocations, from absolute inequality to absolute equality.

	Allocation				
Subject	I	II	III	IV	V
Person i	0	1	25	40	50
Person j	100	99	75 60	50	
Ratio	0	1/99	1/3	2/3	1/1

Table 19. Sequence of allocations with steadily improving ratios.

	Allocation				
Subject	I	II	III	IV	V
Person i	1	10	100	1000	1,000,000
Person j	10	90	800	7000	6,000,000
Ratio	1/10	1/9	1/8	1/7	1/6

Table 20. Median household incomes by race, 1950 and 1975, in constant 1967 dollars.

Year	Median income for blacks	Median income for whites	Ratio (b/w)	Difference
1950	$2,592	$4,778	0.50	$2,186
1975	$5,452	$8,860	0.61	$3,408

Net equalization of ratio, 1950–75 = .11
Net disequalization of constant dollar difference = $1,222

Source: Dorn, *Rules and Racial Equality,* pp. 34–35.

a criterion of equality. But notice that the ratio criterion will count each of the allocations in Table 19 as more equal than its predecessors. In Table 19 the ratios are improving by steady increments, while the differences expand by alarming increments. This is, in fact, an exaggerated version of what has happened to median incomes for black and white American households, as indicated in Table 20. The ratio is moving fitfully up toward 1/1 (that is, the black median/white median ratio rises from .50 to .61), while the difference (even in constant, inflation-free dollars) has risen apace. Some authors, like Dorn, reckon this an instance of rising inequality, whereas others, like James P. Smith and Finis Welch,[7] interpret it as indicating a steady trend toward relative equality between these two racial blocs.

Which view is right depends on the difference between the ratio criterion and the least difference criterion. *The least difference criterion says that any allocation that decreases the absolute difference between the greater entitlement and the lesser is more equal.* Whereas division regulated the ratio criterion, this criterion is regulated by subtraction. We simply subtract the amount held by a disadvantaged party from the amount held by an advantaged party, seeking to minimize the result in moving toward equality. This criterion defines our objection to the ratio criterion by asserting that absolute differences—not just ratios—are important. In absolute equalities, the ratio and least difference criteria converge precisely: any ratio of 1/1 will also have a difference of zero. But once this rare case is breached, the two considerations are utterly distinct. We can diminish the ratio while increasing the difference and we can increase the ratio while diminishing the difference, provided only that the ratio is not 1/1 and the difference is not zero when we begin.

A fourth and last version of relative equality, the minimax criterion, corresponds to the leveling impulse often associated with egalitarian tyranny, as in Tocqueville's analysis: "There is indeed a manly and legitimate passion for equality which rouses in all men a desire to be strong and respected. This passion tends to elevate the little man to the rank of the great. But the human heart also nourishes a debased taste for equality, which leads the weak to want to drag the strong down to their level and which induces men to prefer equality in servitude to inequality in freedom."[8] This principle requires no direct taste for tyranny,[9] and could be better said without the sexist metaphor, but it does attack advantage. *The minimax criterion says that any allocation that diminishes the entitlement of the more advantaged subject is more equal* ("minimax" standing for "minimize the maximum"). This is, of course, the hard edge of egalitarianism, the edge most obviously fostered by envy rather than nobler sentiment; however, in one very special circumstance (constant sum allocation) this principle is equivalent to other more generous ones.

6.2.2.1   *Constant Sum and Redistributive Allocations.* When the sum being distributed remains constant, the four criteria of relative equality are all exactly equivalent. Table 21 shows an example of this equivalence. This is a constant sum allocation—there are always 100 units

Table 21. Constant sum allocation.

Subject	Allocation				
	I	II	III	IV	V
Person i	100	99	75	51	50
Person j	0	1	25	49	50

being divided. The maximin criterion recommends each move from I to II to III to IV to V, since each raises the minimum. The ratio test recommends each of the same moves because each pushes the ratio (j/i) toward unity. The least difference criterion favors this sequence, since each move diminishes the top-to-bottom difference. Finally, the minimax criterion urges the same series of choices, since the advantaged subject's take declines as we move from I toward V.

But an example is not a demonstration, and for that we must turn to diagrams. In Figures 8–11 we represent each of these criteria by an indifference curve.[10] In each case, the less advantaged party's entitlement is shown on the vertical axis and the more advantaged party's allocation is shown on the horizontal axis. The shaded areas lying generally above and to the left of X—between it and the line of absolute equality—constitute relatively equal policies compared to the starting point X according to the four criteria. Now turn to Figure 12. Here the four indifference curves from Figures 8–11 have been superposed, and a line representing the possible allocations of a constant sum has been added (broken line). All the points on this line divide the same fixed sum. Note that all of the points above and to the left of X on the constant sum line (AX), up to absolute equality, are preferable to X according to all four criteria. This is shown by the fact that all four indifference curves meet at X and commend all points to its northwest (the shaded zone north of the maximin line and west of the minimax line). All the constant sum points northwest of X up to absolute equality fall into this larger set, and must therefore be preferred over X by all four criteria. Look now to the points southeast of X on the constant sum line (XB). All of these must be inferior to X according to all four criteria, on reasoning mirroring the reasoning just given above. Since nothing here depends on the location of the particular point X chosen, the demonstration is general. If (and only if) a point Y on the constant sum line is more equal than a point X according to any criterion, it must be preferable according to *all* four.

The convergence is actually much more general than it so far

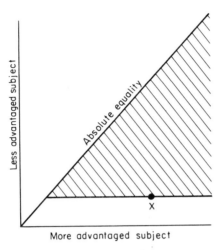

Figure 8. Maximin criterion.

seems. Instead of the restrictive set of constant sum allocations, we can speak of all strictly *redistributive* outcomes. These are outcomes in which one person's entitlement is increased and the other's is decreased—though not necessarily by the same amount.[11] Thus, one subject might gain a hundred units while the other loses just one; or

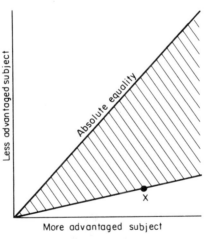

Figure 9. Ratio criterion.

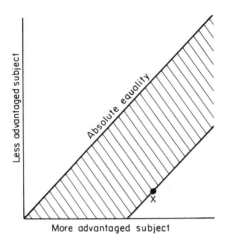

Figure 10. Least difference criterion.

one might lose ten thousand units while the other gains eleven. This class is equivalent to "Pareto-undecidable" allocations. The Pareto principle states that any move that increases the utility of at least one person while decreasing the utility of no one increases the aggregate welfare and is therefore preferred to the status quo. In Figure 13, any move to the northeast of X (shaded area) is Pareto-preferred to X.

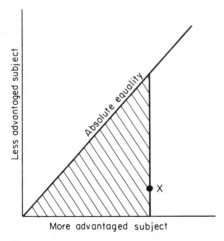

Figure 11. Minimax criterion.

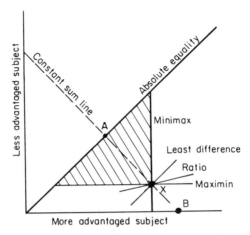

Figure 12. Four indifference curves, with constant sum line.

Similarly, moves in the opposite (southwest) direction are clearly rejected by the Pareto principle. Moves to the northwest and southeast, however, are redistributive moves, involving a gain in utility to one person and a simultaneous (but not necessarily corresponding) loss in utility to the other. Utility is not interpersonally comparable, so we cannot know whether these moves increase or decrease aggregate welfare, whether the gainer gained more than the loser lost. Such moves are therefore "Pareto-undecidable."

The class of redistributive outcomes is also equivalent to the sets of points northwest and southeast of X in Figure 12. These two sets are both bounded by the maximin and minimax criteria in that figure.

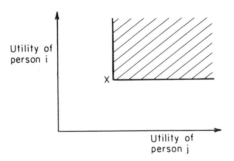

Figure 13. The Pareto principle.

This general class is the one for which our reasoning held good, and it would be incorrect to confine its implications to the special case of constant sum allocation. The general proposition, already demonstrated, is this: *Consider any two allocations X and Y to be redistributive (or Pareto-undecidable) if one subject is better off in X than in Y and another subject is better off in Y than in X. Then if Y is recommended by the maximin criterion, or the ratio criterion, or the least difference criterion, or the minimax criterion, then it must also be recommended by all three of the remaining criteria. If Y is not recommended by at least one criterion, then it will be recommended by none of the other criteria.* The main interpretation of this proposition is that upward redistributions will be opposed and downward redistributions will be endorsed by all four criteria of relative equality. It therefore does not really matter which criterion we choose—provided we are dealing in a two-sided redistributive economy.

6.2.2.2   Relative Equalities for Allocations with Growth or at Least without Mutual Loss. Let us turn now to a broader class of allocations than the one just analyzed, namely, to the class of allocations in which we have *either* redistribution *or* mutual gain (but not mutual loss) in a purportedly equalizing allocation. This broader class of cases is represented in Figure 14 by the unshaded area, which includes the fan of logically nested rules given by our four criteria of relative equality.

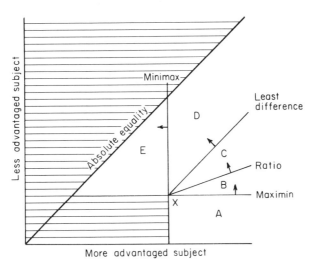

Figure 14. Allocation without mutual loss.

Look at areas A through E in the diagram to see which criteria of relative equality approve of each:

Zone	Is more equal than X according to
A	No criterion
B	Maximin
C	Maximin and ratio criterion
D	Maximin, ratio criterion, and least difference
E	Maximin, ratio criterion, least difference, and minimax

Every outcome not involving mutual loss falls into one of these five zones. (The area beyond absolute equality may be put aside, since it would give more to the disadvantaged than to the advantaged and therefore is analytically nothing but a permutation of identities.[12] This makes our demonstration general.) This tabulation is equivalent to a Venn diagram with the form of a bullseye, as shown in Figure 15. This warrants the following general conclusion: *Consider any two allocations X and Y such that Y is not worse for both subjects. Then if Y is more equal than X according to the minimax criterion, it must also be more equal according to least difference; and if it is more equal according to least difference, it must also be more equal according to the ratio criterion; and if it is more equal according to the ratio criterion, it must also be more equal according to*

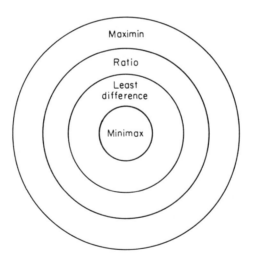

Figure 15. Zones for outcomes without mutual loss.

Table 22. Leveling up.

Subject	Allocation	
	I	II
Person i	100	1,000
Person j	90	100

maximin; and if it does not satisfy maximin, then it does not satisfy any of the four criteria. The most important implication of this conclusion is that "leveling up"—using growth to bring up the bottom while avoiding painful redistribution down from the top[13]—is a very weak form of relative equality. As Table 22 illustrates, one can satisfy this urge, thus fulfill maximin, and still have less equal ratios than before, greater differences than before, and larger entitlements for the previously advantaged. This may not seem very likely but it illustrates the general point, and a vast number of other examples could be supplied. The key to this finding is, of course, the prospect of mutual gain; when that is gone, everything is reversed.

6.2.2.3   Relative Equalities for Allocation with Shrinkage or at Least without Mutual Gain. We now consider a final and obverse class of allocations which are either redistributive or entail mutual *loss* (but not mutual gain). We wish to demonstrate that this allocative circumstance also produces a strict hierarchy of stringency among relative equalities, but that the order is precisely *reversed* from that above. Look at the unshaded portions of Figure 16 and at the five zones defined by the indifference curves depicting our four criteria of relative equality:

Zone	*Is more equal according to*
A	No criterion
B	Minimax
C	Minimax and least difference criterion
D	Minimax, least difference, and ratio criterion
E	Minimax, least difference, ratio criterion, and maximin

This follows by reasoning that is literally the mirror image of the reasoning just given for expansive allocative circumstances, and it precisely turns the bullseye inside out (see Figure 17). The general conclusion is, not surprisingly, inverted. *Consider any two allocations X and Y such that Y is not better for both subjects. Then if Y is more equal than X ac-*

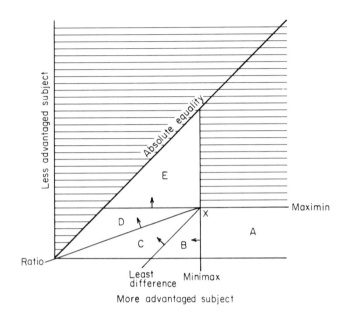

Figure 16. Allocation without mutual gain.

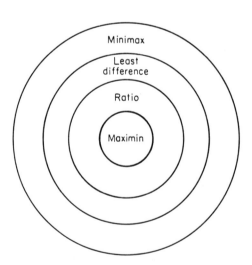

Figure 17. Zones for outcomes without mutual gain.

cording to the maximin criterion, it must also be more equal according to the ratio criterion; and if it is more equal according to the ratio criterion, it must also be more equal according to least difference; and if it is more equal acccording to least difference, it must also be more equal according to minimax; and if it does not satisfy minimax, then it does not satisfy any of the criteria. In short, the maximin criterion is no longer permissive but restrictive, and what satisfies this test under an economy without mutual gain must satisfy all the other criteria as well.

These criteria of relative equality do not lack a coherent hierarchy of stringency, but the hierarchy wholly depends upon the nature of the allocative choice. Under strictly redistributive circumstances, all four criteria coincide. Under "favorable" (mutually beneficial) circumstances and "unfavorable" (mutually harmful) circumstances their hierarchical rankings, from most to least stringent, are:

Mutually beneficial	*Mutually harmful*
Minimax	Maximin
Least difference	Ratio criterion
Ratio criterion	Least difference
Maximin	Minimax

6.2.2.4   How Social Scientists Resolve All of the Above by Means Well-Known to Ostriches. These interactions among the principles of relative equality depend upon the possibility of mutual gain or loss, which depends in turn upon the possibility of fluctuation in the total to be divided. Suppose we wanted to simplify matters greatly in order to set up a single and universal index for relative (in)equality. How would we hide fluctuations in the total from our own attention? We would simply *normalize* everyone's entitlement by treating it as a proportion of the total or (what does the same work) as a proportion of the mean entitlement. Thus a 7:3 division and a 7,000:3,000 division are alike reduced to being divisions in the proportion .7:.3 or 70%:30%. With this disposal of seemingly irrelevant information, every allocative choice looks like the constant sum case (discussed in Section 6.2.2.1), with the result that all four criteria of relative equality coincide. This maneuver underlies just about every important analytic index for relative equality or inequality known to economic and social science.[14] Its apparent purpose is to simplify analysis without putting aside any "useful" information, and it does exactly that. It does it, however, in the style of ostriches. On the normalized data, all rules of relative equality will agree. In the one case where the normalization changes nothing (constant sum allocation) this apparent agreement represents an actual agreement of judgments; in all other cases, it masks conflicts among the criteria by removing information needed to see conflict. Thus, for example, we might be shown the move from allocation I to allocation II in Table 23 as an instance of relative equalization, and we will agree that this modest alteration is to be counted as an increase of the minimum, an improvement of the ratio, a diminution of the difference, and a diminution of the maximum—all of these at once, and all because of each. But it may *not* increase the minimum if the total shrinks from I to II (see Table 24). It may not diminish differences, or lower the maximum, if the total expands from I to II (see Table 25). Only the ratio is preserved in this normalized conception, and the remaining criteria are forced to function as if they were surrogates for the ratio. Thus, conflicting notions of relative equality

Table 23. Relative equalization on normalized data.

| Subject | Allocation | |
	I	II
Person i	.33 (33%)	.35 (35%)
Person j	.67 (67%)	.65 (65%)

Table 24. Relative equalization with decreasing total.

| Subject | Allocation | |
	I	II
Person i	330	175
Person j	670	325
Total	1000	500

Table 25. Relative equalization with increasing total.

| Subject | Allocation | |
	I	II
Person i	330	700
Person j	670	1300
Total	1000	2000

continue to conflict in an unnormalized world but coincide happily in a normalized analysis of it.[15]

6.2.2.5   *An Invariant but Partial Notion of Relative Equality.* All the criteria so far discussed silently ask us to conceive the idea "more equal than" as a complete ordering: for any pair of allocations X and Y, either X is more equal or Y is more equal or the two are equally (un)equal. But as others have already suggested, this may be a distortion. Here, for instance, is the view of Amartya Sen: "The very idea of inequality seems to have a quasi-ordering framework. The concept is not geared to making fine distinctions and comes into its own with sharper contrasts."[16] Even after all this discussion, we have remained captives of dichotomous thought at a second level of abstraction, in assuming that just the right idea of relative equality will produce a universally applicable and categorical series of answers. It is quite likely that this cannot be attained, and that a partial or quasi-ordering idea of relative equality is all that we can expect.

One could assert that relative equality exists only when all four criteria point in the same direction. This would be equivalent to saying that *both* maximin and minimax must be met if an allocation is to count as more equal, no matter what the economic circumstance (expansion, constancy, shrinkage). As we have seen, any outcome meeting both of these criteria will meet the remaining criteria of difference and ratios.[17] A slightly less rigid (but broadly equivalent) test would require that the maximum be diminished without the minimum being diminished or that the minimum be increased without the maximum being increased. This would mean that many or even most allocative choices would lead to *no* judgment about relative equality. It would actually mean that the Pareto principle and equality would divide life between them: equality would say nothing about mutual gain or loss while the Pareto principle continued its silence about redistribution. The division of a two-dimensional commodity space would be as shown in Figure 18.

6.2.3   *Relative Equality in General*

Equality seems two-sided: this group being equal with that group, this person equal with that person. This two-sidedness is symbolized in the conventional notation of arithmetic with one term on each side of "=". One seldom sees a three-sided equality expression, to say

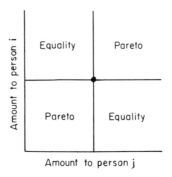

Figure 18. Division of a two-dimensional commodity space.

nothing of a six-sided one (Figure 19). Three or more terms may be equal, each with all the rest, but this will be interpreted as a claim about pairs of terms—it will be decomposable into an array of binary relations. Combining pairwise equalities to form more elaborate ones presents no difficulty so long as equality is conceived dichotomously as holding or not holding in each pair. But the general problem of relative equality involves degrees of equality and therefore requires extension beyond the simple pairwise relation to which the notion applied itself so nicely. We are thus compelled to consider two things at once: (1) the degree to which any given pairs approach equality, and (2) the extent to which any given degree of equality is spread over the putatively equal pairs of subjects. This requires us to combine two independent desiderata in judging the relative equality of any two distributions, as in Table 26. Which of the allocations in the table *is* more equal? Or is neither more equal than the other? The difficulty is that allocation I is more equal when we consider degrees of equality in given pairs, and II is more equal when we consider the spread of equality among pairs. Allocation I offers great equality to fewer people; II offers less equality spread a bit further. This problem faces all general ideas of relative equality, and it suggests that no fully general

Figure 19. Multi-sided expressions of equality.

Table 26. Relative equality of two allocations.

| | Allocation | |
Subject	I	II
Person i	60	80
Person j	60	50
Person k	60	40
Person l	0	10

idea will prove satisfactory. Still, let us examine the problem a little further.

The usual approach is to construct an index of equality or inequality that first measures (in)equality between each pair of subjects and then averages over all pairs. A main example is the Gini index of inequality, which nicely illustrates the best and worst of its genre. While the Gini index is often depicted as an extension of the Lorenz curve—that is, an olgive, or cumulative curve, showing what proportion of a total domain is held by each given proportion of a population (see Figure 20)—its fundamental structure is actually based on pairwise comparisons. Following Sen's notation,[18]

$$G = \frac{1}{2n^2 \cdot u} \sum_{i=1}^{n} \sum_{j=1}^{n} |y_i - y_j|$$

where n is the number of subjects, u is the arithmetic mean of their entitlements, y_i and y_j are the entitlements of persons i and j. We begin by constructing a tableau of all absolute pairwise differences. Thus, for instance, we might begin with allocation II above, and arrive at the pairwise differences shown in Table 27. The grand total of pairwise differences in the table amounts to 440 units. Given four subjects, with a mean entitlement of 45 units, the arithmetic is:[19]

$$\frac{1}{2 \cdot 4^2 \cdot 45} \cdot 440 = \frac{440}{1,440} = .305$$

If we conduct this calculation for distribution I in Table 26, it turns out that its Gini index value is .250—considerably lower than the value for II just calculated. This lower value tells us to think that allocation I is less unequal or more equal than II.

But imagine that we are hired as consulting magicians by Mr. i, whose 80-unit entitlement inclines him to favor allocation II. He

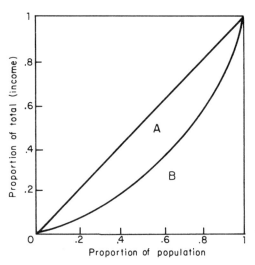

Figure 20. Cumulative curve on household incomes for OECD countries. (*Source:* Based on data for Australia, Canada, France, West Germany, Japan, the Netherlands, Norway, Spain, Sweden, the United Kingdom, and the United States. The curve is for an unweighted average of post-tax income based on standardized household sizes. The bottom-to-top income shares by decile are: 2.2, 8.8, 5.3, 6.7, 8.1, 9.4, 10.8, 12.7, 15.6, 25.4, as given in table 10 of Sawyer, *Income Distribution*. The Gini index may be interpreted as the ratio of area A to area A-plus-B in the Lorenz diagram.)

Table 27. Absolute pairwise differences.

| | Subject | | | |
Subject	i	j	k	l
Person i	0	30	40	70
Person j	30	0	10	40
Person k	40	10	0	30
Person l	70	40	30	0

would like us to defend that allocation in the name of equality—to reverse the judgment just given against it by the Gini index. The task is easy, for we need only propose that relative inequality is properly defined by the mean difference from the mean entitlement, yielding:

Allocation I has a mean difference from the mean of 22.5 units, which norms to .500 when divided by the mean entitlement.

Allocation II has a mean difference from the mean of 20 units, which norms to .444 when divided by the mean entitlement.

While the first (Gini) measure told us one thing, this one tells us another. The implication should be obvious, for it is *easy* to engage in moral gerrymandering of this sort, and it is impossible to say categorically which of two views of relative equality is best or which distribution is most equal. A difficult problem in the simplified case of two-sided comparisons becomes an intractable one in the many-sided case.

The ease of this gerrymandering is alarming *only* if one takes the indices in question as serious *definitions* of (in)equality and not as tentative hints about the shape of an overall distribution. If one takes them in this lighter way, and is willing to surrender any universal scope for equality, it is possible to accept Amartya Sen's wise conclusion:

> *Inequality as a notion does not have any innate property of "completeness."* In a trivial sense it is, of course, the case that one can define "inequality" precisely as one likes, and as long as one is explicit and consistent one may think that one is above criticism. But *the force of the expression "inequality," and indeed our interest in the concept, derive from the meaning that is associated with the term, and we are not really free to define it purely arbitrarily.* And—as it happens—the concept of inequality has different facets which may point in different directions, and sometimes a total ranking can not be expected to emerge. However, each of the standard measures does yield a complete chain, and arbitrariness is bound to slip into the process of stretching a partial ranking into a complete ordering. It is arguable that each of these measures leads to some rather absurd results precisely because each of them aims at giving a complete-ordering representation to a concept that is essentially one of partial ranking.[20]

If Sen is to be believed, we must restrict the concept of relative equality; we must look askance at the many efforts to devise a single, best index of equality,[21] and focus on those cases in which we can make unambiguously equalizing changes, typically by the redistribution of things from the top toward the bottom of society.[22] But we will in any case need to ask ourselves about the *level* at which equality is to be achieved.

6.3   The Level at Which Equality Is to Be Attained

Imagine a hopeless cripple who yearns to play soccer as an equal in a crowd of healthy soccer-loving athletes. We try to promote person-regarding equality by granting him special training and special equipment (say, an electric wheelchair with pneumatic kicking devices) so as to increase his mobility, but every such effort fails. Is equality therefore unattainable? Not at all: we could cripple the healthy athletes since we cannot "uncripple" the cripple. This *will* implement equality. Our cripple will now play on even terms with the others, even though the level of soccer played may be greatly diminished.[23] By slight extension, equality of a sort might be attainable under any circumstances; equality of a more final sort will be attained for all of us. In Colonel George Mason's well-worn epigram, "We came equals into this world and equals we shall go out of it."[24]

However, most advocates of equality would not promote equality at just any level, but rather at a level helpful to its beneficiaries. If I have an income of 10 cents and you have an income of $100,000, my advocacy of equality very likely entails an increase in my income. Yet, strictly speaking, my advocacy of *equality* alone would compel me to choose Allocation I over Allocation II in Table 28. This is because almost every standard of relative equality will pick out allocation I as more equal than II. Since this is surely not what egalitarianism really seeks, we are forced to conclude that some aggregative principles are at least implicitly mixed with any direct demand for equality.[25]

The maximin criterion for relative equality is this sort of compromise and has been proposed as a criterion of social justice by John Rawls.[26] It provides both Rawls' basic concept of justice and his specific rule for material allocation (as the "difference principle"). One

Table 28. Sample allocations.

Subject	Allocation	
	I	II
You	$0	$60,000
Me	0	40,000

way to interpret this principle is to say that we should pursue equality until it begins to hurt those it should help most—those who are least advantaged by existing inequalities. Another (complementary) interpretation is to say that society should let inequalities stand but only if they are advantageous to their victims. Thus we might allow certain inequalities of income if these appeared to offer incentives for work, risk-taking, or capital accumulation that would actually promote the welfare of society's least advantaged members—those without work, without assets to risk, without the possibility of accumulating capital. To attack such inequalities would (for Rawls) be unjust and (for the poor) unprofitable.

If, instead, we leave equality a purely distributive notion,[27] the problem of the level of equality presents itself as a "tradeoff" or conflict of values pitting equality against efficiency or against utilitarian maximization. In the framework of market economics, it thus appears that, as Arthur Okun says, "we can't have our cake of market efficiency and share it equally."[28] He suggests that more equality usually means more government drag on production, lessened incentives for risk, work, and investment, and so on. Yet, as Okun recognizes, more equality may imply more efficiency, and it is often argued that (for a fixed total of commodities or wealth) an equal or nearly equal distribution maximizes total welfare.[29]

While the analytical and empirical complexities of this point are great, they need no resolution here—for our point is simple: no generous or humane view of equality can be merely a view of equality. It must see equality within constraints, above some floor. Equality itself is as well pleased by graveyards as by vineyards.

6.4   Summary

We have dealt with three topics here. First, we have sketched the important difference between absolute and relative equalities. Second, we have analyzed some main criteria of relative equality and have shown how their relations with one another depend upon allocative circumstance. We have also suggested, with Amartya Sen, that relative equality is not a universal relation applicable to any two arbitrarily chosen distributions. Finally, we have noted that equality itself is no respecter of human prosperity, being as well served by total poverty as by universal wealth.

7 Endings

WE END as we began, with Tocqueville's prophetic dread:

> The gradual progress of equality is something fated. The main features of this progress are the following: it is universal and permanent, it is daily passing beyond human control, and every event and every man helps it along. Is it wise to suppose that a movement which has been so long in train could be halted by one generation? Does anyone imagine that democracy, which has destroyed the feudal system and vanquished kings, will fall back before the middle classes and the rich? Will it stop now, when it has grown so strong and its adversaries so weak? . . . This whole book has been written under the impulse of a kind of religious dread inspired by contemplation of this irresistible revolution advancing century by century over every obstacle and even now going forward amid the ruins it has itself created.[1]

While we do not wholly share Tocqueville's anxiety, we have never escaped the ken of his prophecy. It is possible indeed to construe our analysis as an exercise in pettifoggery against Tocqueville—caviling over the details lying beneath his necessarily abstract prophecy. But the pettifogger traffics in trivial details, whereas we have dealt in ones that matter greatly in practice. Policies that treat individuals equally differ significantly from those treating blocs of individuals equally. The difference between dividing a marginal increment equally and dividing things in a way that leads to global equality matters greatly to the eventual meaning of Tocqueville's prophecy. There is a vast difference between equal opportunity and a less mercurial equality of result, just as there is between equal means and equal prospects of advancement. It is one thing to make women and men more equal than once they were, and quite another to make them equal. It is one thing to give people equal lots in society and something very different to give them lots of equal value. Each distinction amends Tocqueville's monumental idea, but only as the world already requires. Each distinction thus models a complication that would have to occur if the prophecy were to pass from theory to practice, from abstract simplicity to empirical complexity, from program to policy, from policy to behavior. In this measure our task is done and the analysis speaks for itself.

But we have yet to connect our analysis with the obvious questions about equality's alleged conquest of the world:

1. Is equality the name for one coherent program or is it the name for a system of mutually antagonistic claims upon society and government?
2. Everywhere one hears praise for the idea of equality, yet inequality persists. How can we explain the disjunction?
3. Equality is the simplest and most abstract of notions, yet the practices of the world are irremediably concrete and complex. How, imaginably, could the former govern the latter?

It is very nice to model the structure of an idea as we have done, but it remains to assess the portent of this analysis. These three questions must be answered by such an assessment, and they are the business that remains.

7.1   Equality: Equalities

The very success of equality requires the idea's accommodation to life's buzzing complexity. How different this is from the simple march described by Tocqueville and parodied in our imaginary Society E. There, society is one undivided mass; allocation occurs in a single stroke, for all time; goods are divisible like peanut butter (and not like babies); people are so like one another in their wants, needs, and ends that their differences never affect value; and thought is dichotomously structured. This is a society without structural complexity. It is therefore a society in which equality could and would retain its simplicity as it was put into practice. Indeed, Society E could admit just one notion of equality, meeting the following specifications:

1. Its subject would be (universally) inclusive, and individual-regarding. (No markers exist for segmentation, for bloc formation, or for the exclusion of any members.)
2. Its domain would be all-inclusively broad and allocation would be

straightforward. (The allocation of everything all at once rules out marginal and global variation.)

3. It would equalize life's results rather than its opportunities. (As a consequence of one-time allocation there would be no opportunities, and without "lumpiness" opportunity-regarding surrogates for more direct equality have no place.)

4. Its value structure would be lot-regarding, but would satisfy person-regarding criteria of equality as well. (Without personal differences, identical lots are of equal value to all.)

5. It would be an absolute equality (or no equality at all in a dichotomizing logic).

This is one form of equality, the simplest and perhaps the most complete, and the only form of equality that could arise in Society E. It is cousin to the equality for which Gracchus Babeuf died in 1796: "Let there be no other difference between people than that of age or sex. Since all have the same needs and the same faculties, let them henceforth have the same education and the same diet. They are content with the same sun and the same air for all; why should not the same portion and the same quality of nourishment suffice for each of them?"[2]

This notion of equality—embracing a uniform division of all things for all persons—may be what lay at the end of Tocqueville's projected history, and may be what he most dreaded. It is certainly part of the general vision that so terrified his aristocratic and bourgeois admirers. But this equality arises naturally not from societies we know but only from a society we can scarcely imagine. It arises as a controlling conception of equality in a mechanically simple context without variation or history, without differentiation or life. Society E is too simple even to describe the communal organization of bees. In any real historical context *no* single notion of equality can sweep the field. Because the structure of human societies is complicated, equality must be complicated if it is to approach practice.

Equality splits itself into many distinct notions, each an element in its grammar. Equality's subject may be individual-regarding, bloc-regarding, or segmental; its domain may be straightforward, marginal, or global; the idea of equality may be applied directly (equal results) or may be a version of equal opportunity (which in turn may equate means or prospects); equality may be based on uniform lots or on lots equally accommodating differences; it may be absolute or relative (and, if relative, based on any of several distinct notions of relative equality). There are, moreover, many subordinate points of structural differentiation, such as the distinction between inclusive and exclusive subjects, or between the two strategies for global equality—compensatory inequality and redistribution of domains.

These distinctions must be combined with one another if equality is to be made flesh. It is meaningless to prescribe "equality for all j's" without defining the domain of their equality, its value structure, its treatment of results and opportunities, its absoluteness or relativity. It is likewise meaningless to demand "equal X" without saying who will be the subject of this equality, on what treatment of value, and with what response to X's lumpiness. These partial views of equality would be like sentence fragments lacking subjects or verbs and therefore lacking the minimum of structure required for communication. Confining attention to basic structural distinctions, we would need to answer each of the following queries to analyze any single instance of equality:

1. Is the subject of this equality simply individual-regarding, segmental, or bloc-regarding?
2. Is the domain of this equality straightforward, marginal, or global?
3. Is this equality direct, or is it means-regarding equal opportunity, or prospect-regarding equal opportunity?
4. Is this a lot-regarding or a person-regarding equality?
5. Is this equality relative or absolute?

Two rabbits can populate a vast continent in a few years, and a small squadron of English sparrows did indeed so populate North America within a single decade. Should it be a surprise that five splittings of equality yield a vast array of meanings of that idea? Without reaching for secondary distinctions, the five grammatical components yield three subject structures, three domain types, three treatments of opportunity and result, two value structures, and two main outcomes of the absoluteness-relativity distinction. In generating combined types, these terms multiply one another, yielding:

$$3 \cdot 3 \cdot 3 \cdot 2 \cdot 2 = 108$$

structurally distinct interpretations of equality. If we include the four subspecies of relative equality, admit of the difference between inclusive and exclusive subjects, and reckon with two strategies of globalism, the number of distinct formulas skyrockets.[3] Attending to tertiary distinctions would quickly push the total to four or perhaps five digits.

These many ways of structuring equality to accommodate it to the form of actual societies have been our subject all along. We are now interested not so much in their existence as in their relationships with one another, particularly the ways in which these different structures may support or antagonize one another. We simplified this concern in Chapter 1 by juxtaposing two polar views—that equality spawns a single coherent program, or that it spawns a system of mutually antagonistic claims upon society and government. According to the first view, each variant of equality would be consistent with every other, and each would play its assigned role just as the parts of a great cathedral fit into a single whole. According to the second view, each form of equality would conflict with every other, so that a commitment to any one equality would rule out a commitment to any other equality. Erecting one wall of the cathedral would topple another. Both of these simplifications are, of course, wrong, and equalities are capable of having many different kinds of relationships to one another. We will survey the main cases one at a time, beginning with those most favorable to equality as a single program and finishing with those most favorable to the view that equality is a system of mutually antagonistic themes.

7.1.1 Convergence

Two very different notions of equality may converge in practice, so that differences of underlying structure are effaced. For instance, in Figure 21 there are two differences between outcome 2 and outcome 3. The two differences may offset one another so that one practical prescription suits both simple person-regarding equality (outcome 2) and segmental lot-regarding equality (outcome 3). There is no necessity in this, but it can happen if the segmenting criteria of the subject in outcome 3 correspond to the same differences of need, end, or want implicated in a simple person-regarding structure like structure 2. Thus, we might demand hemodialysis for all kidney patients and diets for all fat people, then interpret this pairing of treatments as either structure 2 or structure 3. The two structural combinations are not equivalent in general, for structure 2 will usually represent a humane egalitarianism of the kind that Tawney tried so valiantly to promote, while structure 3 can describe the basis of all systematic in-

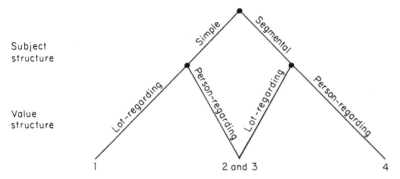

Figure 21. Outcomes with different underlying structures.

equality—such as caste society, racism, or any other arrangement that uses that (segmental) equality precisely to systematize inequality itself.[4] The convergence constitutes an exceptional case in which a segmental subject structure is made to do the work of a person-regarding value structure.

A similar convergence may occur among equalities of opportunity. A scheme of compensatory inequality applied to means-regarding equal opportunity may generate something equivalent to prospect-regarding equal opportunity. Thus, for example, a Headstart program of early education for disadvantaged children may be seen as compensatory inequality of means, yet turn out also to approximate equal prospects between advantaged and disadvantaged kids. Or a quota-based system of recruitment may promote both bloc-regarding equality of prospects and segmental equality of means. This will occur if quotas are proportionate to the relevant populations of aspirants (hence equal prospects by bloc) and if a means-regarding equality of opportunity prevails within each of the quota pools (hence a segmental equality of means).

A convergence of equalities appears in justifications of social democracy and the welfare state (Section 5.4). The downward redistribution of income, and progressive taxation to pay for universally available social services, are among the important features of social democracy, at least as imagined in the ideal.[5] These are justifiable in part as providing relative equality of lots—that is, reduced differences in material circumstance. They are also, and quite differently, justifiable on person-regarding grounds, since they give special attention to the more urgent needs of the poor—taxing away baubles from the rich to provide food for hungry children. The services provided by the welfare state likewise respond to special personal needs arising from illness, age, illiteracy, bad housing, unemployment, and so on. One can interpret the same policies as specimens of utilitarian equality— total welfare is maximized by attending to the special needs of the disadvantaged, since greater marginal utility results from this than from less egalitarian allocations: potatoes do more for the poor than yachts do for the rich.[6] Finally, one can regard many of the same welfare state policies as ameliorations for stunted opportunities of poor children. By improving their health and housing, we make their means and prospects of advancement less distinctly inferior than they would be otherwise. The convergence of all these qualities in one set of policies helps in part to explain the confused complexity of our thought on the welfare state, and it also helps account for the welfare state's resistance to criticism based on a failure to promote equality in any one sense.

These patterns of convergence do not indicate any real amalgamation of structurally distinct equalities; they instead indicate that under specific contingencies different forms of equality find common satisfaction in a single program. In each case, one structural difference offsets another in its effect upon practice, so as to produce a marriage of convenience. This marriage is always a fragile one, quickly dissolved when the relevant contingency is removed. This fragility is especially striking in the convergence of relative equalities. So long as all allocative choices are strictly redistributive (without mutual gain or loss), then relative equalities converge perfectly. If a distributional change raises the minimum or lowers the maximum, or if it improves the ratio or reduces the difference between two subjects of equality, then it must, of logical necessity, also satisfy all of the remaining tests for relative equality.[7] The four all amount to the same thing. But let there be the slightest divergence from the relevant contingency—let there be mutual gain or mutual loss—and the relative equalities immediately diverge.

7.1.2 Strong versus Weak Alternation

A first hint of discord is heard when equality presents a choice between "strong" and "weak" variations. For example, the subject may be inclusive (strong) or exclusive (weak), as with the difference between equality for Americans and equality for, say, white male

Americans. The strong variant can be attained only with the weak, but the weak can be attained without the strong. Thus (strong) equality for Americans can be attained only with equality for white male Americans, but (weak) equality for white male Americans can be attained without any more inclusive equality involving women and blacks. Strong implies weak, whereas weak fails to imply strong.[8]

Another especially obvious instance of this relationship appears between relative and absolute equalities: given an initial inequality, greater equality can be attained without absolute equality, but absolute equality surely presupposes relatively greater equality. If your income is ten times mine at the start, any diminution of the ratio will constitute relative equality, but only a tenfold diminution will bring us to absolute equality. More subtly, one notion of relative equality may be stronger (or weaker) than another. In an expanding economy, the four notions of relative equality fall into a hierarchy, from strong to weak, of: (1) minimax, (2) least difference, (3) ratio criterion, and (4) maximin. Any change that satisfies a higher ranking test also satisfies all lower ranking tests (see Section 6.2.2.2). In a shrinking economy, the opposite hierarchy takes over.[9] The important point is not the detail of ordering, but the existence of a choice between stronger and weaker equalities.

The most important cases of this type center upon subject structure. Assuming a total subject population of given size, we may take a simple individual-regarding structure as strong in relation to either a bloc-equal or segmental structure, both of which weaken the former. A segmental structure requires only that persons belonging to the same segment be equals; persons belonging to different segments—races, castes, educational strata, classes—may be unequal. The simple structure treats everyone as equal with everyone, whereas the segmental structure requires only that some be equal with some. Any practice that meets the test of a simple equality will—for a given population—always meet any segmental test, but many practices meeting a segmental test will violate a simple one. This is a classic case of strong-weak alternation.

The parallel case of simple versus bloc-regarding subject structures is still more important. Simple equality preempts the demand for bloc-regarding equality, because the elimination of inequalities between persons must a fortiori eliminate inequalities across blocs of persons. Insofar as Americans are treated as equals, then American men and women are necessarily equal, American blacks and whites are necessarily equal, native Americans and immigrant Americans are necessarily equal. The obverse is patently false. One can equalize the incidence of inequality upon two blocs without making *any* progress toward equality of a simple individual-regarding sort. No program of affirmative action, no matter how complete its scope and arduous its execution, will promise the slightest easing of inequality among persons.[10] The incidence of inequality will fall less regularly upon women and minorities, but the old differences between winners and losers will remain. The shift from individuals to blocs is profoundly a shift from strong to weak equality. We will pick up this thread again in Section 7.2.

7.1.3 Mutual Exclusion

A more obdurate deviation from unitary egalitarianism arises when equalities rule each other out: either this or that or neither, but not both. This is a more serious obstacle than strong-weak alternation, because mutual exclusion does not allow for a reconciliation like that provided by strong equalities. No resolution will accommodate two exclusive equalities at once.

A main case of mutual exclusion arises from the two value structures. Treating people alike—with lot-regarding equality—will promote an equality that rules out envy. Nobody will gain from trading his lot for someone else's. Treating people in a way that serves equally well their differing wants, ends, or needs will rule out the former equality: we can have lot-regarding equality or person-regarding equality (or neither) but not both at once. Equality of lots requires English- and Spanish-speakers alike to speak English, allows one vote for conformist and rebel alike, one tax for rich and poor alike, one God for Christian and Jew alike. Equality of persons allows English for some and Spanish for others, one sort of "vote" for the conformist and another for the rebel (hard to arrange, eh?), different gods for different faiths. The choice presents itself again and again wherever equality travels.

Similarly, the two forms of equal opportunity—equality of means and equality of prospects—generally rule out one another. Uniform means, presented to persons of unequal talent, constitute a certain formula for inequality of prospect. And, in general,[11] systems that equalize prospects do so by presenting superior means to persons of inferior talent. The matter is, as we have already shown at length,[12] much more complex than that, but it remains a choice between two antagonistic conceptions of equality. And these two are nested within a simpler pairing—direct equality versus equal opportunity—whose elements also generally exclude one another.

Just as important is the disjunction between marginal and global equalities. Given an initial inequality, one can either allocate equally or allocate so as to make equal. This may at first appear to be weak-strong alternation: marginal equality seems weak in being cheap (less costly to the beneficiaries of prior inequality) and global inequality seems strong (costly to the denizens of privilege). But cost is not the test. In choosing marginal equality, we forsake global equality; in choosing globalism we violate marginal equality. Neither of the two provides a strong resolution, and we have a case of mutual exclusion.

None of these is quite the garden variety of mutual exclusion suggested by common sense (for example, having one's cake versus eating it). They are *contingent* relations of mutual exclusion, surmountable by altering some relevant contingency. Let us call two equalities E_1 and E_2, and imagine an unspecified contingency C. When C is satisfied, we can have both E_1 and E_2 at once, or neither, or only one; any combination is possible. Without C, we can have E_1, or E_2, or neither equality, but we cannot have both E_1 and E_2 simultaneously. When the contingency is not satisfied, the two equalities are incompatible.

Substituting real equalities for the formal E_1 and E_2, for the three main cases we have:

Equality 1	Equality 2	Contingency making them compatible
Person-regarding equality	Lot-regarding equality	Persons must have relevantly similar wants, needs, and ends
Means-regarding equal opportunity	Prospect-regarding equal opportunity	Persons must have relevantly similar talents and resources
Marginal equality	Global equality	Domains of allocation must be straightforward[13] or there must be no prior inequalities

These logical relations tell us a little about how incompatibilities among equalities are created by social structure. The structural simplicity of Society E kept equality simple; we see here how some features of non-E society make equality more complex and *continue* to create incompatibilities among equalities. In a society where persons are alike in needs, ends, and wants—in a society of denatured clones—it is possible simultaneously to achieve person- and lot-regarding equality. (And by making people more alike society could alleviate the tension between these two notions of equality.) Similarly, the incompatibility of means-regarding and prospect-regarding equal opportunity arises from human differences (for example, of talent). Again, this incompatibility could be reduced by making people more similar. The tension between marginal and global equality arises from the combination of prior inequality with divided or trivial control over allocation.

The interesting implication is that *inequality itself plays a role in promoting the incompatibility of equalities.* This is not an iron law (and it is not very precise), but it is quite real. Why, to take a main example, do people's wants, needs, and ends differ so much? In part, these differences arise from a division of labor, from differences of power and dependency, from differences of education and access to technology, from differences in income and control over the labor of others—in a word, from inequality. We do not say that human differences arise *only* from social inequality, or that all such differences are eradicable by egalitarian change: both claims are patently false. We do suggest, nevertheless, that some such differences arise from inequality and that some of them are therefore reversible by means of egalitarian change. The same line of thought applies with even greater force to the incompatibility of means-regarding and prospect-regarding equalities of opportunity. A chief source of differing talents and resources is inequality in prior generations, including inequality in naming the talents and resources that will be the criteria for admission into the present generation's winners' circle. Finally, with perfectly direct inference, there can be an incompatibility between marginal and global equality only if inequality already exists, and the importance of this incompatibility must vary directly with the importance of those inequalities. The next phenomenon to be discussed also has inequality as its precondition.

7.1.4 Sisyphean Equality (within One Structure)

It is quite possible to settle upon one structure of equality without attaining coherence. Bloc-regarding equality applied to one system of blocs—say, races—is certainly coherent. But we could invoke other cleavages based upon sex, region, class, blood type, religion, age, sexual proclivity—endlessly. And each bloc-regarding equalization will get in the way of all others, so that the rock of Sisyphus rolls up one hill only to roll down another. This is the pinwheel effect described in Section 2.2.2, and it is part of the complexity that underlies the enormously troublesome doctrine of affirmative action in current practice. It does, of course, have a solution: simple individual-regarding equality trumps the need for bloc-regarding equality.

7.1.5 Compound Differentiation among Equalities

Two or more of these relations among equalities may arise simultaneously. When this occurs, the individual problems interact with one another to create compounds of mind-boggling complexity. Such compounding arose in the lawsuit *Fullilove* v. *Klutznick* (1980). The case centered upon a species of affirmative action known as the "M.B.E. (Minority Business Enterprise) 10-percent set-aside" of the 1977 Public Works Employment Act. This required that 10 percent of all public works contracting be reserved for firms owned by minorities, leaving the remaining 90 percent open to competitive bid. The case reveals a compound of disagreement over nearly every egalitarian structure, but we need only a few disagreements to illustrate our present point. In his dissent (the majority upheld the 10-percent set-aside) Justice Potter Stewart argued:

> On its face, the minority business enterprise provision at issue in this case denies the equal protection of the law. The Public Works Employment Act of 1977 directs that all project construction shall be performed by those private contractors who submit the lowest competitive bids and who meet established criteria of responsibility. One class of contracting firms—defined solely according to the racial and ethnic attributes of their owners—is, however, excepted from the full rigor of these requirements with respect to a percentage of each Federal grant. The statute, on its face and in effect, thus bars a class to which the petitioners belong from having the opportunity to receive a Government benefit, and bars the members of that class solely on the basis of their

race or ethnic background. This is precisely the kind of law that the guarantee of equal protection forbids.

The Fourteenth Amendment was adopted to ensure that every person must be treated equally by each State regardless of the color of his skin. The Amendment promised to carry to its necessary conclusion a fundamental principle upon which this Nation had been founded—that the law would honor no preference based on lineage. Tragically, the promise of 1868 was not immediately fulfilled, and decades passed before the States and the Federal Government were finally directed to eliminate detrimental classifications based on race. Today, the Court derails this achievement and places its imprimatur on the creation once again by government of privileges based on birth.[14]

Here, by way of contrast, is Justice Thurgood Marshall's opinion upholding the set-aside provision:

It is indisputable that Congress' articulated purpose for enacting the set-aside provision was to remedy the present effects of past racial discrimination. Congress had a sound basis for concluding that minority-owned construction enterprises, though capable, qualified, and ready and willing to work, have received a disproportionately small amount of public contracting business because of the continuing effects of past discrimination. Here as in *Bakke,* "minority underrepresentation is substantial and chronic, and . . . the handicap of past discrimination is impeding access of minorities to" the benefits of the governmental program. In these circumstances, remedying these present effects of past racial discrimination is a sufficiently important governmental interest to justify the use of racial classifications.

It is clear to me that the racial classifications employed in the set-aside provision are substantially related to the achievement of the important and congressional articulated goal of remedying the present effects of past racial discrimination.

Today, by upholding this race-conscious remedy, the Court accords Congress the authority to undertake the task of moving our society toward a state of meaningful equality of opportunity, not an abstract version of equality in which the effects of past discrimination would be forever frozen into our social fabric. I applaud this result.[15]

These two views diverge, first, between global and marginal constructions of equality. For Marshall, it is essential to "remedy the present effects of past discrimination," and to eschew "an abstract version of equality in which the effects of past discrimination would forever be frozen into our social fabric." Marshall, in effect, conceives of the contracts governed by the 1977 act as a small domain of allocation set beside the base domain of account presented by American history: the set-aside helps to promote equality in this global sphere. Stewart, taking the marginal perspective, rejects the law for its better-than-equal treatment of minority contractors (and its consequently less-than-equal treatment of majority contractors) within the immediate domain of public works contracts. He makes no connection with the larger (global) domain picked out by Marshall. The opinions diverge again in subject construction. Stewart harps upon equality among persons: "every person must be treated equally." This is the individual-regarding equality of Harlan's dissent in *Plessy* v. *Ferguson.* Marshall, however, entertains a bloc-regarding subject, under which one bloc of contractors is brought more nearly even with another. Moreover, the two opinions construe equal opportunity differently, Stewart taking a means-regarding view and Marshall the prospect-regarding one.

In these opinions, conceptual crowding threatens to overdetermine the justices' arguments, and makes equality—even its special embodiment in the Fourteenth Amendment—seem far from coherent. When several pairs of differences coincide, as in *Fullilove,* each is complicated by each of the rest, and one is left without even a clearcut contradiction. This was evident in the cases of language rights and kidney trouble with which we began (Section 1.3) and it is true here as well.

7.1.6 Simplism

In the midst of complexity, someone can always be counted upon to step forward with some heroic simplification. Instead of many layers of structure, one dichotomy or trichotomy is proposed. Thus, for example, we might seize upon one distinction—say, equal opportunity versus equal results—and imagine this to be the only or the main source of variation among equalities.[16] The resulting bed of Procrustes must compel many quite different equalities to take on a single shape, which of course promotes nothing so much as confusion.

Daniel Bell—who should know better just from reading his own work—declares that "there are, logically speaking, three dimensions of equality: *equality of condition, equality of means,* and *equality of outcomes.*"[17] While no very rigorous criteria are given,[18] each of the three is sketched by example:

1. *Equality of condition.* "Equality before the law," "equality of movement in public places," "one man one vote," "political and civil
rights."
2. *Equality of means.* "Equality of opportunity" (presumably means-
equal, not prospect-equal).
3. *Equality of outcomes.* "Status," "income," "authority" (presumably
made equal).

Now, first of all, these are not so much dimensions as they are sub-
types based on topical differences. Second, they hardly cut at the
joints of structure. Third, they would seem to overlap. (For example,
don't many equalities of condition turn out also to be equalities of opportunity as soon as one looks beneath the surface?)[19] Fourth, they
fail to live up to the generality Bell seems to advertise for them
("There are, logically speaking, [only?] three . . ."). One might almost
as well claim that all things are heavy, sweet, or female; or, perhaps,
that living things are all coconuts, animals, or professors of sociology.

It is less our aim to criticize the internal details of Bell's classification than to point out the necessary futility of its *genre.* Every thought
is, of course, a falsification of the world's full complexity. But to boil
things as complex as equality down to two or three headings is inevi-
tably too far from the truth to serve even as a sensible approximation.

7.2   Taming Equality

We have already passed from our first question, about the coherence
of equality, to the second: "Everywhere one hears praise for the idea
of equality, yet inequality persists. How can we explain the disjunction?" Our views of the first partly answer the second: because of the
antagonisms between one equality and another, *there must always be
some inequalities.* For any society with structural complexity, there
must be choices among equalities, hence equalities left out. That
much we had said already.

But we began with a broader and somewhat more cynical hypothesis about the way in which society might alter a dangerous and expensive ideal so as to tame and cheapen it:

If applied without differentiation—without the complexities that concern us—equality would sweep away class differences, level market
economies, bleach away the variation of human experience. This was
the fate that Tocqueville so dreaded.

The vast majority of human societies have in one way or another been busy with the tasks of equality. Colonial revolutions are common-place; Marxism-Leninism is by now so institutionalized that it is often an apology for ruling classes; and the emancipation of racial and ethnic minorities is a prime activity of liberal reform. Almost everyone seems somehow a partisan of equality. Yet *in*equality in society is as recognizable today as it was in Tocqueville's time. Equality is perhaps less dangerous and less expensive—one almost says less egalitarian—than it once seemed. This may occur because the grammar of equality allows society to choose facets of equality that evade danger, cut costs, and perhaps indeed vitiate the dangerous ideal before it comes to the point of practice.[20]

These cynicisms conjoin two quite different suspicions, which we must pull apart. There is, first of all, a *structural* point about the ease with which equality may be tamed and cheapened. There is, second, a *motivational* point about the reasons why people might actually exercise the resulting opportunities to tame equality. Structural opportunity might meet with no motive (as, say, it seems to have in the case of Gracchus Babeuf and his Conspiracy of the Equals).[21] Similarly, the motive to tame equality might meet with no structural opportunity to do so (as would be the case in Society E).

7.2.1   The Structural Opportunity to Tame Equality

Imagine a simple game with two players, Red and Black. It is a game in which each player must accomplish a different end in order to win. Red's aim is to make equality turn out to be a "radical" idea that greatly diminishes existing inequality. Black's aim is to make equality turn out to be a "nonradical" idea that does not greatly diminish existing inequality. Superficial inspection would suggest that this is a fair game in which Red and Black face equally difficult tasks. This is false: the game is stacked in Black's favor. Black can concede almost all the game's moves to Red—give her almost all the game's power—and still win handsomely. Let us imagine the game as having five moves. In each move, one player unilaterally specifies a main feature of equality: (1) its subject, (2) its domain, (3) its treatment of opportunity, (4) its value structure, and (5) its treatment of relativity and absoluteness. Our thesis then is this: even if Red controls all but one of these moves, Black can use the one remaining move to vitiate Red's radicalizing effort. It does not matter which move is left to Black, for he can use *any* one move to accomplish his end and win.

There are five distinct scenarios to consider, one for each of the moves Red might concede to Black.

Scenario 1. Black controls only the subject:
RED: The domain is to be broadly inclusive (or utterly global), so that everything is subject to equality. The domain itself is to be directly equal (as opposed to opportunities being equal). The value structure is to be lot-regarding: the same bundle of goods for every equal. Equality is to be absolute, not relative.
BLACK: Agreed in every particular, but for the subject. I will let you choose even that, so long as the subject is either: (a) individual-regarding but narrowly exclusive, or (b) bloc-regarding, or (c) segmental, and, of course, so long as I am allowed to define the blocs or segments.

Here, if Red chooses a segmental subject, Black can make it a systematic, hierarchical form of inequality. If she opts for a bloc-regarding subject, Black can make this work simply to redistribute the incidence of inequality.[22] If the subject is individual-regarding, Black can narrow it down to the ken of an already privileged class. All the other features of rigorously radicalizing equality are trumped by Black's choice of subject. Let us turn now to a second, even more clearcut case.

Scenario 2. Black controls only the domain:
RED: The subject is to be universally inclusive and simply individual-regarding. Equality is to be direct (not opportunity-regarding). The value structure is to be lot-regarding. Equality is to be absolute, not relative.
BLACK: Agreed and trivial! The domain is to be narrowly marginal—equality of very little for very many!

The third case is no more complex and even more familiar.

Scenario 3. Black controls only treatment of opportunity:
RED: The subject is to be universally inclusive and simply individual-regarding. The domain is to be broadly inclusive (or utterly global). The value structure is to be lot-regarding. Equality is to be absolute.
BLACK: Fair enough, provided that you mean to talk only of opportunities for acquisition, not acquisition itself. And to rub salt in the wound, I will specify means-regarding equal opportunity with the criteria of excellence chosen by me!

And (perhaps a little less trivially) Black wins a fourth case.

Scenario 4. Black controls only the value structure:
RED: The subject is to be universally inclusive, and simply individ-ual-regarding. The domain is to be broadly inclusive (or utterly global). We are to have direct equality, not equal opportunity. Equality is to be absolute.
BLACK: Well and good, provided that the value structure is person-regarding, and that the ends, needs, and wants of rich folks turn out to be very, very expensive.[23]

A fifth and last case requires little reflection indeed.

Scenario 5. Black controls only the treatment of relatives and absolutes:
RED: I can see it coming: I create the bull of equality by demanding a universal subject with direct attention to individuals, requiring a global domain, spitting out this rubbish of opportunities, and avoiding the special pleading you just used against me; then, you castrate him by making it all relative to a horribly unequal status quo.
BLACK: Right, and done.

There is *one* fully radical configuration for equality: its subject is universally inclusive; its domain global; it equalizes life's results, not its opportunities; its value structure is lot-regarding; it is absolute. This is precisely the same equality as would arise in Society E, and it is subject to deradicalizing alteration when *any* of its features are complicated. These are the very same complications that actuality invites by its own complexity—by its own failure to resemble Society E. If a person has any power at all, and has any (direct or indirect) motive to deradicalize equality, then this complexity gives him some-thing more than a fighting chance. We turn, therefore, to the problem of motive.

7.2.2   The Motive to Tame Equality

No very powerful motive is required to explain why a trenchantly radical conception of equality does not predominate in history. If the relevant decisions were made by accident—by dice or by drunks—one would expect the vast majority of egalitarian demands and efforts to be tolerably tame. The odds are, as we have just demonstrated, quite heavily stacked in that direction.

That bloc-regarding equalities often displace simpler and more dangerous ones need not imply the sinister intelligence of a ruling class working to bring this about. That marginal equalities—of rights to rent hotel rooms and use bus station toilets—often displace global alternatives need not lead us to conclude that a bourgeois elite has planned it this way. That progress toward greater equalities is usually relative need not implicate the state in a conspiracy against the poor. The more striking events (which invite explanation) are those that run against the odds and demand dangerously untamed equality.

We therefore have no more need to *rely upon* a sociology of knowledge than we have need to *reject* such a sociology. We may remind ourselves of a famous epigram: "The ideas of the ruling class are in every epoch the ruling ideas, i.e., the class which is the ruling *material* force of society is at the same time its ruling *intellectual* force."[24] And we may remind ourselves further that a sort of universalistic equality is integral to the pattern of domination that Marx and Engels have in mind: "Each new class, which puts itself into place of one ruling before it, is compelled, merely in order to carry through its aim, to present its interests as the common interests of society . . . Every new class . . . achieves domination only on a broader base than that of the class ruling previously."[25] Far from contradicting Tocqueville, these authors are *agreeing* that a march toward equality is history's way. A diversified, structurally nuanced system of equalities would serve admirably as an ideological medium for such a progression.

The taming of equality, however, requires no such far-reaching scheme of explanation. All that is required is the hypothesis that *advantaged groups do not act under an impulse for self-destruction.* This does not assume that they are highly rational, and does not suggest that they are cunningly self-interested. The groupings might just as well be represented by thinkers who are slow of wit and, within limits, neglectful of their own interests. They need only be free of any well-developed Masada complex.[26] Under these assumptions, we may expect two simple behaviors from relatively advantaged groups and their intellectual representatives, both of these behaviors negative (that is, avoiding something dangerous).

These groups will, first, fail to directly oppose equality in general. Tocqueville's prophecy may be read as a statement of the *rules of rhetoric* for justifying other beliefs, policies, and programs. Only what is consistent with equality in at least one of its structural elaborations can pass through the rhetorical screen that Tocqueville saw being constructed. These may actually be views promoting the efficient exploitation of labor or the stabilization of a government, but they must also be subject to a construction consistent with equality—say, as means-regarding equal opportunity or universal suffrage.[27] To be avoided is the disaster of delegitimation that would follow from opposition to an ascendant *idea*. This rule of conduct is sometimes violated, but seldom violated without cost.

They will, second, avoid the one configuration of equality—reminiscent of Society E—that would unalterably transform society and that would cost them most dearly. Some costs may be paid, for not all "tame" equalities are utterly tame. But by wit or by accident, they will confine themselves to those equalities that are not utterly destructive of advantage. These are many, and the others few. Only a quick-witted impulse of self-destruction could consistently produce the wrong result.

Even the victims of inequality cannot be expected to choose the most radical of equalities. This is partly because even a very inefficient pattern of manipulation from above would rule that out. It is partly because radical equality would imperil everything familiar and would subject everyone to well-advertised risks. In Tawney's telling: "Given five fat sheep and ninety-five thin, how induce the ninety-five to resign to the five [the] richest pastures and shadiest corners? By [somehow] convincing them, obviously, that, if they do not, they will die of rot, be eaten by wolves, and be deprived in the meantime of such pastures as they have ... for there is nothing which frightens thin sheep like the fear of being thinner."[28] But, more important, the victims of inequality will find themselves surrounded by equalities of such bewildering variety and abundance that it will seem superfluous to look for other, less handy, more dangerous and conflictual doctrines as well. It will, perhaps, be noticed that inequalities also persist, but it will appear that remedial efforts are in progress.

Finally, it may be correctly noted—by rich or poor, advantaged or disadvantaged—that radical equality flies in the face of society's established structure and complexity. Only by effacing social pluralism, by attacking the division of labor, by centralizing allocation in unprecedented and perhaps unimaginable degree, by smoothing out all the "lumps" that distinguish one status or plot of land or baby from another, by ignoring or bleaching out all differences of human need, homogenizing all human ends, mixing all human tastes, by insisting on absolutes—only then can the most radical equality ever be brought into practice. It is a daunting prospect.

7.3 Equality and Complexity

We return to the third of our initial questions: Equality is the simplest and most abstract of notions, yet the practices of the world are irremediably concrete and complex. How, imaginably, could the former govern the latter? It cannot. We are always confronted with more than one practical meaning for equality and equality itself cannot provide a basis for choosing among them. The question "Which equality?" will never be answered simply by insisting upon equality. This point, already substantiated by the body of our essay, has one further implication. Intellect resists equality by counterposing rival ideas such as efficiency, freedom, and order. Actuality is smarter, for it chooses the one idea that is more powerful than order or efficiency or freedom in resisting equality. That idea is, of course, equality itself.

Notes

Bibliography

Index

Notes

1. Tocqueville's Dread

1. Alexis de Tocqueville, *Democracy in America*, tr. George Lawrence, ed. J. P. Mayer (New York: Doubleday, 1969), p. 12.

2. For an overview of the historical expansion of equality as a political claim, see Sanford Lakoff, *Equality in Political Philosophy* (Cambridge, Mass.: Harvard University Press, 1964). For the American case, see J. R. Pole, *The Pursuit of Equality in American History* (Berkeley: University of California Press, 1978).

3. Tocqueville, *Democracy in America*, p. 12. Italics added.

4. For a similar argument, that it is a mistake to view history as a movement toward ever greater "equality" as one essential idea, see S. I. Benn and R. S. Peters, *The Principles of Political Thought* (New York: Free Press, 1959), ch. 5, esp. pp. 131–140. Their argument is more explicitly historical than ours, saying that as soon as one generation eliminates one inegalitarian distinction, the next generation creates a new one. For example, equality of opportunity arose as a weapon to attack ascriptive distinctions; it in turn is attacked as inegalitarian by socialists' claims for equal response to need. A rather caustic version of the same claim appears in Pole, *The Pursuit of Equality:* "The evolutionary survival of the idea of equality in America has owed much to its pioneer ability to adapt to varied and often hostile environments by meaning different things to different minds, and furnishing rival interests with equally satisfying terms of moral reference—all of which throws some doubt on the immutable character claimed by the Republic's founders for human rights determined forever by the laws of nature" (p. 1).

For the opposing view, that equality is a single value whose "ideal limit" is a society in which natural differences will have been ironed out, see Isaiah Berlin, "Equality," *Proceedings of the Aristotelian Society*, n.s., 56 (1955–56): 301–326.

5. When we trace the "movement of an idea" from a place called "theory" toward a place called "practice," we understand this to be a loose metaphor, not a reified journey. Of course, human reasoning often makes the opposite journey, from what is concrete to what is abstract.

6. Others who discuss the formal emptiness of equality, and the changes it must undergo to move from principle to practical application, include R. E. Flathman, "Equality and Generalization," in *NOMOS IX: Equality,* ed. J. Roland Pennock and John W. Chapman (New York: Atherton Press, 1967); and John R. Lucas, *The Principles of Politics* (Oxford: Clarendon Press, 1966).

7. More exactly, Bakke expected equality in the sense that the list of persons admitted would not be conditional upon ascriptive identifications—for example, sex, race, family, and so on. Briefly, Bakke, a white applicant, sued the University of California at Davis, which had denied him admission to its medical school, charging that the school's preferential admissions policy for minority students violated Title VI of the 1964 Civil Rights Act and the Equal Protection Clause of the Fourteenth Amendment. The Supreme Court ruled that numerical quotas were in violation of Title VI, but that race could be taken into account in admissions policies (*University of California* v. *Bakke,* 98 S CT 2733 [1978]). For discussions of the *Bakke* case, see John C. Livingston, *Fair Game?* (San Francisco: W. H. Freeman, 1979); Allan P. Sindler, *Bakke, DeFunis, and Minority Admissions* (New York: Longman, 1978); and United States Commission on Civil Rights, *Toward an Understanding of Bakke* (Washington, D.C.: U.S. Government Printing Office, 1979).

8. Plato, *Laws,* tr. Thomas L. Pangle (New York: Basic Books, 1980), p. 143, reference line 757. Also see T. N. Davis, "Justice as the Foundation of Human Equality in Ancient Greece," in *Aspects of Human Equality* (Fifteenth Symposium of the Conference on Science, Philosophy, and Religion), ed. Lyman Bryson, Clarence H. Faust, Louis Finkelstein, and R. M. MacIver (New York: Harper, 1956), pp. 207–220.

9. Or rather, is relevantly subdivided in only one way—that is, by individuals.

10. *New York Times,* March 7, 1976, sect. 6, p. 41.

11. Ibid.

12. *New York Times,* September 25, 1975, p. 24.

13. *New York Times,* September 29, 1975, p. 25.

14. *New York Times,* June 30, 1975, p. 55.

15. And in at least one British clinic, "laborers were [excluded for treatment] because physical strain made treatments less likely to work in them than in, for example, academics." See Guido Calabresi and Philip Bobbitt, *Tragic Choices* (New York: W. W. Norton, 1978), p. 185.

16. *New York Times,* January 14, 1973, sect. 4, p. 16.

17. *New York Times,* March 7, 1976, sect. 6, p. 41.

18. Gerald W. Scully, "Discrimination: The Case of Baseball," in *Government and the Sports Business,* ed. Roger Noll (Washington, D.C.: Brookings Institution, 1974), p. 257.

19. Ibid., p. 250.

20. Ibid.

21. Ibid., p. 261. Italics added. This is not the case for performance levels below those required for retention in the majors.

22. That is, at a .450 slugging percentage.

23. Scully, "Discrimination," p. 263.

24. Ibid., pp. 261–263.

25. Ibid., p. 250.

26. *Newsweek,* September 5, 1977, p. 38.

27. *New York Times,* April 3, 1977, p. 3.

28. John Meisel, *Working Papers on Canadian Politics* (Montreal: McGill-Queens University Press, 1975), p. 189.

29. Ibid.

30. Tocqueville, *Democracy in America,* p. 41. Tocqueville cites various other laws in the same legal code of Connecticut. For example, "Blasphemy, sorcery, adultery and rape are punished by death; a son who outrages his parents is subject to the same penalty." Nor was Connecticut unique. In Massachusetts, a law imposing the death penalty for adultery permitted a couple who had been lovers before the woman's husband had died and the couple had married to be thrown into prison and . . . very near[ly] . . . condemned to death." Catholic priests were subject to the death penalty if they returned to Massachusetts after once being banished. Connecticut severely punished lying and the use of tobacco; Massachusetts banned long hair. (Tocqueville, *Democracy in America,* pp. 41–43.) The point of these examples is not to show how repressive our forbears were, but to underline the fact that even repressive laws represent a particular type of equality: everyone is equally subject to the same moral code. The alternative equality—equal value for recipients—is best expressed by George Bernard Shaw's gloss on the Golden Rule: "Do not do unto others as you would that they should do unto you. Their tastes may not be the same." See his "Maxims for Revolutionists," in *Man and Superman* (Harmondsworth, England: Penguin, 1946, 1972; originally published in London, 1903), p. 251.

31. Immanuel Kant, "On the Common Saying: 'This May Be True in Theory, But It Does Not Apply in Practice' " (1793), reprinted in *Kant's Political Writings,* ed. Hans Reiss (Cambridge: Cambridge University Press, 1970), pp. 61–92, quoted passage on p. 61.

32. The term "grammar" is used here in a serious but nontechnical sense. We are serious about the central place of language as the decisively human medium; it is a central metaphorical construction in our work. We are more specifically influenced by Wittgenstein's *Verwendung* philosophy of

language, ascribing meaning to the actual use of words and sentences, and asserting that the meaning of words is created in use. See his *Philosophical Investigations*, ed. G. E. M. Anscombe (Oxford University Press, 1953). We are not, however, content with ordinary language analysis, for we wish to see the specific relationship between features of a word's use and salient features of a polity—that is: (1) the five structural facts enumerated in Section 1.3, and (2) attempts in actual politics, economics, and societies to impose "equality" as a policy. See, for metaphorical uses of grammar, Paul L. Holmer, *The Grammar of Faith* (San Francisco: Harper and Row, 1978); and Harold J. Laski, *A Grammar of Politics* (New Haven: Yale University Press, 1938).

33. Thus, at least one political philosopher, Thomas Nagel, classifies views of equality by topic: "Contemporary political debate recognizes four types of equality: political, legal, social and economic." See Nagel, *Mortal Questions* (Cambridge: Cambridge University Press, 1979), p. 106. Although this classification is quite serviceable for Nagel's immediate purpose, it fails to produce insights unavailable to a superficial observer. It is a classification convenient for one purpose, but only one.

34. Note that our grammar of equality corresponds exactly to the grammar of a spoken or written language in one way. Formal English grammar was "discovered" and formalized after many generations had already learned to speak *as if* they knew that grammar by heart. There is, to our knowledge, no evidence that Shakespeare was tutored in English grammar, yet he wrote as if governed by an admirably disciplined respect for such a grammar. This historical sequence contrasts with that of arithmetic, in which the formal "grammar" of the axiomatic system precedes ordinary usage, and provides a deductive foundation for the practice of arithmetic. Our "grammar of equality" is in this particular like the natural grammar of English and not like that of arithmetic: people were *already* working out the grammar of equality long before this problem occurred to us. Their work consisted not in analysis but in practical argument about politics, society, and economy. Their practice precedes our theory, and provides whatever foundation the theory may possess.

35. Max Weber, *Economy and Society*, ed. Guenther Roth and Claus Wittich (Berkeley: University of California Press, 1978), vol. 1, p. 15.

2. The Subject of Equality

1. More exactly, let us define a *class of equals,* S, to be the subject for a given relation of equality. S is a "class" less in the Marxian sense than in the mathematical sense: it is a bounded set of elements, the elements being in a relation of equality in some yet-unspecified way. Now, a simple individual-regarding equality is defined by the requirement of *pairwise equality among all the elements of set S.* Suppose, for instance, that only Mr. i and Ms. j

belong to a given class of equals: then we have only one pairwise relation of equality to consider (i = j). Suppose, instead, that persons i, j, and k are members of S: then we must have equality between i and j, between i and k, between j and k. If there are "n" subjects of equality in this sense, then there are n!/2[(n − 2)!] pairwise relations of equality to consider. The factorial symbol "!" instructs us to multiply the given number by all smaller positive integers—for example, 4! would read $4 \cdot 3 \cdot 2 \cdot 1 = 24$. This point of calculation is important only because it suggests the very rapid factorial rise in equality relations as the subject class S is expanded. Thus, for instance, a class of 5 equals would entail 10 pairwise relations of equality, a class of 10 equals would entail 45 such relations, and a class of 20 equals would entail 190 such relations. The numbers quickly get out of hand.

2. Isaiah Berlin, "Equality," in *Proceedings of the Aristotelian Society*, n.s., 56 (1955–56):301–326, reprinted in Berlin, *Concepts and Categories: Philosophical Essays* (London: Hogarth Press, 1978), pp. 81–102, quoted passage on p. 84. Hugo Bedau also defines equality as the distribution of identical shares to discrete individuals. See Bedau, "Egalitarianism and the Idea of Equality," in *NOMOS IX: Equality*, ed. J. Roland Pennock and John W. Chapman (New York: Atherton Press, 1967), pp. 3–27.

3. Berlin, "Equality," pp. 84–85. See also Section 5.2.3.

4. See George Henrik von Wright, *Norm and Action* (London: Routledge and Kegan Paul, 1963).

5. Note that even one-word criteria may entail more than one criterion. Thus, for example, "veteran" entails (for purposes interesting to the U.S. Veteran's Administration) both having served in one or more of the navy, army, air force, and so on, and having been granted an honorable discharge. Or consider the notion of a "qualified voter," as this relates to place of residence, criminal record, compliance with registration laws, and the like. It would thus be a mistake to rest any great weight upon the idea of a simple or unitary boundary criterion. This point underscores the distinction between grammar in our structural sense and grammar as defined by reference to language itself (Section 1.4).

6. Such would be the society of the children of God as described by Saint Paul: "There is no such thing as Jew and Greek, slave and freeman, male and female; for you are all one person in Christ Jesus." Letter of Paul to the Galations 3:28, *New English Bible* (New York: Oxford University Press, 1961). And this vision, of course, does not describe any society that we know.

7. So that if Messrs. a, b, and c are subjects of equality in both Class One and Class Two, while d, e, and f are subjects of equality in Class One only, it follows that Class One is inclusionary vis-à-vis Class Two in the strict sense we intend.

8. For example, see Berlin, "Equality."

9. Matthew 20:1–16, *New Oxford Annotated Bible*, ed. Herbert G. May

and Bruce M. Metzger (New York: Oxford University Press, 1973), p. 1197.

10. Another point needs brief mention. The moral appeal of a claim to equality depends not on any one element of its construction—such as its subject—but on an ensemble of such elements (in this case, the domain and the subject need to be considered together). See Chapter 3.

11. For an official attempt to so justify "separate development," see Information Service of South Africa, *Progress through Separate Development* (New York, 1973), especially ch. 1, "Concepts and Objectives," by J. S. F. Botha.

12. See Immanuel Wallerstein, *The Capitalist World-Economy* (Cambridge: Cambridge University Press, 1979). For data on income distributions in Western nations, see Malcolm Sawyer, "Income Distribution in OECD Countries," *OECD Economic Outlook, Occasional Studies*, 1976. For measures that include more nations but that are much rougher estimates, see Harold Lydell, *The Structure of Earnings* (Oxford: Oxford University Press, 1968); Frederic Pryor, *Property and Industrial Organization in Communist and Capitalist Nations* (Bloomington: Indiana University Press, 1973); and Peter Wiles, *Distribution of Income: East and West* (Amsterdam: North-Holland, 1974).

13. See Chapter 1, n. 7, and Section 2.4.1.

14. But on the other hand, this point could buttress a case for interference in market operations on behalf of relatively greater equality. Minimum wage legislation is a familiar example of such a restriction. The underlying issue here is the incompatibility of certain kinds of economic equality with economic efficiency or productivity. See Arthur Okun, *Equality and Efficiency: The Big Trade-Off* (Washington, D.C.: Brookings Institution, 1975), for an economist's analysis of this issue.

15. For example, much of the impetus for and opposition to welfare reform in the United States in the 1970s stemmed from the fact that Aid to Families with Dependent Children (AFDC) payments, the level of which is set by each state, range from a maximum of $60 a month for a family of four in Mississippi to a maximum of $533 for the same family in Hawaii. Both the Family Assistance Plan proposed in 1969 by President Nixon, and the Better Jobs and Incomes Act proposed in 1977 by President Carter, called for the federal government to set a national minimum level of payment. See Daniel P. Moynihan, *The Politics of a Guaranteed Income* (New York: Random House, 1973); Vincent Burke and Vee Burke, *Nixon's Good Deed* (New York: Columbia University Press, 1974); James Storey, R. Harris, F. Levy, A. Fechter, and R. Michel, *The Better Jobs and Income Plan* (Washington, D.C.: Urban Institute, 1978); Margaret Sulvetta, *The Impact of Welfare Reform on Benefits for the Poor* (Washington, D.C.: Urban Institute, 1978)

16. *Serrano* v. *Priest* 5 Cal. 3d 584, 487, P.2d. 1241 (1971). See David L.

Kirp, "Judicial Policy-Making: Inequitable Public School Financing and the *Serrano* Case," in *Policy and Politics in America,* ed. Allan Sindler (Boston: Little, Brown, 1973).

17. Note also that inclusivity and exclusivity do not at all exhaust the possible relations between two classes. Indeed, for two nonidentical sets, a and b, we may have the following four basic relations:

1. b is wholly included in a.

2. a is wholly included in b.

3. a and b have some elements in common, but neither is wholly included in the other.

4. a and b have no elements in common.

Only the first two figure in our current discussion. The other relations do occur among classes of equals and would-be-equals. We have merely singled out a particularly salient special case in this section.

18. That is, inclusion in the subject class of a general rule (Section 2.2.1). Some demands for equality are demands for explicit inclusion in a class of equals from which the demander of equality is not explicitly excluded. The proposed Equal Rights Amendment to the Constitution would perform precisely this function—it would explicitly state that the class of all citizens to be guaranteed "equality of rights under the law" *includes women,* even though currently standing constitutional formulations do not explicitly *exclude* women (for example, the Preamble begins "We, the people . . ." not "We, the men . . .").

19. We assume $X \cup \sim X$ exhausts S, and that $X \cap \sim X$ is empty.

20. That is, without some such internal equality, a "tier" and a "level" would cease to be "level."

21. Medieval political theory, captured by the phrase "the great chain of being," is based on exactly this system of segmented equality. All existence, from the lowliest plant to God, has its appointed place. Just as the soul dominates the body and the heavens rise over the earth, so is the pope superior to the king, the clergy to the laity, and the nobility to the peasantry. Each class has specified powers, privileges, duties, and obligations which its members share equally. See Ewart Lewis, *Medieval Political Ideas,* 2 vols. (New York: Knopf, 1954); A. O. Lovejoy, *The Great Chain of Being* (Cambridge, Mass.: Harvard University Press, 1936); Paul Sigmund, "Hierarchy, Equality, and Consent in Medieval Christian Thought," in *NOMOS IX: Equality.* Although the idea reached its height in feudal society, it began much earlier and persisted much later. Aristotle argued that "equality must be equal for equals" (*The Politics,* tr. T. A. Sinclair [New York: Penguin Books, 1962], bk. 3, ch. 12, p. 128), and even more explicitly, "It is clear then that by nature some are free, others slaves, and that for these it is both right and expedient that they should serve as slaves" (bk. 1, ch. 5, p. 34), and again, "As between male and female the former is by nature superior and rules, the latter inferior and subject" (bk. 1, ch. 5, p. 33).

Edmund Burke's theory exemplified a secularized view of the great chain of being, and the belief persists in contemporary arguments for secure and honorable statuses. See Eric Nordlinger, *The Working Class Tories* (Berkeley: University of California Press, 1967); Robert McKenzie and Allan Silver, *Angels in Marble* (Chicago: University of Chicago Press, 1968); David Potter, *People of Plenty* (Chicago: University of Chicago Press, 1954); and Duane Lockwood, "Sources of Variation in Working Class Images in Society," *Sociological Review* 14 (November 1966): 249–267. Note that segmental equality need not imply degradation or self-abnegation of segments below the top. Deferential Englishmen feel themselves the moral, if not social, equals of the elite because "they appear to accept the classic doctrine that all who properly fulfill their stations in life contribute worthily to the public good" (McKenzie and Silver, *Angels in Marble*, p. 249). See also Frank Parkin, *Class Inequality and Political Order* (New York: Praeger, 1971), p. 84.

22. For a discussion of the role of status (segmentation) in determining allocations, see Torstein Eckhoff, *Justice: Its Determinants in Social Interaction* (Rotterdam: Rotterdam University Press, 1974), pp. 234–242.

23. Though not as simply as one might imagine. See Max Weber, *Economy and Society*, ed. Guenther Roth and Claus Wittich (Berkeley: University of California Press, 1978), esp. vol. 1, pp. 255–266.

24. This discussion, of course, gives Marx's interpretation neither the credit nor the criticism it deserves. In fact, the question of what to say on this point would divide the authors of this essay against one another. We do, however, agree that a reading of volume 1 of *Capital* is the best foundation upon which to begin such a discussion. See also Perry Anderson, "The Antinomies of Antonio Gramsci," *New Left Review* 100 (1976): 5–78. Anderson argues that political and legal equality through representative democracy "is the principal ideological lynchpin of western capitalism" because "the state 'represents' the totality of the population *abstracted* from its distribution into social classes, as individual and equal citizens . . . The economic divisions within the citizenry are masked by the juridical parity between" wealthy and poor. The distinction between economic inequality and political equality "is then constantly presented to the masses as the ultimate incarnation of liberty."

It is also interesting to note that people seem to create their own masking system, by making equality-inequality or "relative deprivation" comparisons only within relatively short intervals above and below their own place in a system of unequal distribution. See W. G. Runciman, *Relative Deprivation and Social Justice* (Berkeley: University of California Press, 1966); Robert Lane, *Political Ideology* (New York: Free Press, 1962); and J. Nagel, "Inequality and Discontent: A Nonlinear Hypothesis," *World Politics* 26 (July 1974): 453–472. See also, for more recent evidence, Martin Harrop, *Equality and Democracy* (diss., Yale University, 1979). Social psychologists discuss the same phenomenon as social comparison theory. See Leon Festinger, "A Theory of Social Comparison Processes," *Human Relations* 7 (1954): 117–140; and Thomas Pettigrew, "Social Evaluation Theory," in *Nebraska Symposium on Motivation,* vol. 15, ed. David Levine (Lincoln: University of Nebraska Press, 1967), pp. 241–318.

25. Quality within each such category then serves as another segmenting criterion—for example, shortstops hitting .220 are segmented from shortstops hitting .300. See Gerald W. Scully, "Discrimination: The Case of Baseball," in *Government and the Sports Business,* ed. Roger Noll (Washington, D.C.: Brookings Institution, 1973).

26. See especially Ralf Dahrendorf, *Class and Class Conflict in Industrial Society* (Stanford: Stanford University Press, 1959); Anthony Giddens, *The Class Structure of the Advanced Societies* (New York: Harper and Row, 1973); David Apter, *Choice and the Politics of Allocation* (New Haven: Yale University Press, 1971); and Milovan Djilas, *The New Class* (New York: Praeger, 1957).

Some writers have mistakenly argued that because the United States has eliminated the identifiable segments of inherited class or caste, it thereby provides simple individual-regarding equality for its citizens. Tocqueville, for example, looking at the United States with the eyes of a post–French Revolution aristocrat, was struck by the absence of primogeniture, sumptuary laws, and other evidence of rigid classes. He was mistaken, however, in equating this lack of segmentation with near-complete "equality of condition" among all white American men. Because of his amazement at America's lack of segmental equality, with the *in*equality between certain pairs of persons that it implies, he systematically missed evidence of the absence of simple equality in America. See Alexis de Tocqueville, *Democracy in America,* tr. George Lawrence, ed. J. P. Mayer (New York: Doubleday, 1969).

Seymour Martin Lipset makes the same mistake more subtly in his argument that "cross-cutting bases of cleavages make a more vital democracy." American society is fluid enough that important interests and commitments held by many citizens cut across class lines, thereby decreasing the dangers of underclass radicalism and upperclass elitism. By equalizing some things across classes, or by setting up compensatory inequalities, the United States dissolves segmental equality, with its implied class inequality. Lipset goes wrong, however, in his additional argument that once class differences are broken down, individuals are made equal to one another. He makes the unwarranted inference that eliminating a segmental structure is sufficient, as well as necessary, to give each citizen an equal role in a democracy. See Lipset, *Political Man* (Garden City, N.Y.: Doubleday, 1960), pp. 77–96, quoted passage on p. 90.

27. See our discussion of person-regarding value structures in Chapter 5.

28. *Plessy* v. *Ferguson* 163 US 537 (1896). Of course, much more than rail transit was actually at issue, for the doctrine of "separate but equal" treatment was spreading across the South, and had come to center upon the crucial issue of segregationist schooling. And one must in retrospect reject the Supreme Court majority's good faith in blithely imagining that segregation and equality could coexist. See Wallace Mendelson, *The American Constitution and the Judicial Process* (Homewood, Ill.: Dorsey Press, 1980), pp. 535-538, for majority and dissenting opinions in *Plessy*.

29. Mendelson, *The American Constitution*, p. 538.

30. Gunnar Myrdal, with the assistance of Richard Sterner and Arnold Rose, *An American Dilemma: The Negro Problem and American Democracy* (New York: Harper and Row, 1944, 1962).

31. A point analyzed with great insight in Edwin Dorn's *Rules and Racial Equality* (New Haven: Yale University Press, 1979), esp. pp. 42-45, 28-36.

32. Nevertheless, observations made here do not depend on the difficulties associated with the measurement of central tendency. We could make all of our important points here if bananas were *identically distributed* in each of the two blocs. For a more elaborate view of bloc-equality see Dorn, *Rules and Racial Equality*.

33. In 1974 Marco DeFunis, a white applicant, charged that the University of Washington Law School had discriminated against him with its preferential admissions policy for minority applicants. The case went to the Supreme Court but was rendered moot (*Marco DeFunis et al.* v. *Charles Odegaard* 416 U.S. 312 [1974]). See Robert M. O'Neil, *Discriminating against Discrimination* (Bloomington: Indiana University Press, 1975), for a detailed discussion.

34. See Austin Ranney, *Curing the Mischiefs of Faction* (Berkeley: University of California Press, 1975), esp. pp. 111-115, for a discussion of the issues faced by the McGovern-Fraser Commission in its concern for bloc-equality in delegations to Democratic Party conventions, and especially the problem of rival bases for representation—that is, candidate preference versus a multitude of (themselves competing) demographic characteristics.

35. In actual policy determinations, a central problem with bloc-regarding claims is the absence of criteria for assigning priority to one bloc over another. Not only may efforts to achieve bloc-regarding equality between races conflict with efforts to achieve equality between the sexes, but our subject grammar does not give us any substantive basis for deciding which bloc-equality should be pursued first.

One reader points out that demands for bloc-equality may be intended to equalize, or may have the effect of equalizing, among individuals. The reasoning is as follows: whites will not tolerate much more internal inequality among whites than already exists, so that raising the status of blacks will not lead to an equal but opposite lowering of the status of whites. Thus, the outcome pictured in Table 5 "is an unlikely consequence of equalizing advantages between blacks and whites, although it might (and sometimes does) serve as a scare tactic used by the most advantaged whites to keep" less advantaged whites from joining with blacks in demanding reform.

We do not deny the possibility that bloc-equalization may have the incidental effect of promoting simple individual-regarding equality. We are merely pointing out that this effect would be incidental, not essential. We also have at least anecdotal evidence that the pinwheel effect does operate in practice, and that advantaged whites are just as likely to pit disadvantaged groups against one another as to raise them all to the level of the least advantaged white males. One author of this book has been asked several times how an employer or graduate admissions committee should choose between a white woman and a black man for a coveted slot. An excellent historical survey of the tensions between white women and blacks is Catharine Stimpson, " 'Thy Neighbor's Wife, Thy Neighbor's Servants': Women's Liberation and Black Civil Rights," in *Women in Sexist Society*, ed. Vivian Gornick and Barbara Moran (New York: New American Library, 1971), pp. 622–657.

36. In recent policy discourse, the bloc-regarding approach to equality has been complicated by the appearance of new candidates for recognition as blocs requiring equal (or special) treatment with respect to rival blocs. Thus, claims are made on behalf of neighborhoods and geographic regions (for example, the Sunbelt versus the Frostbelt versus the Sagebrush region). The question then arises whether to accord these purported blocs the same standing in allocative deliberations as the previously identified blocs based on personal characteristics like race and sex. For a not-very-helpful discussion of this problem, see Daniel Bell, "On Meritocracy and Equality," *The Public Interest* 29 (Fall 1972), esp. pp. 29–30. But this question of how "real" any particular bloc is points to the more difficult question of the extent to which any bloc definition captures the subjective identity and affiliation of an individual. Further, the inclusion of these purported blocs adds to the number of cleavages in our pinwheel of blocs and reinforces the problem of ordering the claims of rival blocs.

37. "Inclusive" here means in relation to the advantaged class of equals in the original, preemancipatory state of things. While the advantages of membership would presumably decline, the boundaries would expand. Notice that the inclusive-exclusive distinction is most readily formulated for claims that are of simple individual-regarding structure, but can also be applied to the segmental and bloc-regarding structures. Thus, say, we might require bloc-equal treatment for Yale undergraduate men and women (very exclusionary), then expand this to New Haven's men and women (inclusionary), then to all the world's men and women (even more inclusionary).

If the reasoning of Note 35 is correct—that white men will not permit other white men to fall as low as blacks and women have been permitted to lie—then changing the characteristics of members in the advantaged and disadvantaged classes (as in Section 2.3.1) may lead toward greater simple equality of subjects. Thus, the two choices may not be as stark as they are portrayed here.

38. The power of emancipation depends not only on the subject of equality, but also on its domain, a point to which we return in Chapter 3.

39. Note that this doctrine may not have been implemented inclusively—say, for all blacks and rural dwellers—but its thrust was clear.

40. See Section 2.2.2. Although *Plessy* v. *Ferguson* was substantively concerned with racially segregated railway accommodations, the ruling relied in part on the assumption that racially segregated public schools did not violate the Equal Protection Clause of the Fourteenth Amendment, and itself provided the basis of the Court's 1927 ruling in *Gong Lum* v. *Rice* (275 US 78 [1927]), which upheld school segregation. See Arvo Van Alstyne, Kenneth Karst, and Jules Gerard, *Sum and Substance of Constitutional Law* (Inglewood, Calif.: Center for Creative Educational Services, 1979), p. 326; and Mendelson, *The American Constitution*, pp. 535–538.

41. *Brown* v. *Board of Education of Topeka* (I) 347 US 483 (1954). See Van Alstyne et al., *Sum and Substance of Constitutional Law*, pp. 327–329; and Mendelson, *The American Constitution*, pp. 538–544.

42. See Chapter 1, n. 7 for a brief explanation of the case, the details of which are greatly complicated, and arguable if inspected closely. Indeed, the *Bakke* case may be described as a Rorschach test of equality, and so may the Court's decision. Depending on one's attitudes about the desirability of bloc-regarding equality per se and about the proper strategy for government to follow in promoting equality, one can see many different things in Davis Medical School's procedures and in the Court decision.

43. Quoted in J. Harvie Wilkinson III, *From Brown to Bakke* (Oxford: Oxford University Press, 1979), p. 304.

44. See, for example, Terry Eastland and William J. Bennett, *Counting by Race* (New York: Basic Books, 1979); Joel Dreyfuss and Charles Lawrence III, *The Bakke Case* (New York: Harcourt, Brace, Jovanovich, 1979); Allan P. Sindler, *Bakke, DeFunis and Minority Admissions* (New York: Longman, 1978); and Wilkinson, *From Brown to Bakke*.

3. The Domain of Equality

1. Thomas Nagel, *Mortal Questions* (Cambridge: Cambridge University Press, 1979), p. 106. One of the authors of this book also discusses the kind of distributive justice appropriate to different topics of distribution according to the political beliefs of wealthy and poor Americans. See Jen-

nifer Hochschild, *What's Fair?* (Cambridge, Mass.: Harvard University Press, 1981).

2. Note the following superficial complication for this definition. Does "everything" and "some of the things" refer to exactly named particulars, or do they refer to kinds of things? Do we require that a broad domain contain, say, precisely the same nuggets of gold contained in a narrower domain, or merely that it contain an equal quantity of gold? At least in dealing with homogeneous commodities (for example, wheat or gold), we believe it would be silly to insist upon identity of particulars, and intend to require only inclusion of kind.

3. Or a market-exchange criterion might be adopted. If domain I could be traded for domain II with something extra left over, then domain I would be considered broader. Thus, in our example, 100 tons of gold could certainly be traded for one peanut with something left over, and is thus plausibly considered a broader domain of equality.

4. John Locke, "The Second Treatise of Government," in *Two Treatises of Government,* ed. Peter Laslett (New York: New American Library–Mentor, 1960), ch. 6, sect. 54 (quoted in full), p. 346.

5. Similarly, since the New Deal, public facilities and services have increasingly been provided to citizens on an equal basis: highway systems, social security, health care (as in Medicare and Medicaid), public parks and various public utilities, such as rural electrification in the 1930s and as seemingly mundane but necessary a service as sewage systems in modern suburbs. These expanded services clearly represent only part of government activity. The question remains: Why should more facilities and services not be distributed equally?

6. See Milton Friedman, *Capitalism and Freedom* (Chicago: University of Chicago Press, 1962); Robert Nozick, *Anarchy, State, and Utopia* (New York: Basic Books, 1974); and Murray Rothbard, *Left and Right* (San Francisco: Cato Institute, 1979). See also Friedrich Hayek, *Law, Legislation, and Liberty,* 3 vols. (Chicago: University of Chicago Press, 1976). Okun argues this point explicitly, saying that the proper domain of equality is the domain of rights. He distinguishes himself from Friedman and company by arguing for an extension of the domain of (equal) rights to cover the "right to survival," setting a floor on consumption levels. Arthur M. Okun, *Equality and Efficiency: The Big Trade-Off* (Washington, D.C.: Brookings Institution, 1975).

7. Perhaps because the market liberals' limited sort of equality plays so central a role in Marx's theory of capitalist exploitation (for example, the thesis of vol. 1 of *Capital*), many Marxian thinkers are inclined to treat narrow equalities of right as evils *in themselves,* which almost certainly was not Marx's own view. Others dismiss them as unimportant, according to Miliband, who notes "a permanent Marxist temptation to devalue the distinction between bourgeois democratic regimes and authoritarian ones."

Ralph Miliband, *Marxism and Politics* (Oxford: Oxford University Press, 1977), p. 83.

8. See C. B. MacPherson's analysis of Locke's theory of property rights in *The Political Theory of Possessive Individualism* (Oxford: Oxford University Press, 1962), ch. 5; Frank Parkin, *Class Inequality and Political Order* (New York: Praeger, 1971); and Charles H. Anderson, *The Political Economy of Social Class* (Englewood Cliffs, N.J.: Prentice-Hall, 1974).

9. Thus, we disagree with, for example, Joseph Tussman and Jacobus Tenbrock when they argue that "nothing in the annals of our law better reflects the primacy of American concern with liberty over equality than the comparative careers of the due process and equal protection clauses of the Fourteenth Amendment." See "The Equal Protection of the Laws," *California Law Review* 37 (September 1949): 341–380. Note that we do not assert the primacy of equality over liberty, but rather assert that this is the wrong way to think about the question.

Furthermore, our discussion of bloc-regarding equality resolves their "paradox," described as follows: "The equal protection of the law is a 'pledge of the protection of equal laws.' But laws may classify. 'And the very idea of classification is that of inequality' " (Ibid., p. 344).

Examples of theories stating that the ultimate values of freedom and equality necessarily conflict include H. J. McCloskey, "Egalitarianism, Equality and Justice," *Australasian Journal of Philosophy* 44 (May 1966): 50–69; E. Kühnelt-Leddihn, *Liberty or Equality: The Challenge of Our Time* (Caldwell, Idaho: Caxton Printers, 1952). Carritt, on the other hand, notes that those who defend liberty against equality nevertheless argue, usually, for equal liberty, and he asks, "What then is the equality with which freedom is supposed to be incompatible?" E. F. Carritt, "Liberty and Equality," *Political Philosophy*, ed. A. Quinton (London: Oxford University Press, 1967), p. 127.

Two ways in which our analysis of the difference between "conservatives" and "leftists" is too simple are as follows. First, conservatives such as Nozick want to guarantee only an equal right to be involved in the processes of society; they argue that if the procedures are just, the results are just, whatever they happen to be. Marxists are more concerned about good outcomes, and seek to devise and manipulate processes in order to achieve just outcomes. Second, conservatives seek equality among things that do not require a constant sum game. Rights are such things: expanding some people's right to trade or vote does not require taking it away from others. Leftists seek equality among things that are more susceptible to a constant sum game. The amount of money in the world is not fixed, but at any particular moment significant equalization of incomes would require taking money away from some in order to give it to others.

10. Babeuf is among the very few political thinkers who have actually advocated such a broad domain of equality: "Let there be no other differ-

ence between people than that of age or sex. Since all have the same needs and same faculties, let them henceforth have the same education and the same diet. They are content with the same sun and the same air for all; why should not the same portion and the same quality of nourishment suffice for each of them?" From François Noël Babeuf, "Manifeste des égaux" (1796), tr. in Steven Lukes, "Socialism and Equality," *Dissent* 22 (1975): 155.

11. A class X covers a class Y if every element included in Y is also included in X. This is the strict definition, but a slightly broader definition is actually intended. Some elements may be interchangeable (as are, say, dollar bills), so we should say, "Class X covers class Y if every element in Y has a distinct counterpart in X." Thus, "this pile of silver dollars" might be covered by another at least equal pile of silver dollars, even if the second pile did not actually contain the specific coins in the first stack (see Note 2 above). Or, more broadly, the "market test" sketched in Note 3 above could be employed.

12. See Section 2.5.

13. Brian Barry, *Political Argument* (London: Routledge and Kegan Paul, 1965). "Within the total area of want-regarding principles," Barry writes, "I draw a distinction between those which direct attention to the distribution of want-satisfaction among people and those which do not . . . More precisely: an aggregative principle is one which mentions only the total amount of want-satisfaction among the members of a reference group, whereas a distributive principle requires for its statement a mention of the way in which want-satisfaction is to be divided among the members of a reference group" (p. 43). Note that the distributive principle of equality entirely divorced from aggregative considerations implies an *undefined* domain of account, and indifference to its extent (even an empty domain is acceptable).

14. The residue could be evenly divided, in which case we may revert to the straightforward case since it is as if nature or society has extended our egalitarian domain of allocation to make it cover. This case belongs to the family of man-bites-dog stories.

15. To see this, let B's initial holding be greater than fifty.

16. This pattern of marginally equal "small" taxes is strikingly pervasive in American government, with its fragmentation of political jurisdictions and reliance on a wide range of piecemeal taxes. In a public realm of 50 states, 3,000 countries, 18,000 municipalities, and 50,000 other units of local government, the fragmentation of the domain of allocation is obviously enormous. More important, an individual is likely to be taxed by multiple jurisdictions and to incur various "small" taxes even within a single jurisdiction. Depending upon her place of residence, an individual may pay state income taxes, city income taxes, state sales taxes, city sales taxes, local property taxes, payroll taxes, water taxes, and user charges for

various public utilities. See Michael W. Danielson et al., *One Nation, So Many Governments* (Lexington, Mass.: D.C. Heath, 1977), p. 9.

17. One should note, however, that it is *more* equal (in a global sense) than what might actually occur, namely an equal *percent* raise, whereby

$$\frac{X_2 - X_1}{X_1} = \frac{Y_2 - Y_1}{Y_1}$$

A 1 percent raise to each would increase the income of X by $1,000 and the income of Y by only $10. The old inequality ($X_1$ versus Y_1—$100,000 versus $1,000) justifies the new one ($X_2 - X_1$ versus $Y_2 - Y_1$—$1,000 versus $10). This is an example of Aristotle's proportionate equality, discussed in Section 3.2.2.

18. This is not an imaginary example. In the spring of 1980, for instance, Yale University announced that its junior faculty would receive a full 13 percent raise, while its senior faculty would be granted only a 10.5 percent raise. The former, with salaries averaging about half the latter, would thus receive dollar amounts running about 35 percent lower than their elders. Note also that inflation complicates the interpretation of these data considerably. A related illustration occurred in 1877 when a 10 percent wage cut was allegedly matched by a 10 percent reduction in the salary of the president of an American railroad. See Philip S. Foner, *The Great Labor Uprising of 1877* (New York: Monad Press, 1977), p. 53.

19. See Section 2.3.1.

20. For a claim that the government should take this strategy, at least for blacks, see Boris Bittker, *The Case for Black Reparations* (New York: Vintage, 1973); and idem, "Manifesto of the Black Economic Development Conference," *New Republic* 21 (June 1969): 19–21. Of course, affirmative action policies are often justified through this line of thinking.

21. See, for example, David R. Cameron, "Economic Inequality in the United States," unpublished paper, Midwest Political Science Association, 1979.

22. The most compelling of these other justifications is probably the "equal sacrifice" doctrine, discussed in Chapter 5. See F. Y. Edgeworth, "The Pure Theory of Taxation," *Economic Journal* 7 (1897): 46–70; and Walter J. Blum and Harry Kalven, *The Uneasy Case for Progressive Taxation* (Chicago: University of Chicago Press, 1953).

23. For arguments on both sides of the ethical issue of the justifiability of compensatory inequality in the form of preferential treatment for minorities and women in education and employment, see Thomas Nagel, "Equal Treatment and Compensatory Discrimination," *Philosophy and Public Affairs* 2, no. 4 (Summer 1973); Judith Jarvis Thomson, "Preferential Hiring," *Philosophy and Public Affairs* 2, no. 4 (Summer 1973); Robert Simon, "Preferential Hiring: A Reply to Judith Jarvis Thomson," *Philoso-*

phy and Public Affairs 3, no. 3 (Spring 1974); and George Sher, "Justifying Reverse Discrimination in Employment," *Philosophy and Public Affairs* 4, no. 2 (Winter 1975). All are collected in *Equality and Preferential Treatment*, ed. Marshall Cohen, Thomas Nagel, and Thomas Scanlon (Princeton: Princeton University Press, 1977).

24. See Gary Orfield, *Must We Bus? Segregated Schools and National Policy* (Washington, D.C.: Brookings Institution, 1978).

25. Cited and discussed in Nathan Glazer, *Affirmative Discrimination: Ethnic Inequality and Public Policy* (New York: Basic Books, 1975), pp. 44–45.

26. The implication if that compensatory inequality between W's and L's, which would imply a simple subject structure, is preferred. This will rule out the perverse misclassification of Lα's and Wβ's. Note the related issue discussed in Section 2.2.2.

27. This reaction to programs of compensatory inequality may be rooted in a sense of relative deprivation (although in reference to marginal, not global, distribution), so that residents of middle-income neighborhoods complain that City Hall ignores the potholes in their community while it mounts one new program after another in poor neighborhoods. Similarly, the Commission on the Humanities recently recommended that "grade schools and high schools cut back on special programs for backward and disadvantaged children" because "more literate students are being short-changed and need more attention" (*Newsweek*, June 16, 1980, p. 21). See W. G. Runciman, *Relative Deprivation and Social Justice* (Berkeley: University of California Press, 1966), for a thorough study of the subjective experience of social inequalities.

28. American public policy has seldom involved the redistribution of domains. Among the few exceptions are inheritance taxes, the substitution of national-level financing for local financing in certain New Deal programs, and the exercise of the right of eminent domain (although the purpose is generally to build a dam or highway, not to redistribute wealth). There is nothing in the American experience comparable to British policy decisions involving the nationalization of industries. The most recent American policy move into the arena of domain redistribution has occurred in school finance. In *Serrano v. Priest* (5 Cal 3d. 584, 487 P.2d. 1241 [1971]) the California Supreme Court held that the level of local school financing "may not be a function of wealth." This decision paved the way to a redistribution of local domains of allocation but did not compel any strict egalitarian formula of allocation. See David L. Kirp, "Judicial Policy-Making: Inequitable Public School Financing and the *Serrano* Case" (1971), in *Policy and Politics in America*, ed. Allan P. Sindler (Boston: Little, Brown, 1973), p. 105. As it stands, powerful tools of domain redistribution certainly exist (and are in use in other countries) but are rarely employed in American public policy.

29. Miliband, *Marxism and Politics*, p. 10.

30. See Robert Dahl, "On Removing Certain Impediments to Democracy in the United States," *Political Science Quarterly* 92 (Spring 1977): 1–20; and Hochschild, *What's Fair?*

31. Or, more generally, a good may be distributed in a certain ratio to preserve an existing relation. An initial condition of equality would be preserved by an equal distribution under the principle discussed here, just as an unequal initial condition is preserved by an unequal distribution.

32. Aristotle, *Nicomachean Ethics,* tr. Martin Ostwald (New York: Bobbs-Merrill, 1962), bk. 5, ch. 3, p. 118, ll. 10, 20.

33. Aristotle, *The Politics,* tr. Warrington (London: Everyman's Library, 1959), as quoted in John Rees, *Equality* (London: Macmillan, 1972), p. 92.

34. Aristotle, *Nicomachean Ethics,* bk. 5, ch. 3, pp. 118–119, l. 25.

35. The distinction between proportionate equality and segmental equality blurs at the edges. Fines for speeding that charge $10 for every 5 m.p.h. excess of the speed limit could be seen as an instance of proportionate equality, each speeder fined in proportion to her speed, or of segmental equality, each rank of speeder charged a different amount, and all individuals within a rank charged the same amount.

36. Aristotle, *Nicomachean Ethics,* bk. 5, ch. 3, p. 119, l. 25.

37. "If one man is outstanding superior in flute-playing, but far inferior in birth or good looks (even supposing that birth and good looks are a greater good than flute-playing, and greater in proportion than the superiority of this player over the rest), even then, I say, the good player should get the best instrument. For superiority is only relevant when it contributes to the quality of the performance, which wealth and good birth do not do at all." Aristotle, *The Politics,* tr. T. A. Sinclair (Harmondsworth, England: Penguin Books, 1962), bk. 3, ch. 12, p. 128.

38. Aristotle used a similar example: "It can certainly be said that it is not just that out of a sum of a hundred pounds he that contributed one pound should receive equal shares with him who found the remaining ninety-nine, and this applies equally to the original hundred pounds capital and any profits subsequently made." Aristotle, *The Politics,* tr. Sinclair, bk. 3, ch. 9, p. 119.

39. It is, however, precisely consistent with the slogan "Equal pay for equal work," and it would serve as a critique for many relatively vulgar patterns of economic discrimination. Herbert Gans, among others, treats this by distinguishing equality (sameness of results) from equity (compensation for productivity or effort). See Herbert J. Gans, *More Equality* (New York: Vintage Books, 1968), pp. 73–77.

40. Social psychologists have done elaborate research on the human desire (or lack thereof) for this form of equity, which they define as the same ratio of inputs to outputs for each actor. See Elaine Walster, Ellen

Bersheid, and G. W. Walster, "New Directions in Equity Research," *Journal of Personality and Social Psychology* 25 (1973): 151-176; and Leonard Berkowitz and Elaine Walster, eds., *Equity Theory*, vol. 9 of *Advances in Experimental Social Psychology* (New York: Academic Press, 1976). Perhaps the strongest contemporary philosophical argument for this equality of transaction is Joel Feinberg, *Social Philosophy* (Englewood Cliffs, N.J.: Prentice-Hall, 1973).

41. The original inequality (ratio of extent of contribution) is still being preserved. The move appears compensatory because the initial inequality looks like an unequal sharing in a burden, rather than in some benefit or some positive personal attribute.

42. See Leszek Kolakowski, *Main Currents of Marxism*, tr. P. S. Falla (Oxford: Oxford University Press, 1979), vol. 1, pp. 193-216.

43. Furthermore, markets may reward talents or activities that have no "real"social value, in the eyes of at least some observers. Are prize-fighters worth millions of dollars more than schoolteachers? For an answer that unearned unequal advantages may legitimately lead to unequal rewards, see Nozick, *Anarchy, State, and Utopia,* esp. pp. 149-182.

44. In American policy, a special reliance has been placed on education as a way of cutting through causal strings of allocation. In the nineteenth century, public education was supposed to assimilate immigrants, provide basic skills for employment, and provide the critical path for upward mobility out of the slum. (That American schools did not always fulfill this ideal of education as a magic carpet that lifts individuals above poverty, ethnic discrimination, and sharply restricted career horizons is another story. See Colin Greer, *The Great School Legend* [New York: Basic Books, 1972].) More recently, the same extraordinary dependence on schooling to remedy all manner of inequalities is evident in Headstart programs, desegregation plans, and the open admissions policy of the City University of New York.

45. These data are derived from the original work of William Bowens and Glenn Pierce, as reported in Peter Ross Range, "Will He Be First?" *New York Times Magazine,* March 11, 1979, p. 78. The same point is analyzed in Douglas Rae, "The Egalitarian State: Notes on a System of Contradictory Ideals," *Daedalus* 108 (Fall 1979): 37-54.

4. Equalities of Opportunity

1. Ralph W. Emerson, "The Fortune of the Republic," in *Miscellanies,* vol. 11 of *Works of Emerson,* ed. Edward W. Emerson (New York: Houghton, Mifflin, 1904; reissued New York: AMS Press, 1968), p. 541. Note that *opportunity* of civil rights seems a weak promise indeed.

2. Note that the ends-means distinction implied here is not so simple

or unproblematic as may be imagined. Few things fall categorically on one side or the other of this distinction. See John Dewey, *Theory of Valuation* (Chicago: University of Chicago Press, 1939), pp. 40–50.

3. Edwin Dorn, *Rules and Racial Equality* (New Haven: Yale University Press, 1979), esp. pp. 107–121.

4. Immanuel Wallerstein, *The Capitalist World-Economy* (Cambridge: Cambridge University Press, 1979), p. 49.

5. R. H. Tawney describes the preference for inequalities based on merit (rather than on race, or class origin, or religion, or some other ascriptive trait) as follows: "The inequalities of the old regime had been intolerable because they had been arbitrary, the result not of personal capacity, but of social and political favouritism. The inequalities of industrial society were to be esteemed, for they were the expression of individual achievement or failure to achieve. They were twice blessed. They deserved moral approval, for they corresponded to merit. They were economically beneficial, for they offered a system of prizes and penalties. So it was possible to hate the inequalities most characteristic of the eighteenth century and to applaud those most characteristic of the nineteenth. The distinction between them was that the former had their origin in social institutions, the latter in personal character." See Tawney, *Equality* (London: Unwin Books, 1931), p. 102.

6. According to Williams, equality of opportunity is introduced in political discussion when there is a question of the distribution of goods that (1) are desired by large numbers of people in all segments of society, (2) are said to be earned or achieved, and (3) are limited in that not all who desire them can have them. Goods may be limited (a) by their very nature (for example, prestige), (b) contingently, available to all who fulfill certain conditions that not everyone will fill (for example, university education), or (c) fortuitously, in absolute shortage of supply. Bernard Williams, "The Idea of Equality," *Philosophy, Politics and Society,* ser. 2, ed. Peter Laslett and W. G. Runciman (Oxford: Blackwell, 1962), pp. 124–125.

7. For example, when X could be attained in varied quantities or degrees, each such degree or quantity would be assigned a probability by such a function.

8. Or, where X comes in degrees, an "expected value" function, relating degrees of X to the chance of attaining each, would be substituted here.

9. Fred Hapgood argues that, in some circumstances, a lottery is the only fair way to resolving the injustice of cumulative inequalities inherent in any system of (means-regarding) equal opportunity. Lotteries do not change the unequal distribution of wealth and power, but they give everyone an equal chance to receive valued goods. See Hapgood, "Chances of a Lifetime," *Working Papers for a New Society* 3 (Summer 1975): 37–42.

John M. Taurek argues that an equal concern for the lives of individuals requires giving to each an equal prospect of survival so that, faced with a choice between saving the life of one person or the lives of five people (but unable to save all six), the decision would be made by lottery, the toss of a coin. The five do not outweigh the one. See his "Should the Numbers Count?" *Philosophy and Public Affairs* 6, no. 4 (Summer 1977): 293-316.

Torstein Eckhoff argues for lotteries from a somewhat different view of equality. In some circumstances an identical distribution of goods (or bads) is desirable but unattainable, because the good is indivisible. Thus a lottery gives everyone an equal chance at an unequal outcome. See Eckhoff, *Justice: Its Determinants in Social Interaction* (Rotterdam: Rotterdam University Press, 1974), pp. 303-305. This is apparently what the Dutch had in mind when they instituted a lottery (slightly modified by being weighted toward those with higher grades) to select students for medical school. This policy replaced open admissions when the demand for places exceeded the universities' capacity. See Lynn Payer, "Dutch Choosing Medical Students by Lottery," *The Chronicle of Higher Education,* January 30, 1978, p. 3.

10. See Stanley Greenberg, *Race and State in Capitalist Development* (New Haven: Yale University Press, 1980), for a subtler and more complex view of this and related problems.

11. Among the most important of such studies is that of Peter M. Black and Otis Dudley Duncan, *The American Occupational Structure* (New York: John Wiley, 1967). They conclude that "(1) continuity between father and son in general occupational level is more common than would be expected if one's origin did not affect one's destination, but that (2) there is a considerable amount of mobility in our society, and that (3) upward mobility is more common than downward mobility," but the "general pattern of upward mobility . . . is largely the result of changes in the occupational structure itself"—that is, higher occupational levels are expanding while lower levels are contracting. From Alan C. Kerckhoff, *Socialization and Social Class* (Englewood Cliffs, N.J.: Prentice-Hall, 1972), pp. 9-10. Also see Christopher Jencks et al., *Inequality: A Reassessment of the Effect of Family and Schooling in America* (New York: Basic Books, 1972); and James E. Rosenbaum, *Making Inequality: The Hidden Cirriculum of High School Tracking* (New York: John Wiley, 1976), for studies of the effect of education on mobility. And see Joseph Kahl, *The American Class Structure* (New York: Holt, 1953).

12. Vilfredo Pareto, *Manual of Political Economy,* tr. Ann S. Schwier, ed. Ann S. Schwier and Alfred N. Page (New York: Augustus Kelley, 1970), p. 288. For a most amusing *reductio* of Pareto's view and of strict means-regarding equal opportunity, see Michael Young, *Rise of the Meritocracy* (Harmondsworth, England: Penguin Books, 1959).

Richard Herrnstein argues that equal opportunity, meritocratic selection procedures, and the heritability of intelligence are combining in advanced industrial societies to produce a rigid caste system: "By removing arbitrary barriers between classes, society has encouraged the creation of biological barriers. When people can freely take their natural level in society, the upper classes will, virtually by definition, have greater capacity than the lower." Herrnstein, "IQ," *Atlantic* 228 (September 1971): 43–64, quoted passage on p. 64. Bell criticizes this view, as do Block and Dworkin. See Daniel Bell, "On Meritocracy and Equality," *Public Interest* 29 (1972): 29–68; and H. J. Block and Gerald Dworkin, "IQ, Heritability and Inequality," pt. 1, *Philosophy and Public Affairs* 3, no. 4 (Summer 1974): 331–409, pt. 2, *Philosophy and Public Affairs* 4, no. 1 (Fall 1974): 40–97.

13. This point is quite explicit in Mill's discussion of meritocratic competition: "Whoever succeeds in an overcrowded profession or in a competitive examination, whoever is preferred to another in any contest for an object which both desire, reaps benefit from the loss of others . . . But it is, by common admission, better for the general interest of mankind that persons should pursue their objects undeterred by this sort of consequences. In other words, society admits no right, either legal or moral, in the disappointed competitors to immunity from this kind of suffering." See John Stuart Mill, *On Liberty* (Indianapolis: Bobbs-Merrill, 1956), p. 115.

14. For an elegant analysis of related issues, to which our analysis owes a clear debt, see Kenneth Arrow, "A Utilitarian Approach to the Concept of Equality in Public Expenditure," *Quarterly Journal of Economics* (1971). Reprinted in E. S. Phelps, ed., *Economic Justice* (Harmondsworth, England: Penguin Books, 1973).

15. See Arthur M. Okun, *Equality and Efficiency: The Big Trade-off* (Washington, D.C.: Brookings Institution, 1975).

16. There exists a most complex *l*iterature on testing and test-I.Q. For a biased sample, see Arthur Jensen, *Bias in Mental Testing* (New York: Free Press, 1979).

17. See Ralf Dahrendorf, "On the Origin of Inequality among Men," in Dahrendorf, *Essays in the Theory of Society* (Stanford: Stanford University Press, 1968), pp. 151–178.

18. This doctrine is discussed in Robert Freeman Butts and Lawrence A. Cremin, *A History of Education in American Culture* (New York: Holt, Rinehart and Winston, 1963; first published in 1953), pp. 384, 390.

19. John Schaar, "Equality of Opportunity and Beyond," in *NOMOS IX: Equality*, ed. J. Roland Pennock and John W. Chapman (New York: Atherton Press, 1967), pp. 228–250, passage quoted on p. 231. A similar view is incorporated in a larger frame of argument in Schaar, "Some Ways of Thinking about Equality," *Journal of Politics* 26 (1964): 867–895.

20. John Rawls, *A Theory of Justice* (Cambridge, Mass.: Harvard University Press, 1971).

21. Ibid., p. 73.

22. Ibid., emphasis added.

23. Ibid., p. 75. This is the Democratic Equality interpretation of the two Principles of Justice, the interpretation that Rawls favors.

24. See Section 2.2.1 on segmental structure.

25. For example, consider Bell's judgment that "the purpose of societal arrangements is to allow the individual the freedom to fulfill his own purposes" (Bell, "Meritocracy and Equality," p. 40); or Giovanni Sartori, who sees the principle of "equal opportunity to become unequal" as desirable and beneficent within the framework of his liberal interpretation of life and society (*Democratic Theory* [Detroit: Wayne State University Press, 1962], p. 346).

26. For a more rigorous interpretation of this equality, see K. O. May, "A Set of Independent, Necessary and Sufficient Conditions for Simple Majority Decision," *Econometrica* 20 (October 1952): 680-684.

27. Although in an original position characterized by the lack of such information, this is precisely the conclusion we would reach. See Douglas W. Rae, "Decision Rules and Individual Values in Constitutional Choice," *American Political Science Review* 63, no. 1 (March 1969): pp. 40-56.

28. Williams, "Idea of Equality," p. 126.

29. Rosenbaum, *Making Inequality*, quoted passage on p. 40. Rosenbaum analyzes the structure of the tracking system in one high school and concludes that it resembles the model of a tournament rather than an open contest. See also Kaare Svalastoga's discussion of the multiplicative principle in social stratification in Svalastoga, *Social Differentiation* (New York: David McKay, 1965), pp. 12, 93.

30. For discussions of how wealth, status, and position are acquired, and to what extent they are inherited, see John Brittain, *The Inheritance of Economic Status* (Washington, D.C.: Brookings Institution, 1977); John Brittain, *Inheritance and the Inequality of Material Wealth* (Washington, D.C.: Brookings Institution, 1978); Jencks, *Inequality;* Lester Thurow, *Generating Inequality* (New York: Basic Books, 1975), ch. 6; A. B. Atkinson, *Unequal Shares: Wealth in Britain* (London: Penguin Books, 1972); Nicholas Oulton, "Inheritance and the Distribution of Wealth," *Oxford Economic Papers,* n.s., 28 (March 1976): 86-101; Lee Solton, *Toward Income Equality in Norway* (Madison, Wis.: University of Wisconsin Press, 1965); Blau and Duncan, *American Occupational Structure;* and Christopher Jencks, *Who Gets Ahead? The Determinants of Economic Success in America* (New York: Basic Books, 1979).

31. Kurt Vonnegut illustrates such a society in his short story "Harrison Bergeron" in which the United States Handicapper General follows the 211th, 212th, and 213th amendments to the Constitution to create complete equality. She does this by making sure that all television announcers stutter, all ballerinas and athletes wear many pounds of scrap iron, all beautiful women and handsome men wear hideous masks, and all intelligent people wear "mental handicap radios." See Vonnegut, *Welcome to the Monkey House* (New York: Delacorte Press, 1968), pp. 7-13.

Bertrand Russell is less fanciful but equally disparaging of a society that values equality above all else, writing that "it has always been difficult for communities to recognize what is necessary for individuals . . . to make exceptional contributions . . . namely, elements of wildness, of separateness from the herd, of domination by rare impulses of which the utility was not always obvious to everyone." And: "Unjust societies of the past gave to the minority opportunities which, if we are not careful, the new society that we seek to build may give to no one." For example, "If there had not been economic injustice in Egypt and Babylon, the art of writing would never have been invented." Russell concludes that "a society in which each is the slave of all is only a little better than one in which each is the slave of a despot. There is equality where all are slaves, as well as where all are free . . . Equality, by itself, is not enough to make a good society." See Russell, *Authority and the Individual* (Boston: Beacon Press, 1949), quoted passages on pp. 26, 47, 57, 49.

Williams likewise concludes that, in a fantasy world "where everything about a person is controllable, equality of opportunity and absolute equality seem to coincide" (Williams, "Idea of Equality," p. 129).

32. See Richard Sennett and Jonathan Cobb, *The Hidden Injuries of Class* (New York: Vintage Books, 1972); Michael Lewis, *The Culture of Inequality* (New York: New American Library, 1978); and Ely Chinoy, *Automobile Workers and the American Dream* (New York: Random House, 1955).

Matthew Arnold argued that "the religion of inequality has the natural and necessary effect, under present circumstances, of materializing our upper class, vulgarizing our middle class, and brutalizing our lower class. And this is to fail in civilization." Quoted in Henry A. Myers, *Are Men Equal?* (New York: G. P. Putnam's Sons, 1945), pp. 147–148.

And Jerome Karabel writes: "A meritocracy is more competitive than an overtly-based class society, and this unrelenting competition exacts a toll both from the losers, whose self-esteem is damaged, and from the winners, who may be more self-righteous about their elite status than in a more traditional ruling group. Apart from increased efficiency, it is doubtful whether a frenetically inegalitarian society is much of an improvement over an ascriptive society which, at least, does not compel its poor people to internalize their failures." Quoted in Bell, "Meritocracy and Equality," p. 43.

33. See, for instance, James Fallows, "The Tests and the 'Brightest': How Fair Are the College Boards?" *Atlantic* (February 1980): 37–48.

34. *Griggs* v. *Duke Power Company*, 401 U.S. 424 (1971). See the discussion of this case in Dorn, *Rules and Racial Equality*, pp. 129ff.

35. See Nathan Glazer, *Affirmative Discrimination* (New York: Basic Books, 1975), p. 46.

36. For a discussion of how the drive for economic efficiency will eventually eliminate discrimination without government intervention, see Milton Friedman, *Capitalism and Freedom* (Chicago: University of Chicago Press, 1962), pp. 108–118.

37. Bell, "Meritocracy and Equality," p. 36.

38. A more direct approach to realizing means-regarding equal opportunity between an advantaged and a disadvantaged bloc would be a handicapping system. Under such a system, members of a disadvantaged bloc would each get some special advantage (for example, points added to raw test scores) that would offset uncontrolled disadvantages visited upon that bloc. This would, of course, be subject to the criticisms given in Section 3.2.1, for it would wrongly advantage those members of the disadvantaged bloc who were not as individuals disadvantaged, and it would similarly handicap members of the advantaged bloc who were not themselves actually advantaged.

39. Bell makes the following rather polemical points about these ambiguities: "What is the logic of extending the principle only to women, Blacks, Mexicans, Puerto Ricans, American Indians, Filipinos, Chinese, and Japanese (the catgories in the HEW guidelines)? Why not to Irish, Italians, Poles, and other ethnic groups? And if representation is the criterion, what is the base of representation? At one California state college, as John Bunzel reports, the Mexican-Americans asked that 20% of the total work force be Chicanos, because the surrounding community is 20% Mexican-American. The Black students rejected the argument and said that the proper base should be the state of California, which would provide a different mix of blacks and Chicanos. Would the University of Mississippi be expected to hire 37 per cent black faculty because this is the proportion of blacks in the population of Mississippi? And would the number of Jews in most faculties in the country be reduced because the Jews are clearly overrepresented in proportion to their number? ... Governor Reagan of California has said that conservatives are highly underrepresented in the faculties of the state universities ... Should conservatives therefore be given preference in hiring?" Bell, "Meritocracy and Equality," p. 38.

40. For a formal analysis of quotas in the present sense, see Thomas R. Conrad, "The Debate about Quota Systems: An Analysis," *American Journal of Political Science* 20 (1976): 135-149. For a rejoinder to Conrad's view, see Felix E. Oppenheim, "Equality, Groups, and Quotas," *American Journal of Political Science* 21 (1977): 65-69. In this paper Oppenheim seeks to show that a single, value-free conception of equality will account for the emergence of quotas.

41. See Section 2.2.2 and note 29 in Chapter 2.

42. Bell interprets quotas as a substitution of results for opportunities, which is correct in relation to bloc-regarding structures, but not true in relation to individual-regarding ones. See Bell, "Meritocracy and Equality," pp. 40ff. All of this, however, must be viewed on the understanding that "results" are normative claims, not actualities that can be spent for groceries. See, for example, Paul Burstein, "Equal Employment Legislation

and the Income of Women and Nonwhites," *American Sociological Review* 44 (1979): 367–391.

43. See Lester C. Thurow, "A Theory of Groups and Economic Redistribution," *Philosophy and Public Affairs* 9, no. 1 (Fall 1979): 25–41 for a discussion of equal opportunities for groups vs. equal opportunities for individuals.

5. The Value of Equality

1. R. H. Tawney, *Equality*, 4th ed. (London: Allen and Unwin, 1952), pp. 49–50. Similarly, Walzer writes: "What egalitarianism requires is that many bells should ring. Different goods should be distributed to different people for different reasons. Equality is not a simple notion, and it cannot be satisfied by a single distributive scheme." Michael Walzer, "In Defense of Equality," *Dissent* (Fall 1973): 399–408, quoted passage on p. 401. Also see Gregory Vlastos, "Justice and Equality," in *Social Justice*, ed. Richard Brandt (Englewood Cliffs, N.J.: Prentice-Hall, 1962), pp. 31–72; William Frankena, "The Concept of Social Justice," in Brandt, *Social Justice*, pp. 1–29; David Thomson, *Equality* (Cambridge: Cambridge University Press, 1949); Sanford Lakoff, *Equality in Political Philosophy* (Boston: Beacon Press, 1964); Bernard Williams, "The Idea of Equality," in *Philosophy, Politics, and Society*, ser. 2, ed. Peter Laslett and W. G. Runciman (Oxford: Blackwell, 1962); and J. N. Findlay, *Values and Intentions* (London: Allen and Unwin, 1961).

2. Person-regarding value structure is *not* the same as individual-regarding subject structure (see Chapter 2). Person-regarding equality may have an individual- or bloc-regarding subject, but stereotypes may be required to establish person-regarding equality on a bloc-regarding basis. For an implicitly person-regarding argument with a bloc-regarding subject structure, see Elizabeth H. Wolgast, *Equality and the Rights of Women* (Ithaca, N.Y.: Cornell University Press, 1980).

3. See Section 1.2. This is a hyperbolic exaggeration of the homogenized American equality of the melting pot tradition, and some have actually proposed such homogeneity as a necessary condition for the realization of equality. See, for example, J. R. Pole, *The Pursuit of Equality in American History* (Berkeley: University of California Press, 1978), esp. p. 27.

4. We are indebted to James S. Fishkin, Yale University, for this point.

5. Indeed, envy in this sense defines the closely related concept of economic "equity" for such authors as Duncan Foley and Hal Varian. As the latter writes, "If, in a given allocation, agent i prefers the bundle of agent j to his own, we will say that agent i *envies* agent j. If there are no envious agents at allocation x, we will say that x is equitable." See Hal. R. Varian,

"Equity, Envy, and Efficiency," *Journal of Economic Theory* 9 (1974): 63–91, quoted passage on p. 63; and idem, "Distributive Justice, Welfare Economics and the Theory of Fairness," *Philosophy and Public Affairs* 4 (Spring 1975): 223–247. See also Duncan K. Foley, "Resource Allocation and the Public Sector," *Yale Economic Essays* 7 (1967): 45–98. Note, however, that Foley-Varian equity is a more general conception than is lot-regarding equality, for it requires merely that $V_{ii} \geq V_{ij}$, and $V_{jj} \geq V_{ji}$, so that we might have a situation in which agents derived *more* value from their own lots than they would from the lots of others. Note also that lot-regarding equality says nothing about the amount of satisfaction a person gets from his or her lot of goods. Ms. j could absolutely loathe her allocation of food, but if she loathes i's allocation just as much, then their situation is lot-equal.

6. Consider the familiar Edgeworth box with two persons i and j, and two commodities X and Y, as shown in Figure 22. The nonidentical allocation Q gives 10X and 2Y to person i, while person j gets 5X and 8Y. If their indifference curves both pass from Q to its mirror-image, Q', in which j gets 10X and 2Y, while i gets 5X and 8Y, then lot-regarding equality obtains despite nonidentical lots. The intuitive interpretation seems to be that differences in taste simply offset differences in lots. This is, we think, a man-bites-dog case. For a contrasting view and the source of Figure 22, see John E. Roemer, "Inequality, Exploitation, Justice and Socialism: A Theoretical-Historical Approach," *Cowles Foundation for Research in Economics*, discussion paper 545, February 20, 1980.

7. Vilfredo Pareto, *Manual of Political Economy*, tr. Ann S. Schwier, ed. Ann S. Schwier and Alfred N. Page (New York: Augustus Kelley, 1971), p. 45, italics added. An equally important restatement of this view is Lionel Robbins, "Interpersonal Comparisons of Utility," *Economic Journal* 48 (1938): 634–641.

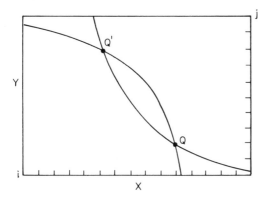

Figure 22. Lot-regarding equality with nonidentical lots.

8. Some argue that interpersonal comparisons are not, at least in theory, all *that* unknowable. A more sophisticated social psychology, for example, would permit us to compare relative degrees of want or need. See Ilmar Waldner, "The Empirical Meaningfulness of Interpersonal Utility Comparisons," *Journal of Philosophy* 69 (February 1972): 87–103; and J. Harsanyi, "Can the Maximin Principle Serve as a Basis for Morality?" *American Political Science Review* 69 (June 1975): 594–606.

9. Varian, "Equity, Envy and Efficiency"; Foley, "Resource Allocation." See note 4 above.

10. See Elisha A. Pazner and David Schmeidler, "A Difficulty in the Concept of Fairness," *Review of Economic Studies* 41 (1974): 441–443. Note that these authors find a difficulty in the concept of fairness, not a difficulty in the concept of efficient production. They later produce a different concept of equality of fairness that fits Paretian efficiency better. See "Egalitarian Equivalent Allocations: A New Concept of Economic Equity," *Quarterly Journal of Economics* 92 (1978): 671–687. It is interesting to compare this spare doctrine about the grounds of envy with the old Calvinist requirement ("rule of equity") that such comparisons of wealth or circumstance as may provoke envy ought to be eschewed. Compare Pole, *The Pursuit of Equality*, p. 63. It is also interesting to compare both these views of envy with the much richer psychological view in Helmut Schoeck, *Envy: A Theory of Social Behavior* (New York: Harcourt, Brace, and World, 1969).

11. For cogent critical discussions of this, see J. E. Meade, *Efficiency, Equality and the Ownership of Property* (London: Allen and Unwin, 1964); Amartya K. Sen, *Collective Choice and Social Welfare* (San Francisco: Holden-Day, 1970), esp. pp. 21ff; and idem, *On Economic Inequality* (New York: W. W. Norton, 1973), esp. pp. 12ff.

12. This same-bundles view seems to lie very close to John Rawls' doctrine of "primary goods," a point that he finesses with some success in *A Theory of Justice* (Cambridge, Mass.: Harvard University Press, 1971). For a critical discussion of this and related matters, see Benjamin R. Barber, "Justifying Justice: Problems of Psychology, Measurement and Politics in Rawls," *American Political Science Review* 69 (June 1975): 663–674.

13. See, for instance, the "Wilt Chamberlain example" in Robert Nozick, *Anarchy, State, and Utopia* (New York: Basic Books, 1974), pp. 161–163.

14. Max Weber, *Economy and Society*, ed. Guenther Roth and Claus Wittich (Berkeley: University of California Press, 1968), vol. 1, p. 636.

15. Karl Marx, *Capital*, ed. Friedrich Engels (New York: International Publishers, 1967), vol. 1, p. 72. This idea is nicely explicated in Leszek Kolakowski, *Main Currents of Marxism*, tr. P. S. Falla (Oxford: Oxford University Press, 1978), vol. 1, pp. 276ff. See also Peter Berger and Thomas Luck-

man, *The Social Construction of Reality* (Garden City, N.Y.: Doubleday, 1966); George Lukacs, *History and Class Consciousness* (Cambridge, Mass.: MIT Press, 1971); and Tim Patterson, "Notes on the Historical Application of Marxist Cultural Theory," *Science and Society* 39 (Fall 1975): 257-291.

16. Marx, however, does note the additional relation of formal equality between market participants as a central mystifying element of capitalist exchange. Marx, *Capital*, esp. ch. 9.

17. That is, personhood is irrelevant to its identical-lots form.

18. Robert A. Dahl and Charles E. Lindblom, *Politics, Economics, and Welfare* (New York: Harper and Row, 1953), p. 44.

19. K. O. May, "A Set of Independent, Necessary and Sufficient Conditions for Simple Majority Decision," *Econometrica* 20 (October 1952): 680-684.

20. See, for example, John Stuart Mill, *Considerations on Representative Government* (London: Longmans Green, 1890); Enid Lakeman and James D. Lambert, *How Democracies Vote* (London: Faber and Faber, 1955); and Douglas W. Rae, *The Political Consequences of Electoral Laws* (New Haven: Yale University Press, 1967).

21. Marx indeed held that "bourgeois rights" are inherently, analytically, linked to such inequalities. See in particular *Critique of the Gotha Programme* (1875; rpt. New York: International Publishers, 1938). See also Ralf Dahrendorf, "On the Origin of Inequality among Men," in Dahrendorf, *Essays in the Theory of Society* (Stanford: Stanford University Press, 1968), pp. 151-178; Carole Pateman, *The Problem of Political Obligations: A Critical Analysis of Liberal Theory* (New York: John Wiley, 1979); and Robert A. Dahl, "On Removing Certain Impediments to Democracy in the United States," *Political Science Quarterly* 92 (Spring 1977): 1-20.

22. Felix E. Oppenheim, "Egalitarianism as a Descriptive Concept," *American Philosophical Quarterly* 7 (1970): 143-152.

23. Isaiah Berlin, "Equality," *Proceedings of the Aristotelian Society*, n.s. (1956), p. 305, italics added.

24. Among activists see, for example, George Bernard Shaw, *The Road to Equality*, ed. Louis Crompton (Boston: Beacon Press, 1971); "The Brook Farm Manifesto," in *American Utopianism*, ed. Robert Fogarty (Itasca, Ill.: F. E. Peacock, 1972), pp. 63-66; Edward Bellamy, *Looking Backward* (Cambridge, Mass.: Harvard University Press, 1967); Huey Long, *Every Man a King* (New Orleans: National Book, 1933); and Upton Sinclair, *I, Governor of California and How I Ended Poverty* (Los Angeles: no publisher, no date).

Among academics, see Herbert Gans, *More Equality* (New York: Pantheon Books, 1973); S. M. Miller and Pamela Roby, *The Future of Inequality* (New York: Basic Books, 1970); and Lester Thurow, "Tax Wealth, Not Income," *New York Times Magazine*, April 11, 1976, pp. 32 ff.

25. Some argue, of course, that the motives of income egalitarians are

not always pure, as is argued in the poem titled "On Communists," by Ebenezer Elliott (*The New Oxford Book of Light Verse* [Oxford: Oxford University Press, 1978], p. 51):

> What is a Communist? One who has yearnings
> For equal division of unequal earnings;
> Idler or bungler, or both, he is willing
> To fork out his penny and pocket your shilling.

26. One can, of course, vary other aspects of work to compensate for differences in work satisfaction. In *Walden Two*, people work only a few hours a day on noxious jobs, and many hours a day in enjoyable jobs (B. F. Skinner, *Walden Two* [1948; rpt. New York: Macmillan, 1962]). In Bellamy's egalitarian utopia, prizes, honors, and prestige are very finely divided and carefully distributed to provide incentives for, and to reward, difficult or unpleasant tasks (Bellamy, *Looking Backward*). And Adam Smith wrote that "the wages of labour vary with the ease or hardship, the cleanliness or dirtiness, the honourableness or dishonourableness of the employment" (Adam Smith, *The Wealth of Nations*, ed. Andrew Skinner [Harmondsworth, England: Penguin Books, 1977], bk. 1, ch. 10, p. 202).

27. See Pazner and Schmeidler, "Concept of Fairness"; and Nozick, *Anarchy, State, and Utopia*, pp. 161–163.

28. Elizabeth H. Wolgast argues, for example, that the interests of women are not served by a demand for equal rights. Men and women differ, and an equal assignment of rights fits women into a Procrustean bed. Her quarrel with egalitarianism is actually with its lot-regarding form and particularly its blindness to human variation; her argument is implicitly person-regarding: "Why not put egalitarian androgynous models aside and look to a social form fitting a species of two sexes, both having their own strength, virtues, distinctive tendencies, and weakness, neither being fully assimilable to the other?" (Wolgast, *Equality and the Rights of Women*, p. 137). An argument of this form is a two-edged sword; the fact of differences between sexes has been used throughout history to justify the domination of women by men.

29. Albert Weale, *Equality and Social Policy* (London: Routledge and Kegan Paul, 1978), p. 47.

30. Sen, *Economic Inequality*, p. 18.

31. What Stanley Benn terms "equal consideration of interests" appears sometimes to be a case of person-regarding equality (that is, $V_{ii} = V_{jj}$) and at other times to be a hybrid conception in the form $V_{ki} = V_{kj}$, where k equally considers i and j. See Benn, "Egalitarianism and Equal Consideration of Interests," in *NOMOS IX: Equality*, ed. J. Roland Pennock and John W. Chapman (New York: Atherton Press, 1967), pp. 61–78. A principle to which Peter Singer gives the same name is essentially

equivalent to the utilitarian proposition that each person counts for one and none for more than one in deciding the desirability of policies. See *Practical Ethics* (Cambridge: Cambridge University Press, 1979), pp. 19 ff. J. L. Mackie's "third stage of universalization" seems equivalent to person-regarding equality without the equality itself. See Mackie, *Ethics: Inventing Right and Wrong* (Harmondsworth, England: Penguin Books, 1977), pp. 292 ff. For a related view, see Ronald Dworkin, *Taking Rights Seriously* (Cambridge, Mass.: Harvard University Press, 1977).

32. It is amusing to see the extent of human variation determined by D. Weschler and reported in Edward L. Thorndike, *Human Nature and the Social Order,* ed. Geraldine Joncich Clifford, abridged ed. (Cambridge, Mass.: MIT Press, 1969), p. 122. The figures are ratios between measurements for the 2nd and 999th individual per thousand: normal body temperature (1.03); calcium content of body fluids (1.16); acidity of blood (1.21 to 1.32); sizes of various body parts (1.26–1.32); number of digits correctly repeated after a single hearing (2.50).

33. Note that with a sufficiently narrow marginal allocation, even great differences among people are of little concern, while with large, global allocations, we care enormously about small differences.

34. Pareto, *Political Economy;* Robbins, "Interpersonal Comparisons"; and see note 5 and Section 5.2.1.

35. Or perhaps i doesn't much *like* pie; or, more complicated, perhaps j has been taught that ladies do not have large appetites.

36. To make matters worse, Richard McKelvey has shown that *no* institutional device can be devised that will prevent such manipulation. See McKelvey, "Intransitivities in Multidimensional Voting Models and Some Implications for Agenda Control," *Journal of Economic Theory* 12 (1976): 472–482.

37. Two other problems with interpersonal comparisons of utilities are relative deprivation (see note 24, Chapter 2) and false consciousness (see note 53, this chapter). Neither of these deals with the problem of *interpersonal* comparisons; both call into question the validity of the individual's assessment of his or her own utility. Thus W. G. Runciman can argue that "dissatisfaction with the system of privileges and rewards . . . is never felt in an even proportion to the degree of [objective] inequalities to which the various members [of a society] are subject." Runciman, *Relative Deprivation and Social Justice* (Berkeley: University of California Press, 1966), p. 3.

38. As quoted in Robbins, "Interpersonal Comparisons," p. 637.

39. Robert Nozick, *Anarchy, State, and Utopia;* Charles Fried, *An Anatomy of Values* (Cambridge, Mass.: Harvard University Press, 1970); and Bruce Ackerman, *Social Justice in the Liberal State* (New Haven: Yale University Press, 1980).

40. Ackerman, *Social Justice,* p. 11.

41. Ibid., p. 44.

42. J. N. Findlay addresses the problem of "deeply rooted wants" and "shallowly planted" ones in *Values and Intentions*. Similarly, T. N. Scanlon discusses the urgency of preferences and the appropriate social response to ends with varying degrees of urgency in "Preference and Urgency," *Journal of Philosophy* 72 (November 1975): 655–669. So, more polemically, does Theodore Lowi in *The End of Liberalism* (New York: W. W. Norton, 1969, 1979).

43. But note that a *fickle* person's announced ends may be mercurial enough to merge with his or her subjective wants so that utility-based and ends-based comparisons are no longer distinct.

44. *Wisconsin* v. *Yoder* 406 U.S. 205 (1972).

45. We are indebted to Carol Dunahoo for her informative unpublished course paper "An Enquiry into Equality" for the analysis of this case. Yale University, fall term, 1979.

46. Opinion of the Court, delivered by Chief Justice Warren E. Burger, p. 220.

47. Note that even the arch-pluralist James Madison gives no more than a contingent justification for religious toleration, as he affirms that "whilst we assert for ourselves a freedom to embrace, to profess and to observe, the Religion which we believe to be of divine origin, we cannot deny equal freedom to those whose minds have not yet yielded to the evidence which has convinced us. If this freedom be abused, it is an offense against God, not against man." One is tempted to wonder *whose* God will take offense at the violation of whose freedom and how much simpler it would be if all had the same God. Quoted from Pole, *The Pursuit of Equality*, p. 83.

48. In other words, rather than making a collective decision about the use of joint resources, individuals reveal their preferences (and satisfy their aims) by "voting with their feet." See Charles Tiebout, "A Pure Theory of Local Expenditures," *Journal of Political Economy* 64 (October 1956): 416–424. For an excellent discussion, see Dennis C. Mueller, *Public Choice* (Cambridge: Cambridge University Press, 1979), pp. 126–129. Also see Albert O. Hirschman, *Exit, Voice and Loyalty* (Cambridge, Mass.: Harvard University Press, 1970).

49. There are many important borderline cases, including the insanity defense for murder, the desires of a sexual maniac, and the behavior of addicts.

50. Vlastos, "Justice and Equality," p. 41.

51. Marx, *Critique of the Gotha Programme*, p. 10.

52. In other words, with this conception of needs, "a claim that X's interests are served does not require a claim that (at least some of) his actual wants, aims, or preferences are satisfied." Such a theory would justify paternalistic inferences. James S. Fishkin, *Tyranny and Legitimacy* (Balti-

more: Johns Hopkins University Press, 1979), pp. 23–24. This line of thought leads us into the murky waters of false consciousness. See Joseph Gabel, *False Consciousness*, tr. Margaret Thompson (New York: Harper and Row, 1975).

Social scientists who have tried to define universal human needs include Abraham Maslow, *Toward a Psychology of Being* (New York: Van Nostrand, 1962); Alfred Schutz, "Equality and the Meaning Structure of the Social World," in *Aspects of Equality*, ed. L. Bryson, C. Faust, L. Finkelstein, and R. M. MacIver (New York: Harper and Bros., 1956), pp. 33–78; and Rawls, *A Theory of Justice*. Without trying to define them very rigorously, L. T. Hobshouse emphasizes the importance of satisfying basic needs in all societies. See *The Elements of Social Justice* (London: Allen and Unwin, n.d.), esp. p. 118.

53. See B. F. Skinner, *Beyond Freedom and Dignity* (New York: Knopf, 1971); see also Skinner, *Walden Two*.

54. Abraham Maslow, "Psychological Data and Value Theory," in *New Knowledge in Human Values*, ed. Abraham Maslow (New York: Harper and Row, 1959), pp. 119–136.

55. Hobshouse, *Elements of Social Justice*, p. 110.

56. Andrew Carnegie, "Wealth," in *Democracy and the Gospel of Wealth*, ed. Gail Kennedy (Boston: D.C. Health, 1949), pp. 1–8, quoted passage on p. 2. A more subtle version of the argument is Kingsley Davis and Wilbert Moore's functional claim for elite privileges. See Davis and Moore, "Some Principles of Stratification" and related articles in *Readings on Social Stratification*, ed. Melvin Tumin (Englewood Cliffs, N.J.: Prentice-Hall, 1970), pp. 367–435.

57. Edmund Burke, "An Appeal from the New to the Old Whigs," in *The Writings and Speeches of Edmund Burke* (Boston, 1901), vol. 4, p. 174, as quoted in Samuel A. Beer, *British Politics in the Collectivist Age* (New York: Knopf, 1966), p. 12.

58. For an example of an economist who assumed the diminishing marginal utility of income, see Ragnor Frisch, *New Methods of Measuring Marginal Utility* (Tübingen: J. C. B. Moha, 1932), and "A Complete Scheme for Computing All Direct and Cross Demand Elasticities in a Model with Many Sectors," *Econometrica* 27 (April 1959): 177–196. For a more theoretical discussion of whether interpersonal comparisons are possible, and thus whether one can discuss issues of diminishing marginal utility, see I. M. D. Little, *A Critique of Welfare Economics* (Oxford: Clarendon Press, 1950).

59. This is because such redistribution takes the punch out of France's joke about laws equal enough to permit rich and poor alike to sleep under bridges.

60. Singer, *Practical Ethics*, pp. 19ff. Steven Lukes makes the same

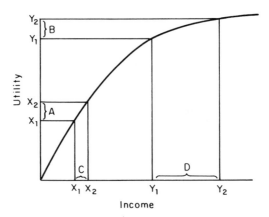

Figure 23. Increase in utility for low-income person X and high-income person Y.

point, from a Kantian and not a utilitarian framework, in discussing what equality of consideration or respect for all humans requires from a policy. Compare Lukes, "Socialism and Equality," *Dissent* 22 (1975): 154–168.

61. Or, more exactly, if the total does not diminish as a consequence of redistribution.

62. The same increase in utility corresponds to a smaller increase in income for a poor person than for a rich one. In Figure 23, if the increase in utility for low-income person X (represented by distance A) is to equal the increase in utility for high-income person Y (distance B), then the increase in income for Y (distance D) must exceed the increase in income of X (distance C): that is, $(A = B) \rightarrow (D > C)$.

63. Abba Lerner, *The Economics of Control: Principles of Welfare Economics* (New York: Macmillan, 1944).

64. And, seen from j's viewpoint, $V_{jj} = V_{ji}$, for all simple equals i and j.

6. Relative Equalities

1. A great many useful points on this subject are to be found in Amartya K. Sen, *On Economic Inequality* (New York: W. W. Norton, 1973), esp. pp. 24–76.

2. Notice that bloc-regarding equality is not an extension of simple equality, because blocs may themselves contain simple inequality while standing in a relation of perfect bloc-regarding equality to one another. An artificial simplification is to treat only central tendencies for each bloc,

then to think of blocs as if all their members stood at this central tendency. Thus, a bloc consisting of Paul Mellon and our reader has a central tendency net worth of at least $50 million. For a more elaborate discussion, see Edwin Dorn, *Rules and Racial Equality* (New Haven: Yale University Press, 1979).

3. Here we presuppose the groundwork given above. One could interpret this question as one of deciding the extent to which a simple individual-regarding equality has been attained. Note that such equalities are implicitly absolute.

4. Felix E. Oppenheim, "Egalitarianism as a Descriptive Concept," *American Philosophical Quarterly* 7 (1970): 143–152, quoted passage p. 145.

5. See Douglas Rae and Michael Taylor, *The Analysis of Political Cleavages* (New Haven: Yale University Press, 1971), ch. 2. For a critical discussion, see Mogens N. Pedersen, "On Measuring Party System Change: A Methodological Critique and a Suggestion," *Comparative Political Studies* 12, no. 4 (January 1980): 387–403.

6. John Rawls, *A Theory of Justice* (Cambridge, Mass.: Harvard University Press, 1971).

7. James P. Smith and Finis Welch, "Race Differences in Earnings: A Survey and New Evidence," Rand Corporation, 1978.

8. Alexis de Tocqueville, *Democracy in America,* tr. George Lawrence, ed. J. P. Mayer (Garden City, N.Y.: Doubleday, 1969), p. 57.

9. It would, however, entail tyranny in the sense of doing harm to some when it would have been possible to harm none. For a development of tyranny in this sense see James S. Fishkin, *Tyranny and Legitimacy: A Critique of Political Theories* (Baltimore: Johns Hopkins University Press, 1979). On this definition, all four principles of relative equality entail tyranny; the minimax criterion is just the most obvious case.

10. These are analogous to the indifference curves of microeconomics. Rather than representing the various combinations of a collection of goods that give equal satisfaction to a consumer, our indifference curves can be seen as representing the various allocational distributions that give equal satisfaction to an ardent egalitarian whose sole consideration is the promotion of one species of relative equality.

11. See Arthur Okun's discussion of the "leaky bucket" in redistributive policies, in Okun, *Equality and Efficiency: The Big Trade-Off* (Washington, D.C.: Brookings Institution, 1975), pp. 91–95.

12. Note that we could perform the same analysis with twice as many lines by labeling the axes with names (like Mr. i or Ms. j) instead of with ranks like more and less advantaged. It seems best to count people's noses instead of counting their feet and dividing by two.

13. See David Potter, *People of Plenty* (Chicago: University of Chicago Press, 1954).

14. These include the Gini index, variance and coefficient of varia-

tion, standard deviation, various logarithmic indices, and the whole series of "normative indices" used in welfare economics. See Sen, *Economic Inequality,* p. 36. See also Malcolm Sawyer, *Income Distribution in O.E.C.D. Countries* (Washington, D.C.: Organization for Economic Cooperation and Development, Occasional Studies, 1976), pp. 6–11.

15. The different results of normalized and nonnormalized measures of inequality are apparent in Kristol's example of equality's ambiguity: "A comparative percentile increase for lower-income groups represents a step toward equality only from a limited, statistical point of view. In another perspective, it can be regarded as a movement toward further inequality. for when a man's income is increased from a million dollars a year to two million (i.e., doubled), while another's income is increased from one thousand to five thousand (i.e., quintupled), it can fairly be said that the rich man has benefited more notably—in absolute magnitudes—than the poor." Whether the second allocation is judged more or less than the first depends entirely upon whether the sizes of the totals divided are taken into account. Irving Kristol, "Equality as an Idea," in *Encyclopedia of the Social Sciences,* ed. David L. Sills (New York: Macmillan and Free Press, 1968), vol. 5, pp. 108–111, quoted passage on p. 110.

16. Sen, *Economic Inequality,* pp. 75–76.

17. This maximin-minimax tells us always that zone E is preferable to X and that X is always preferable to zone A in Figures 14 and 16. Both of the remaining principles must agree in their judgments of these two zones, as will be seen upon inspection of the diagrams.

18. Sen, *Economic Inequality,* p. 31.

19. This is a function of the ratio between the average pairwise difference and the mean—it is actually exactly half that ratio. Thus, the value .305 implies that the average pairwise difference was $.305 \cdot 2 = .610$ of the mean (27.5 units mean difference, divided by 45 units mean entitlement = .610).

20. Sen, *Economic Inequality,* p. 48.

21. For useful surveys of such efforts see Sen, *Economic Inequality;* Sawyer, *Income Distribution;* D. G. Champernowne, *The Distribution of Income between Persons* (Cambridge: Cambridge University Press, 1973); Jan Pen, *Income Distribution,* tr. Trevor S. Preston (New York: Praeger, 1971); and Martin Bronfenbrenner, *Income Distribution Theory* (Chicago: Aldine-Atherton, 1971).

22. For an argument to the effect that such an approach is *unavoidable* for the United States, see Lester C. Thurow, *The Zero-Sum Society* (New York: Basic Books, 1980).

23. See Kurt Vonnegut, "Harrison Bergeron," reprinted in *Welcome to the Monkey House* (New York: Dell, 1968).

24. *The Papers of George Mason, 1725–1792,* ed. Robert A. Rutland (Chapel Hill: University of North Carolina Press, 1970), vol. 1, p. 229.

Cited in J. R. Pole, *The Pursuit of Equality in American History* (Cambridge: Cambridge University Press, 1978), p. 30.

25. We here follow Brian Barry's distinction between aggregative and distributive principles: "An aggregative principle is one which mentions only the total amount of want-satisfaction among the members of a reference group, whereas a distributive principle requires for its statement a mention of the way in which want-satisfaction is to be divided among the members of a reference group." Notice that mixed principles referring both to the total and to their distribution are termed distributive. All of our concepts of relative equality, including those with aggregative features (for example, maximin) are thus distributive for Barry. See Barry, *Political Argument* (London: Routledge & Kegan Paul, 1965), p. 43. For an attempt to devise a measure of relative equality which incorporates aggregative considerations, see Nicholas Rescher, *Distributive Justice* (Indianapolis: Bobbs-Merrill, 1966), pp. 35ff.

26. Rawls, *A Theory of Justice.*

27. There is no such thing in Barry's scheme, and it would be more useful to say that aggregative principles require no mention of distribution, while distributive principles require no mention of totals and mixed principles require both. On this telling, most views of equality become purely distributive, while some (mainly maximin) become mixed.

28. Okun, *Equality and Efficiency.*

29. See Section 5.4.

7. **Endings**

1. Alexis de Tocqueville, *Democracy in America*, tr. George Lawrence, ed. J. P. Mayer (New York: Doubleday, 1969), vol. 1, p. 12.

2. Quoted in Steven Lukes, "Socialism and Equality," *Dissent* 22 (1975): 155. For a brief discussion of Babeuf's egalitarianism, see Leszek Kolakowski, *Main Currents of Marxism: Its Rise, Growth and Dissolution*, tr. P. S. Falla (Oxford University Press, 1978), vol. 1, pp. 184–187.

3. The calculation would not be $108 \cdot 4 \cdot 2 \cdot 2 = 1,728$, since each of the new distinctions is partly redundant of one which came before. The correct calculation is $6 \cdot 4 \cdot 3 \cdot 2 \cdot 5 = 720$, surely enough meanings for one idea.

4. See Section 2.2.1. In the example here: hemodialysis for all kidney patients and sharp sticks in the eye for all fat people.

5. See David Cameron, *Inequality and the State* (forthcoming).

6. This implies a marginal but not a global *in*equality. A policy of person-regarding marginal equality between rich and poor would imply giving *less* to the poor than to the rich, since it takes more marginal increase in, say, money to improve rich people's utility states than it does to

make a corresponding improvement for poor people. If I already have $1,000,000 and you have $10, I may need a further $5,000,000 to get as much added utility as you would derive from $100. See Figure 23.

7. See Section 6.2.2.1.

8. It is possible for both a strong and a weak equality to be attained simultaneously, or for the weak equality to be achieved but not the strong, or for neither to be achieved. It is not possible to attain the strong equality without attaining the weak one. Strong implies weak, but weak does not imply strong.

9. See Section 6.2.2.3.

10. See Sections 2.2.2 and 2.3.

11. The exception is random decision.

12. See in particular Sections 4.2, 4.3, 4.3.1, and 4.3.2.

13. See Section 3.2.

14. Quoted from *New York Times,* July 3, 1980, p. D15.

15. Ibid.

16. For a slightly subtler example, Robert Nisbet sets up equality of opportunity and equality before the law as one equality and opposes this to a "new equality" based on "equality of condition, equality of result." This is *more* complex than many other efforts of the sort. See Robert Nisbet, *Twilight of Authority* (New York: Oxford University Press, 1975), p. 199.

17. Daniel Bell, *The Cultural Contradictions of Capitalism* (New York: Basic Books, 1976), p. 282.

18. Except that for equality of condition, we are told that "the guiding principle here, indisputably, is equal treatment by a common standard." Bell, *Cultural Contradictions,* p. 263. Since this equality fits the other two types of equality, it cuts very little analytic ice.

19. For instance, see Section 5.2.2. Note also the criterion cited in note 18 above.

20. From Section 1.5.

21. Frank E. Manuel and Fritzie P. Manuel, *Utopian Thought in the Western World* (Cambridge, Mass.: Harvard University Press, 1979), pp. 568–577.

22. See Section 2.2.2. In order to accomplish this, Black will just be sure the blocs are not surrogates for advantaged and disadvantaged classes, in which case bloc-regarding equality becomes dangerous.

23. For one example of just such a plea set in a utilitarian framework (and therefore inverted), see F. Y. Edgeworth, *Mathematical Psychics* (London: Kegan Paul, 1881).

24. Karl Marx and Friedrich Engels, *The German Ideology* (Moscow: Progress Publishers, 1964), p. 67. For useful contemporary analyses of Marx's theory of ideas see G. A. Cohen, *Karl Marx's Theory of History* (Princeton: Princeton University Press, 1979); see also Ziyad I. Husami, "Marx on Distributive Justice," *Philosophy and Public Affairs* 8 (Fall 1978):

27–64. A non-Marxian variant of this thesis is presented in Charles E. Lindblom's *Politics and Markets* (New York: Basic Books, 1978)—that is, Lindblom's "circularity" thesis.

25. Marx and Engels, *German Ideology*, pp. 67–68.

26. Kristol, however, reckons that the "new class" does indeed have "an impulse for self-destruction." Irving Kristol, *Two Cheers for Capitalism* (New York: Basic Books, 1978), p. 183.

27. Murray Edelman thus writes that, to reduce political tensions, "it is not uncommon to give the rhetoric to one side and the decision to the other." See Edelman, *The Symbolic Uses of Politics* (Chicago: University of Illinois Press, 1976), p. 39.

28. R. H. Tawney, *Equality*, 4th ed. (London: Allen and Unwin, 1952), pp. 150–151.

Bibliography

Ackerman, Bruce. *Social Justice in the Liberal State*. New Haven: Yale University Press, 1980.

Anderson, Charles H. *The Political Economy of Social Class*. Englewood Cliffs, N.J.: Prentice-Hall, 1974.

Anderson, Perry. "The Antinomies of Antonio Gramsci." *New Left Review* 100 (1976): 5–78.

Apter, David. *Choice and the Politics of Allocation*. New Haven: Yale University Press, 1971.

Aristotle. *Nicomachean Ethics*. Translated by Martin Ostwald. New York: Bobbs-Merrill, 1962.

——— *The Politics*. Translated by T. A. Sinclair. New York: Penguin Books, 1962.

Arrow, Kenneth. "A Utilitarian Approach to the Concept of Equality in Public Expenditure." *Quarterly Journal of Economics,* 1971. Reprinted in E. S. Phelps, ed., *Economic Justice*. Harmondsworth, England: Penguin Books, 1973.

Atkinson, A. B. *Unequal Shares: Wealth in Britain*. London: Penguin Books, 1972.

Barber, Benjamin R. "Justifying Justice: Problems of Psychology, Measurement and Politics in Rawls." *American Political Science Review* 69 (June 1975): 663–674.

Barry, Brian. *Political Argument*. London: Routledge and Kegan Paul, 1965.

Bedau, Hugo. "Egalitarianism and the Idea of Equality." In *NOMOS IX: Equality,* edited by J. Roland Pennock and John W. Chapman. New York: Atherton Press, 1967.

Beer, Samuel A. *British Politics in the Collectivist Age*. New York: Knopf, 1966.

Bell, Daniel. *The Cultural Contradictions of Capitalism*. New York: Basic Books, 1976.

——— "On Meritocracy and Equality," *Public Interest* 29 (1972): 29–68.

Bellamy, Edward. *Looking Backward.* Cambridge, Mass.: Harvard University Press, 1967.

Benn, Stanley. "Egalitarianism and Equal Consideration of Interests." In *NOMOS IX: Equality,* edited by J. Roland Pennock and John W. Chapman. New York: Atherton Press, 1967.

———— and Peters, R. S. *The Principles of Political Thought.* New York: Free Press, 1959.

Berger, Peter, and Luckmann, Thomas. *The Social Construction of Reality.* Garden City, N.Y.: Doubleday, 1966.

Berkowitz, Leonard, and Walster, Elaine, eds. *Equity Theory.* Vol. 9 of *Advances in Experimental Social Psychology.* New York: Academic Press, 1976.

Berlin, Isaiah. "Equality." *Proceedings of the Aristotelian Society,* n.s., 56 (1955–56): 301–326.

Bittker, Boris. *The Case for Black Reparations.* New York: Vintage, 1973.

Black, Peter M., and Duncan, Otis Dudley. *The American Occupational Structure.* New York: John Wiley, 1967.

Block, H. J., and Dworkin, Gerald. "IQ, Heritability and Inequality." Pt. 1, *Philosophy and Public Affairs* 3, no. 4 (1974): 331–409, and pt. 2, *Philosophy and Public Affairs* 4, no. 1 (1974): 40–97.

Blum, Walter J., and Kalven, Harry. *The Uneasy Case for Progressive Taxation.* Chicago: University of Chicago Press, 1953.

Boles, Janet K. *The Politics of the Equal Rights Amendment: Conflict and the Decision Process.* New York: Longman, 1979.

Brittain, John. *The Inheritance of Economic Status.* Washington, D.C.: Brookings Institution, 1977.

———— Inheritance and the Inequality of Material Wealth. Washington, D.C.: Brookings Institution, 1978.

Bronfenbrenner, Martin. *Income Distribution Theory.* Chicago: Aldine-Atherton, 1971.

Burke, Vincent, and Burke, Vee. *Nixon's Good Deed.* New York: Columbia University Press, 1974.

Burstein, Paul. "Equal Employment Legislation and the Income of Women and Nonwhites." *American Sociological Review* 44 (1979): 367–391.

Butts, Robert Freeman, and Cremin, Lawrence A. *A History of Education in American Culture.* New York: Holt, Rinehart and Winston, 1963.

Calabresi, Guido, and Bobbitt, Philip. *Tragic Choices.* New York: W. W. Norton, 1978.

Cameron, David R. "Economic Inequality in the United States." Unpublished paper, Midwest Political Science Association, 1979.

———— Inequality and the State (forthcoming).

Carnegie, Andrew. "Wealth." In *Democracy and the Gospel of Wealth,* edited by Gail Kennedy. Boston: D.C. Heath, 1949.

Carritt, E. F. "Liberty and Equality." *Law Quarterly Review* 56 (1940). Reprinted in *Political Philosophy,* edited by A. Quinton. London: Oxford University Press, 1967.

Champernowne, D. G. *The Distribution of Income between Persons.* Cambridge: Cambridge University Press, 1973.

Chinoy, Ely. *Automobile Workers and the American Dream.* New York: Random House, 1955.

Cohen, G. A. *Karl Marx's Theory of History.* Princeton: Princeton University Press, 1979.

Conrad, Thomas R. "The Debate about Quota Systems: An Analysis." *American Journal of Political Science* 20 (1976): 135–149.

Dahl, Robert. "On Removing Certain Impediments to Democracy in the United States." *Political Science Quarterly* 92 (Spring 1977): 1–20.

———— and Lindblom, Charles E. *Politics, Economics and Welfare.* New York: Harper and Row, 1953.

Dahrendorf, Ralf. *Class and Class Conflict in Industrial Society.* Stanford: Stanford University Press, 1959.

———— "On the Origin of Inequality among Men." *Essays in the Theory of Society.* Stanford: Stanford University Press, 1969.

Danielson, Michael W., et al. *One Nation, So Many Governments.* Lexington, Mass.: D. C. Heath, 1977.

Davis, Kingsley, and Moore, Wilbert. "Some Principles of Stratification." In *Readings on Social Stratification,* edited by Melvin Tumin. Englewood Cliffs, N.J.: Prentice-Hall, 1970.

Davis, T. N. "Justice as the Foundation of Human Equality in Ancient Greece." In *Aspects of Human Equality,* Fifteenth Symposium of the Conference on Science, Philosophy, and Religion. Edited by Lyman Bryson, Clarence H. Faust, Louis Finkelstein, R. M. MacIver. New York: Harper, 1956.

Dewey, John. *Theory of Valuation.* Chicago: University of Chicago Press, 1939.

Djilas, Milovan. *The New Class.* New York: Praeger, 1957.

Dorn, Edwin. *Rules and Racial Equality.* New Haven: Yale University Press, 1979.

Dreyfuss, Joel, and Lawrence, Charles, III. *The Bakke Case.* New York: Harcourt, Brace, Jovanovich, 1979.

Dunahoo, Carol. "An Enquiry into Equality." Unpublished paper, Yale University, 1979.

Dworkin, Ronald M. *Taking Rights Seriously.* Cambridge, Mass.: Harvard University Press, 1977.

Eastland, Terry, and Bennett, William J. *Counting by Race.* New York: Basic Books, 1979.

Eckhoff, Torstein. *Justice.* Rotterdam: Rotterdam University Press, 1974.

Edelman, Murray. *The Symbolic Uses of Politics*. Chicago: University of Illinois Press, 1964.

Edgeworth, F. Y. *Mathematical Psychics*. London: Kegan Paul, 1881.

——— "The Pure Theory of Taxation." *Economic Journal* 7 (1897): 46–70.

Elliott, Ebenezer. "On Communists." *The New Oxford Book of Light Verse*. Oxford: Oxford University Press, 1978, p. 51.

Emerson, Ralph Waldo. "The Fortune of the Republic." *Miscellanies*. Vol. 11 of *Works of Emerson*, edited by Edward W. Emerson. New York: Houghton, Mifflin, 1904; rpt. New York: AMS Press, 1968.

Fallows, James. "The Tests and the 'Brightest': How Fair are the College Boards?" *Atlantic* (February 1980): 37–48.

Feinberg, Joel. *Social Philosophy*. Englewood Cliffs, N.J.: Prentice-Hall, 1973.

Festinger, Leon. "A Theory of Social Comparison Processes." *Human Relations* 7 (1954): 117–140.

Findlay, J. N. *Values and Intentions*. London: Allen and Unwin, 1961.

Fishkin, James S. *Tyranny and Legitimacy*. Baltimore: Johns Hopkins University Press, 1979.

Flathman, R. E. "Equality and Generalization." In *NOMOS IX: Equality*, edited by J. Roland Pennock and John W. Chapman. New York: Atherton Press, 1967.

Fogarty, Robert, ed. *American Utopianism*. Itasca, Ill.: F. E. Peacock, 1972.

Foley, Duncan K. "Resource Allocation and the Public Sector." *Yale Economic Essays* 7 (1967): 45–98.

Foner, Philip S. *The Great Labor Uprising of 1877*. New York: Monad Press, 1977.

Frankena, William. "The Concept of Social Justice." In *Social Justice*, edited by Richard Brandt. Englewood Cliffs, N.J.: Prentice-Hall, 1962.

Fried, Charles. *An Anatomy of Values*. Cambridge, Mass.: Harvard University Press, 1970.

Friedman, Milton. *Capitalism and Freedom*. Chicago: University of Chicago Press, 1962.

Frisch, Ragnor. *New Methods of Measuring Marginal Utility*. Tübingen: J. C. B. Moha, 1932.

——— "A Complete Scheme for Computing All Direct and Cross Demand Elasticities in a Model with Many Sectors." *Econometrica* 27 (April 1959): 177–196.

Gabel, Joseph. *False Consciousness*. Translated by Margaret Thompson. New York: Harper and Row, 1975.

Gans, Herbert J. *More Equality*. New York: Vintage Books, 1968.

Giddens, Anthony. *The Class Structure of Advanced Societies*. New York: Harper and Row, 1973.

Glazer, Nathan. *Affirmative Discrimination: Ethnic Inequality and Public Policy.* New York: Basic Books, 1975.

Greenberg, Stanley, *Race and State in Capitalist Development.* New Haven: Yale University Press, 1980.

Greer, Colin. *The Great School Legend.* New York: Basic Books, 1972.

Hapgood, Fred. "Chances of a Lifetime." *Working Papers for a New Society* 3 (Summer 1975): 37–42.

Harrop, Martin. *Equality and Democracy.* Dissertation, Yale University, 1979.

Harsanyi, J. "Can the Maximin Principle Serve as a Basis for Morality?" *American Political Science Review* 69 (June 1975): 594–606.

Hayek, Friedrich. *Law, Legislation and Liberty.* Chicago: University of Chicago Press, 1976.

Herrnstein, Richard. "IQ." *Atlantic* 228 (September 1971): 43–64.

Hirschman, Albert O. *Exit, Voice and Loyalty.* Cambridge, Mass.: Harvard University Press, 1970.

Hobshouse. L. T. *The Elements of Social Justice.* London: Allen and Unwin, n.d.

Hochschild, Jennifer. *What's Fair?* Cambridge, Mass.: Harvard University Press, 1981.

Holmer, Paul L. *The Grammar of Faith.* San Francisco: Harper and Row, 1978.

Hook, Sidney. *The Paradoxes of Freedom.* Berkeley: University of California Press, 1964.

Husami, Ziyad I. "Marx on Distributive Justice." *Philosophy and Public Affairs* 8 (Fall 1978): 27–64.

Information Service of South Africa. *Progress through Separate Development.* New York, 1973.

Jencks, Christopher, et al. *Inequality: A Reassessment of the Effect of Family and Schooling in America.* New York: Basic Books, 1972.

———— *Who Gets Ahead? The Determinants of Economic Success in America.* New York: Basic Books, 1979.

Jensen, Arthur. *Bias in Mental Testing.* New York: Free Press, 1979.

Kahl, Joseph. *The American Class Structure.* New York: Holt, 1953.

Kant, Immanuel. "On The Common Saying: 'This May Be True in Theory, But It Does Not Apply in Practice.' " 1793; reprinted in *Kant's Political Writings,* edited by Hans Reiss. Cambridge: Cambridge University Press, 1970.

Kerckhoff, Alan C. *Socialization and Social Class.* Englewood Cliffs, N.J.: Prentice-Hall, 1972.

Kirp, David L. "Judicial Policy-Making: Inequitable Public School Financing and the *Serrano* Case." In *Policy and Politics in America,* edited by Allan P. Sindler. Boston: Little, Brown, 1973.

Kolakowski, Leszek. *Main Currents of Marxism: Its Rise, Growth and Dissolution.* Translated by P. S. Falla. Oxford: Oxford University Press, 1979.

Kristol, Irving. "Equality as an Ideal." In *Encyclopedia of the Social Sciences,* edited by David L. Sills. New York: Macmillan and Free Press, 1968. Vol. 5, pp. 108–111.

———— *Two Cheers for Capitalism.* New York: Basic Books, 1978.

Kühnelt-Leddihn, E. *Liberty or Equality: The Challenge of Our Time.* Caldwell, Idaho: Caxton Printers, 1952.

Lakeman, Enid, and Lambert, James D. *How Democracies Vote.* London: Faber and Faber, 1955.

Lakoff, Sanford. *Equality in Political Philosophy.* Cambridge, Mass.: Harvard University Press, 1964.

Lane, Robert. *Political Ideology.* New York: Free Press, 1962.

Laski, Harold J. *A Grammar of Politics.* New Haven: Yale University Press, 1938.

Lerner, Abba. *The Economics of Control: Principles of Welfare Economics.* New York: MacMillan, 1944.

Lewis, Ewart. *Medieval Political Ideas.* New York: Knopf, 1954.

Lewis, Michael. *The Culture of Inequality.* New York: New American Library, 1978.

Lindblom, Charles E. *Politics and Markets.* New York: Basic Books, 1978.

Lipset, Seymour Martin. *Political Man.* Garden City, N.Y.: Doubleday, 1960.

Little, I. M. D. *A Critique of Welfare Economics.* Oxford: Clarendon Press, 1950.

Livingston, John C. *Fair Game?* San Francisco: W. H. Freeman, 1979.

Locke, John. "The Second Treatise of Government." In *Two Treatises of Government,* edited by Peter Laslett. New York: New American Library-Mentor, 1960.

Lockwood, Duane. "Sources of Variation in Working Class Images in Society." *Sociological Review* 14 (November 1966): 249–267.

Long, Huey. *Every Man a King.* New Orleans: National Book, 1933.

Lovejoy, A. O. *The Great Chain of Being.* Cambridge, Mass.: Harvard University Press, 1936.

Lowi, Theodore. *The End of Liberalism.* New York: W. W. Norton, 1969, 1979.

Lucas, John R. *The Principles of Politics.* Oxford: Clarendon Press, 1966.

Lukacs, George. *History and Class Consciousness.* Cambridge, Mass.: MIT Press, 1971.

Lukes, Steven. "Socialism and Equality." *Dissent* 22 (1975): 154–168.

Lydell, Harold. *The Structure of Earnings.* Oxford: Oxford University Press, 1968.

MacCallum, Gerald D., Jr. "Negative and Positive Freedom." *Philosophical Review* 76 (1967): 312–334.

Mackie, J. L. *Ethics: Inventing Right and Wrong.* Harmondsworth, England: Penguin Books, 1977.

MacPherson, C. B. *The Political Theory of Possessive Individualism.* Oxford: Oxford University Press, 1962.

Manuel, Frank E., and Manuel, Fritzie P. *Utopian Thought in the Western World.* Cambridge, Mass.: Harvard University Press, 1979.

Marx, Karl. *Capital.* Vol. 1, edited by Friedrich Engels, translated by Samuel Moore and Edward Aveling. New York: International Publishers, 1967.

———— *Critique of the Gotha Programme.* New York: International Publishers, 1938.

———— and Engels, Friedrich. *The German Ideology.* Moscow: Progress Publishers, 1964.

Maslow, Abraham H. "Psychological Data and Value Theory." In *New Knowledge in Human Values.* New York: Harper and Row, 1959.

———— *Toward a Psychology of Being.* New York: Van Nostrand, 1962.

May, Kenneth O. "A Set of Independent, Necessary and Sufficient Conditions for Simple Majority Decision." *Econometrica* 20 (October 1952): 680–684.

McCloskey, H. J. "Equalitarianism, Equality and Justice." *Australasian Journal of Philosophy* 44 (May 1966): 50–69.

McKelvey, Richard. "Intransitivities in Multidimensional Voting Models and Some Implications for Agenda Control." *Journal of Economic Theory* 12 (1976): 472–482.

McKenzie, Robert, and Silver, Allan. *Angels in Marble.* Chicago: University of Chicago Press, 1968.

Meade, J. E. *Efficiency, Equality and the Ownership of Property.* London: Allen and Unwin, 1964.

Meisel, John. *Working Papers and Canadian Politics.* Montreal: McGill-Queens University Press, 1975.

Mendelson, Wallace. *The American Constitution and the Judicial Process.* Homewood, Ill.: Dorsey Press, 1980.

Miliband, Ralph. *Marxism and Politics.* Oxford: Oxford University Press, 1977.

Mill, John Stuart. *Considerations on Representative Government.* London: Longmans Green, 1890.

———— *On Liberty.* Indianapolis: Bobbs-Merrill, 1956.

Miller, S. M., and Roby, Pamela. *The Future of Inequality.* New York: Basic Books, 1970.

Moynihan, Daniel P. *The Politics of a Guaranteed Income.* New York: Random House, 1973.

Mueller, Dennis C. *Public Choice.* Cambridge: Cambridge University Press, 1979.

Myers, Henry A. *Are Men Equal?* New York: G. P. Putnam's Sons, 1945.

Myrdal, Gunnar, with Sterner, Richard, and Rose, Arnold. *An American*

Dilemma: The Negro Problem and American Democracy. New York: Harper and Row, 1944, 1962.

Nagel, J. "Inequality and Discontent: A Non-Linear Hypothesis." *World Politics* 26 (July 1974): 453–472.

Nagel, Thomas. "Equal Treatment and Compensatory Discrimination." *Philosophy and Public Affairs* 2, no. 4 (Summer 1973): 348–363.

—— *Mortal Questions.* Cambridge: Cambridge University Press, 1979.

Nisbet, Robert. *Twilight of Authority.* New York: Oxford University Press, 1975.

Nordinger, Eric. *The Working Class Tories.* Berkeley: University of California Press, 1967.

Nozick, Robert. *Anarchy, State and Utopia.* New York: Basic Books, 1974.

Okun, Arthur M. *Equality and Efficiency: The Big Trade-Off.* Washington, D.C.: Brookings Institution, 1975.

O'Neil, Robert M. *Discriminating against Discrimination.* Bloomington: Indiana University Press, 1975.

Oppenheim, Felix E. "Egalitarianism as a Descriptive Concept." *American Philosophical Quarterly* 7 (1970): 143–152.

—— "Equality, Groups, and Quotas." *American Journal of Political Science* 21 (1977): 65–69.

Orfield, Gary. *Must We Bus? Segregated Schools and National Policy.* Washington, D.C.: Brookings Institution, 1978.

Oulton, Nicholas. "Inheritance and the Distribution of Wealth." *Oxford Economic Papers,* n.s., 28 (March 1976): 86–101.

Pareto, Vilfredo. *Manual of Political Economy.* Translated by Ann S. Schwier, edited by Ann S. Schwier and Alfred M. Page. New York: Augustus Kelley, 1970.

Parkin, Frank. *Class Inequality and Political Order.* New York: Praeger, 1971.

Pateman, Carole. *The Problem of Political Obligation: A Critical Analysis of Liberal Theory.* New York: John Wiley, 1979.

Patterson, Tim. "Notes on the Historical Application of Marxist Cultural Theory." *Science and Society* 39 (Fall 1975): 257–291.

Pazner, Elisha A., and Schmeidler, David. "A Difficulty in the Concept of Fairness." *Review of Economic Studies* 41 (1974): 441–443.

—— "Egalitarian Equivalent Allocations: A New Concept of Economic Equity." *Quarterly Journal of Economics* 92 (1978): 671–687.

Pedersen, Mogens N. "On Measuring Party System Change: A Methodological Critique and a Suggestion." *Comparative Political Studies* 12, no. 4 (January 1980): 387–403.

Pen, Jan. *Income Distribution.* Translated by Trevor S. Preston. New York: Praeger, 1971.

Pettigrew, Thomas. "Social Evaluation Theory." *Nebraska Symposium on Motivation,* vol. 15, edited by David Levine. Lincoln: University of Nebraska Press, 1967.

Plato. *Laws.* Translated by Thomas L. Pangle. New York: Basic Books, 1980.

Pole, J. R. *The Pursuit of Equality in American History.* Berkeley: University of California Press, 1978.

Potter, David. *People of Plenty.* Chicago: University of Chicago Press, 1954.

Pryor, Frederick. *Property and Industrial Organization in Communist and Capitalist Nations.* Bloomington: Indiana University Press, 1973.

Rae, Douglas W. "Decision Rules and Individual Values in Constitutional Choice." *American Political Science Review* 63, no. 1 (March 1969): 40–56.

———— "The Egalitarian State: Notes on a System of Contradictory Ideals." *Daedalus* 108, no. 4 (Fall 1979): 37–54.

———— *The Political Consequences of Electoral Laws.* New Haven: Yale University Press, 1967.

Rae, Douglas W., and Taylor, Michael. *The Analysis of Political Cleavages.* New Haven: Yale University Press, 1971.

Range, Peter Ross. "Will He Be First?" *New York Times Magazine,* March 11, 1979.

Ranney, Austin. *Curing the Mischiefs of Faction.* Berkeley: University of California Press, 1975.

Rawls, John. *A Theory of Justice.* Cambridge, Mass.: Harvard University Press, 1971.

Rees, John. *Equality.* London: Macmillan Press, 1972.

Rescher, Nicholas. *Distributive Justice.* Indianapolis: Bobbs-Merrill, 1966.

Robbins, Lionel. "Interpersonal Comparisons of Utility." *Economic Journal* 48 (1938): 634–641.

Roemer, John E. "Inequality, Exploitation, Justice and Socialism: A Theoretical-Historical Approach." *Cowles Foundation for Research in Economics,* discussion paper 545, February 20, 1980.

Rosenbaum, James E. *Making Inequality: The Hidden Curriculum of High School Tracking.* New York: John Wiley, 1976.

Rothbard, Murray. *Left and Right.* San Francisco: Cato Institute, 1979.

Runciman, W. G. *Relative Deprivation and Social Justice.* Berkeley: University of California Press, 1966.

Russell, Bertrand. *Authority and the Individual.* Boston: Beacon Press, 1949.

Rutland, Robert A., ed. *The Papers of George Mason, 1725–1792.* Chapel Hill: University of North Carolina Press, 1970.

Sartori, Giovanni. *Democratic Theory.* Detroit: Wayne State University Press, 1962.

Sawyer, Malcolm. *Income Distribution in OECD Countries.* OECD Economic Outlook. Occasional Studies: 1976.

Scanlon, T. N. "Preference and Urgency." *Journal of Philosophy* 72 (November 1975): 655–669.

Schaar, John. "Equality of Opportunity and Beyond." In *NOMOS IX:*

Equality, edited by J. Roland Pennock and John W. Chapman. New York: Atherton Press, 1967.

——— "Some Ways of Thinking about Equality." *Journal of Politics* 26 (1964): 867–895.

Schoeck, Helmut. *Envy: A Theory of Social Behavior.* New York: Harcourt, Brace and World, 1969.

Schultz, Alfred. "Equality and the Meaning Structure of the Social World." In *Aspects of Equality,* Fifteenth Symposium of the Conference on Science, Philosophy and Religion, edited by Lyman Bryson, C. H. Faust, L. Finkelstein, and R. M. MacIver. New York: Harper, 1956.

Scully, Gerald W. "Discrimination: The Case of Baseball." In *Government and the Sports Business,* edited by Roger Noll. Washington, D.C.: Brookings Institution, 1974.

Sen, Amartya K. *Collective Choice and Social Welfare.* San Francisco: Holden-Day, 1970.

——— *On Economic Inequality.* New York: W. W. Norton, 1973.

Sennett, Richard, and Cobb, Jonathan. *The Hidden Injuries of Class.* New York: Vintage Books, 1972.

Shaw, George Bernard. "Maxims for Revolutionists." In *Man and Superman.* Harmondsworth, England: Penguin Books, 1946, 1972.

——— *The Road to Equality.* Edited by Louis Crompton. Boston: Beacon Press, 1971.

Sher, George. "Justifying Reverse Discrimination in Employment." *Philosophy and Public Affairs* 4, no. 2 (Winter 1975): 159–170.

Sigmund, Paul. "Hierarchy, Equality, and Consent in Medieval Christian Thought." In *NOMOS IX: Equality,* edited by J. Roland Pennock and John W. Chapman. New York: Atherton Press, 1967.

Simon, Robert. "Preferential Hiring: A Reply to Judith Jarvis Thomson." *Philosophy and Public Affairs* 3, no. 3 (Spring 1974): 312–320.

Sinclair, Upton. *I, Governor of California and How I Ended Poverty.* Los Angeles: no publisher, no date.

Sindler, Allan P. *Bakke, DeFunis and Minority Admissions.* New York: Longman, 1978.

Singer, Peter. *Practical Ethics.* Cambridge: Cambridge University Press, 1979.

Skinner, B. F. *Beyond Freedom and Dignity.* New York: Knopf, 1971.

——— *Walden Two.* New York: Macmillan, 1962.

Smith, Adam. *The Wealth of Nations.* Edited by Andrew Skinner. Harmondsworth, England: Penguin Books, 1977.

Smith, James P., and Welch, Finis. "Race Differences in Earnings: A Survey and New Evidence." Rand Corporation, 1978.

Solton, Lee. *Toward Income Equality in Norway.* Madison: University of Wisconsin Press, 1965.

Stimpson, Catharine. "Thy Neighbor's Wife, Thy Neighbor's Servants:

Women's Liberation and Black Civil Rights." In *Woman in Sexist Society*, edited by Vivian Gornick and Barbara Moran, pp. 622–657. New York: New American Library, 1971.

Storey, James; Harries, R.; Levy, F.; Fechter, A.; and Michel, R. "The Better Jobs and Income Plan." Washington, D.C.: Urban Institute, 1978.

Sulvetta, Margaret. "The Impact of Welfare Reform on Benefits for the Poor." Washington, D.C.: Urban Institute, 1978.

Svalastoga, Kaare. *Social Differentiation.* New York: David McKay, 1965.

Taurek, John M. "Should the Numbers Count?" *Philosophy and Public Affairs* 6, no. 4 (Summer 1977): 293–316.

Tawney, R. H. *Equality.* Fourth edition. London: Allen and Unwin, 1952.

Thomson, David. *Equality.* Cambridge: Cambridge University Press, 1949.

Thomson, Judith Jarvis. "Preferential Hiring." *Philosophy and Public Affairs* 2, no. 4 (Summer 1973): 364–384.

Thorndike, Edward L. *Human Nature and the Social Order.* Abridged ed., edited by G. J. Clifford. Cambridge, Mass.: MIT Press, 1969.

Thurow, Lester. *Generating Inequality.* New York: Basic Books, 1975.

———— "Tax Wealth, Not Income." *New York Times Magazine,* April 11, 1976.

———— "A Theory of Groups and Economic Redistribution." *Philosophy and Public Affairs* 9, no. 1 (Fall 1979): 25–41.

———— *The Zero-Sum Society.* New York: Basic Books, 1980.

Tiebout, Charles. "A Pure Theory of Local Expenditures." *Journal of Political Economy* 64 (October 1956): 416–424.

Toqueville, Alexis de. *Democracy in America.* Translated by George Lawrence, edited by J. P. Mayer. New York: Doubleday, 1969.

Tussman, Joseph, and Tenbrock, Jacobus. "The Equal Protection of the Laws." *California Law Review* 37 (September 1949): 341–380.

U.S. Commission on Civil Rights. *Toward an Understanding of Bakke.* Washington, D.C.: U.S. Government Printing Office, 1979.

U.S. Department of Commerce, Bureau of the Census. *Current Population Reports,* P. 60, no. 120 (November 1979).

U.S. Department of Labor, Bureau of Labor Statistics. "Employment and Earnings." vol. 27, no. 5, May 1980.

U.S. Department of Labor, Women's Bureau. *The Earnings Gap between Men and Women.* Washington, D.C.: U.S. Government Printing Office, 1976.

Van Alstyne, Aarvo; Karst, Kenneth; and Gerard, Jules. *Sum and Substance of Constitutional Law.* Inglewood, Calif.: Center for Creative Educational Services, 1979.

Varian, Hal R. "Equity, Envy and Efficiency." *Journal of Economic Theory* 9 (1974): 63–91.

———— "Distributive Justice, Welfare Economics and the Theory of Fairness." *Philosophy and Public Affairs* 4 (Spring 1975): 223–247.

Vlastos, Gregory. "Justice and Equality." In *Social Justice,* edited by Richard Brandt. Englewood Cliffs, N.J.: Prentice-Hall 1962.

Vonnegut, Kurt. "Harrison Bergeron." In Vonnegut, *Welcome to the Monkey House.* New York: Delacorte Press, 1968.

Von Wright, George Henrick. *Norm and Action.* London: Routledge and Kegan Paul, 1963.

Waldner, Ilmar. "The Empirical Meaningfulness of Interpersonal Utility Comparisons." *Journal of Philosophy* 69 (February 1972): 87–103.

Wallerstein, Immanuel. *The Capitalist World-Economy.* Cambridge: Cambridge University Press, 1979.

Walster, Elaine; Bersheid, Ellen; and Walster, G. W. "New Directions in Equity Research." *Journal of Personality and Social Psychology* 25 (1973):151–176.

Walzer, Michael. "In Defense of Equality." *Dissent* 20 (Fall 1973): 399–408.

Weale, Albert. *Equality and Social Policy.* London: Routledge and Kegan Paul, 1978.

Weber, Max. *Economy and Society.* Edited by Guenther Roth and Claus Wittich. Berkeley: University of California Press, 1978.

Wiles, Peter. *Distribution of Income: East and West.* Amsterdam: North-Holland Publishing, 1974.

Wilkinson, J. Harvie, III. *From Brown to Bakke.* Oxford: Oxford University Press, 1979.

Williams, Bernard. "The Idea of Equality." In *Philosophy, Politics and Society,* ser. 2, edited by Peter Laslett and W. G. Runciman. Oxford: Blackwell, 1962.

Wittgenstein, Ludwig. *Philosophical Investigations.* Edited by G. E. M. Anscombe. Oxford: Oxford University Press, 1953.

Wolgast, Elizabeth H. *Equality and the Rights of Women.* Ithaca, N.Y.: Cornell University Press, 1980.

Young, Michael. *Rise of the Meritocracy.* Harmondsworth, England: Penguin Books, 1959.

Index